THE ASSISTED REPRODU

THE ASSISTED REPRODUCTION OF RACE

Camisha A. Russell

Indiana University Press

This book is a publication of

Indiana University Press
Office of Scholarly Publishing
Herman B Wells Library 350
1320 East 10th Street
Bloomington, Indiana 47405 USA

iupress.indiana.edu

Library of Congress Cataloging-in-Publication Data

Names: Russell, Camisha A., author.
Title: The assisted reproduction of race / Camisha A. Russell.
Description: Bloomington : Indiana University Press, 2018. | Includes bibliographical references and index.
Identifiers: LCCN 2018019397 (print) | LCCN 2018041360 (ebook) | ISBN 9780253035912 (e-book) | ISBN 9780253035820 (cl : alk. paper) | ISBN 9780253035905 (pb : alk. paper)
Subjects: LCSH: Medical ethics. | Genetics—Moral and ethical aspects.
Classification: LCC R724 (ebook) | LCC R724 .R864 2018 (print) | DDC 174.2—dc23
LC record available at https://lccn.loc.gov/2018019397

1 2 3 4 5   23 22 21 20 19 18

For Mom,
who knew it all along,
even if she couldn't come
this far.

Contents

Acknowledgments

I HAVE MANY people to thank from the early phase of this work. The influence of my academic mentors remains visible in the final product. Robert Bernasconi set high expectations but also did everything he could to ease the way. Without him, I would never have attempted to address the history of race, and without his expert advice, it would not be a history worth reading. Sarah Clark Miller was the person with whom I first began to elaborate the contours of the project as it appears today. She also provided much needed emotional support. If memory serves, she also originated the title. Susan M. Squier wrote the first book Sarah and I read together on the topic of assisted reproductive technologies, *Babies in Bottles*, and it was in the course of a seminar with Susan that I first came to the idea of race as technology. Nancy Tuana helped me frame this project within the larger field of bioethics and lent the endeavor not only her personal support but the formidable aid of the Rock Ethics Institute, of which she was director. I am grateful to the Rock Ethics Institute for both its intellectual support and its financial support in the form of supplemental fellowship during the 2009–2010 academic year, when I began to write this work. I offer my gratitude to the Woodrow Wilson Foundation as well, whose generous Charlotte W. Newcombe Fellowship supported me during the 2012–2013 academic year.

Many people and institutions were also instrumental in the subsequent phases of this book. Dee Mortensen of Indiana University Press has been the best editor for which a first-time author could hope, proving enthusiastic and supportive from our first exploratory meeting, through the reader reports, and all the way to that final push to finish the final draft. I was tremendously fortunate to spend the two years after graduate school on a University of California President's Postdoctoral Fellowship, which provided mentoring, encouragement, and the freedom to focus exclusively on my research and writing. My thanks to David Theo Goldberg and his assistant Arielle Read for hosting me in their UC Humanities Research Institute during that time. I am also grateful to Colorado College as a whole, and the philosophy department in particular, for the Riley Fellowship that followed my time in California and provided still more space in which to finally complete the manuscript.

With respect to the quality of the book, my sincere thanks to Margret Grebowicz and my anonymous second reader, both of whom evinced strong support for the project while suggesting that I strengthen my voice, along with a few other crucial changes. However, my deepest gratitude on this front is reserved for my friend and colleague Laura Beeby, who went through the entire manuscript several times and offered invaluable perspective on how to carry out the final revisions. I probably could have finished the book without her, but you would be reading a lesser version.

On a personal level, I am grateful to my partner, Rebecca Saxon, who had to live with me during most of this process. Her love and faith nourish and sustain me. Together we now raise a son, Addae, who came along in the middle of this whole thing and who lights up both our lives. It is fitting that Addae's feet and Rebecca's hand, along with my own hand, grace the cover of this book. For the artistry of that photograph and for her generous donation of the rights to it, I sincerely thank Anastassia Pronksy of B+N Photography in Mississauga, Ontario.

You will also see both my parents in this book and, in the background, both their parents as well. Thanks to my father for sharing the story of the places in which they grew up and the challenges of their interracial courtship and marriage in 1970s Wyoming. Thanks to his parents and sister and my mother's sister for attending their wedding. Thanks to my dad as well for his appreciation of the value of higher education and heartfelt declarations of pride.

Ultimately, I owe the greatest debt to my mother. I have a distinct visual memory of a gathering she had in her home for some friends during our last year together—the year she was dying of cancer. In the memory she is holding a glass of wine. One of her friends has just asked me what my book is about, and I am trying to offer a nonacademic, friendly description of the project. It's nothing my mother has ever heard before—though we spoke often and at length, it was always more about how I was doing than the content of my academic writings. "I just have one question," she says when I've finished. "How is this different from the way people have always controlled who can have children with whom?" She is, after all, a white woman who married a black man very much against her own mother's wishes. I am the product of that union. "It's not different," I tell her, feeling flushed. "Just continuous." And then she nods her acceptance. "Okay." It was an important point and connection for my work that I have never forgotten since. Though she did not live to see this book finished, let alone the birth of her grandchild, she was there when I started, and I know that her unconditional love and the inner strength that grew from it underlie all of my accomplishments, up to and including this one.

THE ASSISTED REPRODUCTION OF RACE

Introduction: From What Race *Is* to What Race *Does*

In 2002, I was working as a Peace Corps volunteer in a village in the Central Region of Togo, West Africa. I'd been there for a year and a half when my father came to visit. My mother had visited a few months earlier, around Christmas-time. I took my father to a middle school where I'd been working. The principal brought us to talk to the troisième class (roughly ninth grade), and we introduced my father to the students and then asked them if they had any questions.

One boy raised his hand. "How is it that Camisha is white, but her father is black, like us?" he asked. To my surprise, though I grew up black in the United States, I had been white since arriving in Togo. I was still getting used to it. I opened my mouth to answer, but the principal raised his hand to stop me, indicating that he would "take this one."

"You remember when Camisha's mother came to visit?" he asked. The students nodded. "She was short and white." The students nodded again. My mother, though she always imagined herself to be 5'6" was in fact 5'2". My father is 6'6". I am 5'9", which is pretty tall by Togo standards. "And her father," the principal continued, "is tall and black." The students nodded again. I too thought things were going well.

"So you see," the principal concluded, "she got her father's height and her mother's skin."

I once heard someone joke at a conference, "Academics are the only ones who keep asking what race is; everybody else already knows." Apart from very young children or people living within ethnically homogenous and truly isolated populations, I suspect this is true. As my above story illustrates, however, *what* exactly constitutes knowledge of race or correct racial classification most certainly differs around the world. In the United States, the majority opinion is that I am black or mixed race; in Togo, West Africa, the majority opinion is that I am white.

Nevertheless, most people definitely "know" *something* about race, and it probably bears a reasonable resemblance to what the others around them "know." In fact, it is the difference between what any North American who hears my story "knows" about race and what the middle-school principal in Togo "knew" that gives my story its punch line. (It always gets great laughs at parties.) As Paul Taylor puts it, "if a culture distinguishes and categorizes people using methods that appeal in part to such things as the way people look, then we might say of that culture that it has a concept of race."[1]

Still, when writing on the topic of race, there is a temptation to put the word in scare quotes, to make sure that everyone understands that what I mean by "race" isn't what Adolf Hitler meant or what courts and legislators meant in the Jim Crow South. "Of course, race is an illusion," I should say here, "but if you'll just allow me to talk about that illusion for a while, perhaps I can explain how we all got so lost and how we can all find our way back to the light of reason." Such a stance appeals for a variety of reasons. After all, what could be so wrong about refusing to believe in something that has been so harmful for so long? Perhaps it would be naïve to squeeze our eyes shut and pretend *racism* isn't real, but surely it must be admirable to marshal scientific and historical evidence in order to prove rationally and beyond any doubt that everything we think we know about *race* is simply a series of historical and persistent errors based on fear, prejudice, and greed.

Admirable, perhaps, but is this truly an appropriate and effective strategy? It may not be true that there is a single false idea of race or even a larger but still manageable number of false ideas of race residing in people's minds, thus accounting for the continued existence of racism. Even if we could eradicate such a false idea through some sort of mass education campaign, doing so might not eradicate racism. Simply put, adamantly refusing to recognize the existence of race probably won't make it go away.

Overview

Before we begin in earnest, I would like to briefly summarize the project of this book and the task of this introduction. By doing so, I hope to help the reader better track the forthcoming arguments. My central aim here is to explore how notions of race and racial identity function within *assisted reproductive technologies* (ARTs), offering what I believe to be two valuable philosophical contributions. The first contribution is to philosophical and bioethical discussion surrounding ARTs. While feminists and bioethicists have engaged in a variety of critical analyses of ARTs, often exploring their gendered dimensions, the role of race in ART practices remains undertheorized. Much of this work will be found in chapters 1 and 5. The second contribution is to philosophical discussion surrounding race itself. In an effort to shift our thinking on race from debates over *what race is* to investigations of *what race does* (and how), chapter 2 argues that race should be considered technologically. Subsequent chapters, particularly 3 and 5, make use of different (though not fully distinct) conceptions of technology to examine how race might be considered as technology in different (though not fully distinct) contexts. The overarching point of these examinations is to highlight the fact that race is both *produced* and *productive*. Race ideas and racial science are both human inventions and have been used (and continue to be used, consciously or unconsciously) to carry out a variety of political and increasingly personal projects.

To prepare the reader for this work on race and reproductive technologies, I go forward with this introduction by explaining why I have chosen ARTs as a site of investigation for the concept of race. I continue by offering a description of the Critical Philosophy of Race as a framework within which to understand my work. I then provide an overview of late twentieth-century philosophical debates about the reality of race—including the argument for race as a social construction—before stepping back to consider some early to mid-twentieth-century views of race in terms of nature, culture, and politics. These debates about and conceptions of race provide a context for understanding what is to be gained by considering race as technology. Finally, I wrap up this introduction by describing the forthcoming chapters in a bit more detail.

Assisted Reproductive Technologies

As I will discuss later in this introduction, one popular line of attack against race (or, more to the point, against *racism*) involves arguing that our current racial categories lack scientific reality. Today, that line of attack uses the language of genetics (i.e., there is no genetic basis for race). We might imagine, then, that racial categorizations would be least present in scientific contexts—and particularly those focused on genetics. Yet a variety of scholars working in genetics or engaged in the critical study of science and medicine have pointed to the persistence of race as an organizing discourse in these very contexts.[2] If this is surprising or remarkable, we might also be struck by the consistent, central, and unapologetic use of racial categorization in the world of assisted reproductive technologies (ARTs). Then again, we might not.

On the one hand, we might see ARTs as part of reproductive medicine, as medical technologies used to treat infertility. When we hear the language of biological, genetic, or biogenetic relation being used to describe the role of those people who provided the gametes (egg or sperm) used in the creation of a child (who may be raised by other parents)—as in "the biological mother" or "the genetic father"—we might assume that genetic science serves as an important framework for ART practices. On the other hand, we might understand ARTs as technologies that mimic or correct nature in order to create families. When ARTs are seen as an intimate site in which babies and kinship (parents and children) are created, the importance of race may not seem so surprising after all.

Whether we find the importance of race in ARTs fitting or surprising, I believe they offer a significant site for the investigation of questions surrounding race for two principle reasons. First, while ARTs are a contemporary issue of continued and increasing importance, questions of the relationship between race and ARTs have not been sufficiently engaged by philosophers and have even been dismissed as merely contingent or ethically neutral by some bioethicists. Second, because they involve "assistance" or "third-party intervention" in the supposedly natural process of reproduction, ARTs serve as sites where one can see, perhaps more clearly than elsewhere, the construction of race as "natural," precisely (and ironically) *through* social and technological intervention. The realm of assisted reproduction becomes especially interesting in this context because, as Lisa Ikemoto notes, while "we understand technology to be something that humans invent . . . procreative technology use blurs the line implicit in that understanding of technology—the line between human and technology." In other words, "'technology' intervenes, at least temporarily, in our patterned ways of thinking about boundaries of use," allowing us to reconsider our conceptions of the natural and the unnatural, even as it reveals to us the use of those concepts for social and political ends.[3] Thus, we can look to ART practices both to see how race has been understood and deployed in the past and to examine how those understandings and deployments may be shifting to accommodate new contexts, desires, and anxieties.

This work, then, aims both to consider the (heretofore undertheorized) role of race in ARTs and to use ARTs as a context through which to improve our understanding of how race works. The latter will be accomplished through the theoretical lens of *race as technology*.

Critical Philosophy of Race

I consider the following investigation to be a work in the Critical Philosophy of Race. *Critical Philosophy of Race* is a relatively new term but one that describes work that has been going on for some time both within philosophy and in other disciplines. The new title attempts both to bring these various projects together and to place emphasis on certain of their features.

> Critical Philosophy of Race consists in the philosophical examination of issues raised by the concept of race and by the persistence of various forms of racism across the world. It is philosophical not only in employing a wide variety of methods and tools (including interdisciplinary sources) to clarify and scrutinize the understanding of race and racism, but also in its engagement with traditional philosophical questions and in its readiness to engage critically some of the traditional answers.[4]

Broadly speaking, work that qualifies as Critical Philosophy of Race can be seen as doing at least one of two things (and often both). First, it may use the tools of the philosophical tradition to critically examine questions of race, racism, or race thinking. This may include attempts to describe or define one or more of these phenomena, attempts to explain their current form or origin, or attempts to offer new concepts and conceptualizations to allow us to think through or combat them. Second, work in Critical Philosophy of Race may critique philosophical theories, the philosophical canon, the philosophical tradition, or the current discipline of philosophy in terms of race, racism, or race thinking.

Critical philosophers of race may argue, for example, that a philosophical theory of justice is inadequate because it fails to address (or is even incapable of addressing) racial injustice. They may claim that the philosophical tradition has been fundamentally shaped by race thinking and cannot be fully understood without recognizing this fact. They may point out that the philosophical canon is full of figures with troubling racial views that, far from being the only views available at that time, were not shared by those philosophical contemporaries who have been excluded from the canon—and thus that the philosophical canon may be in need of serious expansion or revision. Or they may ask why, compared to other academic disciplines, philosophy has been so woefully inattentive to issues of race. They may ask whether continued inattention to race threatens to render philosophy irrelevant to contemporary academic discourse, let alone the "real world."

While broad enough to encompass a variety of works in philosophical sub-disciplines such as African American philosophy, Africana philosophy, Latino/a philosophy, or whiteness studies, the term *Critical Philosophy of Race* does not imply a focus on the particular experience of or patterns of discrimination against any one racially designated group. Nor does Critical Philosophy of Race imply an exclusive commitment to any one of the major traditions into which philosophy has been divided, such as analytic, continental, American, or history of philosophy. Works in Critical Philosophy of Race can be found in any of these traditions and may, in fact, draw on several at the same time. Like feminist work in philosophy, with which it shares many features, Critical Philosophy of Race is often not only philosophically pluralist but also more broadly interdisciplinary.

What *does* determine whether any particular piece of philosophical work treating the subjects of race, racism, or race thinking counts as Critical Philosophy of Race is precisely the word *critical*, which is adopted from the body of legal scholarship known as *Critical Race Theory* (with its own connections to *Critical Legal Studies*). According to the editors of one influential volume on the subject, "Critical Race Theory embraces a movement of left scholars, most of them scholars of color, situated in law schools, whose work challenges the ways in which race and racial power are constructed and represented in American legal culture and, more generally, in American society as a whole."[5] Denying that there is a canonical set of doctrines or methodologies to which all critical race theorists subscribe, they point to two common interests: (1) "to understand how a regime of white supremacy and its subordination of people of color have been created and maintained in America, and, in particular, to examine the relationship between that social structure and professed ideals such as 'the rule of law' and 'equal protection'" and (2) "a desire not merely to understand the vexed bond between law and racial power but to change it."[6] In contrast to Critical Race Theory, Critical Philosophy of Race is *not* limited to the American context, taking not only an explicitly historical approach to race but an explicitly global one as well. What it does adopt with the word *critical* are (1) the recognition that a regime of white supremacy has been in place during the last several hundred years of philosophizing, (2) the admission that philosophizing has not only been deeply affected *by* white supremacy but also been integral *to* the creation and support of that regime, and (3) an ethico-political commitment not only to exposing but to opposing this state of affairs.

Critical race theorists, like poststructuralists, postmodernists, and many feminists in the philosophical tradition, reject the idea that scholarship should or even *could* be "objective" or "neutral." They recognize that "Scholarship— the formal production, identification, and organization of what will be called 'knowledge'—is inevitably political."[7] For critical philosophers of race, this recognition means both that they will not makes claims of objectivity and neutrality with respect to their own work and that they will challenge past claims to objectivity and neutrality in the philosophical canon, particularly where those claims have been used to entrench and bolster white supremacy. Along with the rejection of objectivity and neutrality in theorizing comes a rejection of any call for impartiality in moral or political reasoning that attempts to equate all race consciousness with racism. Critical Race Theory and Critical Philosophy of Race explicitly *embrace* race consciousness, aiming

> to reexamine the terms by which race and racism have been negotiated in American consciousness, and to recover and revitalize the radical tradition of race-consciousness among African-Americans and other peoples of color—a tradition that was discarded when integration, assimilation and the ideal of color-blindness became the official norms of racial enlightenment.[8]

Thus, rather than assuming that awareness of race is only a social ill, and that race must be overcome to vanquish racism, critical race theorists question "regnant visions of racial meaning and racial power" and "seek to fashion a set of tools for thinking about race that avoids the traps of racial thinking."[9]

Critical Philosophy of Race faces similar struggles against these "official norms of racial enlightenment." Thus it must adopt an explicitly political stance that demands awareness of both the past and continuing importance of race ideas and racialized practices in everything from metaphysics and epistemology to ethics and politics, from the construction of the philosophical canon to the current demographics of the philosophical discipline. But it must do more than challenge or reject these norms; it must also investigate how these norms came to be established and what social and political purposes their establishment has served. It is in order to pay due attention to the social and political purposes that notions of race have served and continue to serve that I will argue (in chapter 2) that we ought to think of race in terms of technology.

The Debate over the "Reality" of Race

By now it is probably already clear that I think one can and should talk about race. I stand with other critical race philosophers and theorists in the belief that race *consciousness* (the recognition of the ways in which the concept of race operates in our nonideal political reality) can be separated from race *thinking* (defined by Taylor as "a way of assigning generic meaning to human bodies and bloodlines"[10]). Nevertheless, I think it will be both instructive and ultimately useful to take time here to look at some of the philosophical debate over the metaphysics of race.

According to Charles Mills, though a consistent terminology in the metaphysics of race has not yet stabilized, one can productively distinguish between three different views in the debate: racial realism or naturalism, eliminativist constructivism, and anti-eliminativist constructivism.[11] A great deal of ink has already been spilled arguing against racial realism or naturalism, but with the help of Paul Taylor (whose *Race: A Philosophical Introduction* helpfully summarizes many of what have become the standard views of race theory), I will spill a bit more, just for clarity. Still, it is worth pointing out at the outset that very few people seriously espouse this view these days and that such people tend not to be well regarded in their professions. Yet racial discrimination and deep structural inequalities between racial groups persist. This, I will argue, suggests that racial realism or naturalism is, and may have always been, a straw man, unworthy of the bulk of our antiracist focus. This is not to say that racial naturalist views did not exist but that we have greatly simplified them in our efforts to banish them.

In any case, *racial naturalism* is the idea that "races are naturally occurring elements of a universe that, in its arrangement and constitution, is utterly indifferent to our systems of meaning."[12] In other words, the racial naturalist believes that people do not create races but rather nature does; human beings simply observe and study naturally occurring races in order to uncover their distinct properties. In the modern era, defined among other things by the positivist belief in the power of science, a naturalistic approach to race thinking evolves into what Taylor calls *classical racialism*, which "tries to reduce social and cultural differences between peoples to the biological and morphological differences between them, and it tries to explain these morphological differences with scientific precision, by appeal to the concept of race."[13] This view, Taylor argues, can be reduced to five central claims: (1) "The human race can be exhaustively divided into a few discrete subgroups"; (2) "Each of these smaller groups possesses a unique set of heritable and physiologically specifiable traits"; (3) "These distinctive sets of physiological traits vary with equally distinctive sets of moral, cognitive, and culture characteristics"; (4) These groups "can be ranked along graduated scales of worth and capacity"; and (5) "The features that distinguish these races are passed down as part of a racial essence that shapes the character, conduct, potential, and value of each individual member of each race."[14]

Committed to placing concepts and uses of race in their historical contexts, Taylor is careful to note that while the idea of race did not have to develop in the way that it did (such development was not *necessary*), it was not mere historical accident. Rather, "Modernity and Race helped bring each other into being, and they sustained and spurred each other on through different stages of development. . . . [For example,] the most successful racializing institution in history prepared the way for today's global economy: the transnational exchange markets and financial frameworks of global capitalism cut their teeth on the transatlantic slave trade."[15] As we will see later in greater detail, race and modern *science* also helped bring each other into being, with concepts like evolution, heredity, and eugenics not only relying on racialist intuitions and "evidence" for their elaboration but also being incorporated back into race thinking to provide it with greater legitimacy and social force.

Insofar as the concept of race itself is equated with and thought to be exhausted by a racial naturalism or realism that inevitably leads to classical racialism, it is easy to see why many scholars or ordinary people feel that we ought to dispense with the notion of race altogether. Those are the scholars (and ordinary people) we might label *eliminativist constructivists*. The eliminativist constructivist can point to any number of rather obvious and well-known problems with realist or naturalist race thinking. Taylor offers us three: First, it operates with a "typological bias," which is to say that "it lumps people into putatively distinct categories on the basis of physiological traits that vary continuously."[16] One such trait is skin color. Human complexions come in a variety of different shades, and people vary enormously within "races." In different places and different time periods, the same complexion might yield a variety of different racial classifications. Moreover, the phenomenon of passing shows that no particular racial ancestry guarantees the "appropriate" appearance. Other common racial markers like hair color and texture or the shape of one's nose also vary along continua. The demarcations that race thinkers attempt to create along these continua never seem to remain as sharp as they are intended to be, often blurring to the point that they must ultimately be seen as arbitrary. Second is the problem of "illusory consistency," referring to the fact that "the traits that are supposed to define races fail to present themselves in reliable clusters."[17] Not only do various racialized physical traits like skin color, hair texture, and facial features fail to appear together consistently and exclusively within their designated racial categories, but the psychological, mental, moral, and cultural traits that are also supposed to be attached to race fail to cluster in individual members of each ostensible race in the ways that race thinking demands. And third, "human heredity is much more complicated than the transmission of racial essences" (which essences are implied by the ideas of "blood" relation, "pure blood," and "mixed blood"), and biological race thinking is "incapable of providing an adequate scientific account of this complexity."[18]

One well-known eliminativist constructivist and proponent of this last point in particular is Anthony Appiah, who points to the following passage from science writer Paul Hoffman's 1994 article "The Science of Race":

> On average there's .2 percent difference in genetic material between any two randomly chosen people on Earth. Of that diversity, 85 percent will be found within any local group of people—say, between you and your neighbor. More than half (9 percent) of the remaining 15 percent will be represented by differences between ethnic and linguistic groups within a given race (for example, between Italians and French). Only 6 percent represents differences between races (for example, between Europeans and Asians). And remember that's 6 percent of .2 percent. In other words, race accounts for only a miniscule .012 percent difference in our genetic material.[19]

For Appiah, this is evidence for the nonexistence of race. Race, he argues, is an essentially biological concept that is supposed to allow for meaningful classification of human beings into scientifically delineable groups such that their shared physiological features (e.g., skin color) would be predictive of other group traits. If we cannot come up with such scientifically delineable groups, or if the groups we can come up with do not allow us to draw any correlations with moral or social traits, then the race concept fails. In other words, if there are no *races*, the *race concept* must be rejected.

Of course, Appiah did eventually amend his original focus on the nonreality of race to allow for the reality of racial *ascription* (e.g., people thinking I'm black) and racial *identification* (e.g., me considering myself black) and for their effects, rarely under an individual's conscious control, on an individual's life paths and life chances (e.g., those two things significantly decreasing my odds of becoming a philosophy professor). Though no biological racial essence can be identified, he argues that if you "understand the sociohistorical process of construction of the race, you'll see that the label works despite the absence of an essence."[20] Until very recently, however, while Appiah was sympathetic to racial identifications and understood why they have been seen as useful in fighting racism and oppression, he did not endorse their continued use, as he found them to be too reliant on false notions of racial (or cultural) essence and too restrictive of individual freedom.

Before we move to the *anti-eliminativist constructivist* position—which is the view of the metaphysics of race that is most in keeping with the commitment to race consciousness in Critical Philosophy of Race and Critical Race Theory—it is worth taking a brief detour. In the early 1990s, a debate central to the formation of Africana philosophy, and following on previous debates in the black scholarly tradition, emerged between Appiah and Lucius Outlaw. Challenging Appiah's insistence on the nonreality of race, Outlaw argued that *raciation* and *ethnicization*—the complicated biological, sociocultural, and historical processes by which populations and subgroups are formed and maintained—"are important aspects of the socially contingent, but anthropologically necessary ways in which we humans, as social animals, organize meaningfully, give order to, and thus define and construct the worlds in which we live."[21] I would like to highlight two key aspects of this view that will be important to my argument for race as technology: First, it places significant emphasis on the processes by which race is made. Second, it deliberately leaves space for positive aspects of racial identification.

However, Outlaw's emphasis on the roles of both necessity and human nature, along with social and historical contingency, may be criticized as an attempt to ground the reality of racial categorization in its inevitability. He argues for "an understanding and appreciation of senses of *belonging* and of a shared *destiny* by which individuals are intimately connected to other individuals in ways that make for the constitution of particular kinds of social collectivities."[22] These collectivities, which Outlaw names *social-natural kinds*, are meant to take the place of biological or material kinds in the concept of race. At the same time, Outlaw takes issue with those who believe that to say that something is socially constructed necessarily implies that thing is not *real*. "Such approaches to the 'socially constructed' involve conceptions of the *real* that are much too simple in that they generally regard only material kinds as real while allowing that the fictive or imagined can and do have real effects when played out through social practices," Outlaw claims. "Approaches of this sort fail to appreciate more fully varieties of kinds of *reals* and the full range of social realities."[23]

As Anna Stubblefield points out, however, these two arguments of Outlaw's—that races are social-natural kinds and that socially constructed things can still be real—are in some conflict. In using the supposedly natural and necessary character of racial categorization and social segregation as a key element of his definition of race, Outlaw implicitly concedes that races must be some sort of *natural* kind in order to count as real. According to Stubblefield, Outlaw's view breaks down to the argument that race is real because it "(1) reflects natural tendencies on the part of human beings to classify each other according to appearance and ancestry; (2) has social, political, and historical importance, such that one's race makes a difference in one's life and how one relates to the world; and (3) reflects cultural differences between members of the groups we call races."[24] Stubblefield argues that the first of these reasons does not hold up well. The second, she believes, is much stronger but would gain force were Outlaw to more specifically challenge Appiah's notion of "reality."

With respect to the third reason, Stubblefield writes: "Outlaw's important contribution to the project of defining race in terms of culture is his proposal that defining race should be a creative, political project. . . . Outlaw's proposal is that we should define race *prescriptively*, rather than *descriptively*. We should focus on how race *should be* defined, not on what it is."[25] Herein lies my primary reason for detouring into the Appiah-Outlaw debate. As Stubblefield points out, the underlying prescriptive nature of debates over race is precisely what gets missed when people (including Appiah and Outlaw themselves) take the debate between them to be "primarily a dispute about the nature of race and how to define it"—in other words, a dispute over *the metaphysics of race*.[26] Appiah and Outlaw use their differing conclusions as to the reality of race to come to differing conclusions about whether we should take race into account in our individual moral reasoning. Ostensibly, the moral arguments about race follow from the ontological ones. Stubblefield believes that in truth the process works the other way around: possessing already their moral commitments to taking race into account (in Outlaw's case) and to *not* taking race into account (in Appiah's), Outlaw and Appiah proceed to argue for the racial ontologies that they believe would best support their moral views. She believes that at its heart, the debate is a consequentialist one over whether taking race into account only perpetuates antiblack oppression or is in fact necessary to effectively combat such oppression. Their accounts, then, are fundamentally prescriptive.

Stubblefield does not intend to criticize either view by calling them prescriptive. Her aim is neither the discovery nor the development of a "grand theory" of race that would "say what race is and how we ought to think about it in all contexts and for all purposes" (something she doubts is even possible). Rather, she aims for a "defensible prescriptive conception of race that helps us to understand anti-black oppression and that allows for the construction of an ethical approach that will be useful in combating anti-black oppression."[27] This aim is "pragmatic" in the sense Iris Marion Young describes in her own efforts to theorize gender—that is, as "categorizing, explaining and developing accounts and arguments that are tied to specific practical and political problems, where the purpose of this theoretical activity is clearly related to those problems" and "is not concerned to give an account of a whole."[28] On this account, the question of how we *should* think about race becomes a legitimate one, and both Appiah's and Outlaw's approaches possess merit insofar as they can argue that considering race as not real or real (in their respective senses) offers a practical advantage in explaining and combating antiblack oppression. Though Appiah, Outlaw, and Stubblefield all seek to construct some sort of ethical approach from their given theories, pragmatic theorizing need not be pragmatic in that specific sense.

A pragmatic theory may also be constructed because it offers explanatory advantages relative to a set of political concerns, even if that explanation will not be used to yield normative claims. Thus, my forthcoming argument that race *should* be thought of as a technology because it helps us to understand the role of race in assisted reproductive technologies (and may be useful in approaching other problems and within other contexts as well) is prescriptive only in that limited sense. It prescribes a course of thought and consideration, not a specific course of action.

Detour complete, let us conclude this summary of the debate over what race *is* with a look at the anti-eliminativist constructivist camp, which includes Mills, Stubblefield, and Taylor. The anti-eliminativist constructivist view can be summarized as follows: "Race is sociopolitical rather than biological, but it is nonetheless real." This view subverts the very terms in which the Outlaw-Appiah debate occurred, arguing that it is "a false dichotomization to assume that the only alternatives are race as nonexistent and race as biological essence."[29] Instead, "reality" here is to be understood in terms of objectivity (or intersubjectivity), with anything that is neither subjective nor relativistic counting as objective (or as having social reality). Certainly, the fact that races have been and continue to be defined in different ways at different times in different cultures serves as empirical evidence of the fact that racial categorizations do not possess an independent, transhistorical reality or essence. To say that they are socially constructed and culturally relativistic in this sense, however, is not to say that race is radically subjective or voluntaristic. Neither individuals in nor subcommunities of a particular society possess the power to choose their race or to choose not to have one at all. Not only does self-definition come up against the ways in which one is defined by others, but not all possible racial self-definitions will be socially intelligible. The very terms available to an individual for her self-definition will be largely determined by her social context. (I cannot, for example, stand in front of an American and claim to be white or give my ethnicity as "Wyoming," even though both my parents were born there.)

A popular analogy for proponents of the anti-eliminativist constructivist view compares race to money. Money is arbitrarily socially constructed and comes in different forms according to time and place, but no individual or even subcommunity has the power to refuse to recognize its meaning or to give it different rules of value. (I cannot decide to pay for my groceries in buttons instead of cash or hand you a dollar bill and tell you that it's equivalent to the one hundred dollars I borrowed from you last week.) Money is therefore both socially constructed and real. As Robert Bernasconi points out, this analogy need not imply that either race or money can only or best be understood as "an invention of the mind." Sartre saw such things rather as "a petrifaction of action," to which he also gave the name "the practico-inert."[30]

Mills cites as a principle virtue of the anti-eliminativist constructivist approach the fact that it "simultaneously recognizes the *reality* of race (causal power, theoretical centrality) and demystifies race (positing race as constructed)."[31] It thus becomes possible to talk about race as something meaningful and real without aligning oneself with biological or essentialist (typically racist and ill-founded) theories of race that see members of racial groups as sharing with each other certain fundamental and heritable physical, moral, and intellectual characteristics. Mills's view, along with Stubblefield's pragmatism and prescriptive focus, also reminds us, as Taylor too emphasizes, that historical and contemporary uses of race and the critiques they have spawned are always deeply political.

Nature, Culture, or Politics?

As we have seen, among those who study race, notions of what race *is* are frequently and often implicitly based on beliefs about the most effective moral or political means of fighting racism, which in turn are based on particular ideas about how racism operates. It turns out that this is by no means a recent phenomenon in the study of race. Bernasconi, in his work on the 1950 UNESCO statement on race, illustrates this process and its dangers. He shows how the official norms and terminology of "racial enlightenment" originated and their effects on the academy. The historical context in which the UNESCO statement was crafted, taken up, and debated is important here. With the rise and fall of Nazi Germany, the evils of race thinking had been dramatically demonstrated to the world, making the issue of racism both morally urgent and politically unavoidable. The Allied powers needed a way to portray their victory and the sacrifices involved as a noble triumph of justice and broader humanity, in spite of the fact that they themselves were countries whose power and wealth "derived from a sordid racist history that embraced the Atlantic slave trade and colonial genocides, and which survived the Second World War in the form of racial segregation in the United States and the imperial dominance claimed by the European powers." This fundamental hypocrisy could be disguised only by defining racism "in such a way that it could be isolated and expunged while everything else remained intact, including a belief in the superiority of the Western philosophical tradition." Thus, particular sociopolitical circumstances conditioned the emergence of a narrow understanding of racism (both assumed and engendered by the UNESCO statement) as "discrimination based on a *belief* in the correlation between, on the one hand, certain unwelcome behavioral patterns, deficient intellectual aptitudes or immoral inclinations and, on the other hand, a certain genetic heritage."[32]

By focusing on racism as a problematic set of *beliefs* rather than a politically powerful set of sedimented social practices, a relatively easy course of remedial action could be mapped. One had simply to disprove the problematic correlation between behavior and biology. This could be done by "highlighting the radical difference between the two spheres across which the alleged correlation had been established: nature and culture," which in turn could be relegated to two "distinct disciplines with very different methodologies: biology and anthropology."[33] Among socially and politically dominant groups, very little needed to be given up with this change. Arguing for a separation of nature (race) and culture (ethnicity) did not require rescinding any notions of superiority on the part of dominant groups; on the contrary, that superiority simply needed to be understood as cultural (behavioral) rather than biological (racial).

Ashley Montagu, the dominant member of the committee that produced the UNESCO statement, had argued in his own work that the idea of "race" (which he placed in scare quotes) was "a culturally produced difference in social status converted into a difference in biological status," which "now turned into a biological difference . . . would serve, it was hoped, to justify and maintain the social difference."[34] Though he urged the UNESCO committee to abandon the language of race altogether, the ultimate phrasing of paragraph 6 of the 1950 UNESCO declaration left open the question of whether a legitimate *biological* concept of race existed:

> 6. National, religious, geographic, linguistic and cultural groups do not neces-sarily coincide with racial groups: and the cultural traits of such groups have no demonstrated genetic connexion with racial traits. Because serious errors of this kind are habitually committed when the term "race" is used in popular parlance, it would be better when speaking of human races to drop the term "race" altogether and speak of ethnic groups.[35]

With the race question handed over to the biologists, the rest of us were advised to follow the anthropologists and stop speaking of race altogether. "By highlighting a failure to draw the nature-culture distinction as the main cause of racism," writes Bernasconi, "it was possible to pretend that the existence at that time of segregation laws in the United States and apartheid in South Africa was not sustained by self-interest or evil intent, but was merely a consequence of muddled thinking, which could be corrected at the educational level at virtually no cost to anyone." Better yet: "Now that the epistemological error had been exposed, the Western academy could be counted upon to herald the way into a new era of enlightenment, thereby restoring its own sense of its moral as well as its cultural superiority."[36]

Though, as already discussed, attempts to challenge *beliefs* in the correlation between genetic heritage and moral, cultural, or intellectual capacities are both well meant and scientifically supported, these attempts leave much unchallenged. They "leave intact a world structured by past racisms that cannot be located at the level of thought because they are now—and probably were always—primarily located within practices that are sustained not so much by individuals, but by institutions, both local and global." Moreover, they prove "inadequate to the task . . . of illuminating the history of racism."[37] To better understand these failings, we might turn from the nature versus culture distinction to a productive and ultimately much more illuminating distinction drawn by Eric Voegelin, a German-born political theorist working in Austria during the rise of National Socialism in Germany. His insights were articulated in the 1930s (well before the UNESCO statement) and, on my account, demonstrate a much sharper understanding of the function of race.

Voegelin distinguishes between race *theory* (an endeavor of the natural sciences) and the race *idea* (a fundamentally political concept). In his exploration of the race *idea*, Voegelin explicitly does not seek a means by which to distinguish members of particular races or a better understanding of interracial relations. "When we speak of the race idea," he writes, "we have in mind chiefly the idea as it is used by modern creeds, of the type of National Socialism, in order to integrate a community spiritually and politically." Thus, his concern is with race as a tool for defining and shaping communities. Contrary to the way discussions of race are often framed (as described above), Voegelin argues that the race idea is not the sort of thing that can be proven true or false. This is because "the race idea with its implications is not a body of knowledge organized in systematic form, but a political idea in the technical sense of the word. A political idea does not attempt to describe social reality as it is, but it set ups symbols . . . which have the function of creating the image of a group as a unit." While Voegelin acknowledges that theories of race have proved empirically unverifiable and believes this to be a valid criticism, he argues that a "symbolic idea like the race idea is not a *theory* in the strict sense of the word." Precisely because the race idea is not a theory, such criticism, while correct, "is without meaning, because it is not the function of an idea to describe social reality but to assist in its constitution."[38] Thus the point of a race idea is not simply to recognize differences between groups but to establish and maintain those differences.

The power of a political idea is not, however, infinite. It is not the case that just "any product of a fertile imagination can serve as a political symbol." Rather, history shows that "social symbols, even when they move very far away from empirical reality, have at least their starting point in it, and that the link to reality cannot be broken without their function being destroyed."[39] In other words, race theories will keep appearing and being rewritten for the express purpose of underwriting the continued symbolic functions of race. For Voegelin, this means that the study of race

> must necessarily be arranged in two parts, one of which deals with race theory and its scientific content, while the other traces the race idea as a political idea in its effectiveness in the construction of a community. The dual arrangement is necessary, since the race idea does not appear as simply a political idea

(or rather, has not yet appeared as such) that shapes the lives of those who belong to it, uniting them while excluding all others; rather, beyond this it claims to result from scientific reflection.[40]

Thus we must recognize that, though use of the race idea purports to be based in and supported by scientific race theory, to criticize the race idea by pointing to the flaws in the supposedly supporting scientific theory is only half the battle—the very well-worn half. As Voegelin notes:

> heated argument is possible about the merits of any symbol. Those who belong to the social group and believe in its existence will always be able to point to the element of reality which is contained in their group symbols, and to prove that their social group is really a unit. Those who are politically opposed to the group in question will always be able to point out the discrepancy between the symbol and the reality which it represents. And, according to their temper and intellectual sophistication, they will stigmatize it as hypocritical, as an ideology, a myth, or an invention of a ruling class to deceive a guileless people. A scientific analysis has to keep clear of both of these fallacies, and to describe realistically the growth and function of the symbol.[41]

The sort of scientific analysis that Voegelin recommends here, then, is *not* one that questions the biological or even the cultural existence or reality of racial groups or racial difference on the basis of empirical data. Rather, he calls for a methodical description and analysis of the development and function of the race idea as a political symbol and as constitutive of social realities within specific historical contexts.[42]

When we view the race idea as a political idea in this way, scientific or pseudoscientific methods of racial *classification* are revealed as largely arbitrary. Racial or racialized identities as *political identities*, however, become crucial to understanding the operation of race as a political symbol within the sociohistorical context under examination. Mahmood Mamdani, for example, working in the context of the 1994 Rwandan genocide, shows how racial and ethnic identities, thought to be natural and cultural respectively, are ultimately two sides of the same coin—political identities operating in shifting sociohistorical contexts to unite and divide different groups and to justify differential allocations of power and resources to members of those groups (frequently enshrined in law). For Mamdani, a claim about race, ethnicity, tribal culture, or other identity classifications is to be understood as political "not because it is not true but because this truth does not reflect an original fact but a fact created politically and enforced legally."[43] He finds the origins of these political claims (and their correlative laws) in the colonial period, when the census in most African colonies classified populations into two broad, overall groups called *races* and *tribes*. Mamdani describe how races and tribes were understood (and the laws and, indeed, legal systems that applied to each), with particular focus on the ways in which ethnicities and their "traditions" were essentialized such that any cultural change or evolution among tribes or ethnicities was deemed inauthentic. He calls this "the technology of colonial rule."[44]

Mamdani does not argue, however, that ethnicities as consensual cultural identities did not exist in Africa before colonial rule. Rather his claim is that when "the political authority and the law it enforces identify subjects ethnically and discriminate between them, then ethnicity turns into a legal and political identity."[45] The Rwandan case, on his account, is unique for its strong *racialization* of the Tutsi and the Hutu identities during the colonial period. While he acknowledges that Tutsi privilege existed before colonialism, he argues that Belgian colonialism changed the justification for this privilege, such that "the terms *Hutu* and *Tutsi* came to identify two groups, one branded indigenous, the other exalted as [racially] alien." Moreover: "As Belgian authorities issued identity cards to the Hutu and Tutsi, Tutsi became sealed from Hutu. Legally identified as two biologically distinct races, the Tutsi as Hamites and the Hutu as Bantu, Hutu and Tutsi became distinct legal identities. The language of race functioned to underline this difference between indigenous and alien."[46] For Mamdani, this language of race is stronger than that of ethnicity. Conflicts between ethnic groups are like conflicts between neighbors. Conflicts between races, by contrast, are conflicts between insiders and outsiders. It is the language of race rather than ethnicity that is most likely to lead to something like genocide. Of course, the Rwandan genocide did not take place under colonialism. Mamdani argues, however, that the racialization of the Hutu and Tutsi must be seen as a distinctly colonial legacy, which was not abandoned by the nationalist projects that ushered in the postcolonial period (though it perhaps should have been). Rather, racial identities were taken up as part of the struggle for justice, where *race-as-nation* became the ideological foundation for revolution.

Voegelin's perspective from Germany under National Socialism and Mamdani's grounding in postcolonial Africa might seem like an odd pairing. They do, however, have some history in common: modern-era conceptions of race and state. Mamdani argues that the modern state

> stands up to time, by giving itself both a past and a future. The production of the past is the stuff of *history-writing*, just as the securing of a future is the domain of *law-making*. Between history-writing and law-making, there is a strategic alliance. Law identifies agency in history. By enforcing group identities on individual subjects, the law institutionalizes group life.[47]

With these insights about the modern state, we are able to adopt a more critical stance toward race ideas and identities, identifying their essence neither as biological nor cultural (in some limited sense) but as political. Thus in both these theories, by contrast to that advanced by UNESCO, the crucial move is *not* to contrast the natural (as that which race would but cannot be) with the cultural (as that which actually accounts for so-called racial difference). Rather, a movement must be made from the belief in race and racial identities as potentially fixed and empirically discoverable to the understanding of race and racial identities as political, as *produced by* and *productive of* social realities.

This realization by no means absolves us of the need to look at questions surrounding race within their specific sociohistorical contexts. Indeed, it calls for precisely such careful investigation. Politics may be everywhere, but they are by no means everywhere the same. Similar terms may be in play, and similar strategies may be adopted, but each context will have particularities that will be the key to antiracist theorizing and action. With this realization, we also find the justification for continued discussion and study of *race* under that very (and variable) term. As Taylor puts it: "The basic reason to go on is that the scientific repudiation of classical racialism didn't lead directly to the abandonment of its social and political uses."[48] As we go on, however, we must make a shift, moving away from an unhelpful focus on what people *believe* about race to how race has been and continues to be *used*. In other words, we must move from the question of what race *is* to what race *does*.

Description of Chapters

Having argued for the importance of examining the function of the race idea in particular contexts, I begin in chapter 1 by examining the role race has played in contemporary ART practices. The chapter also serves as a review of most of the literature that has taken up the question of race and ARTs and could be read on its own as an introduction to the topic. Working with relatively recent practices and examples, I argue that employing insights from the philosophy of technology allows us to make an important move in our discussion of ARTs away from traditional bioethical approaches that seek primarily to justify or condemn their use by particular individuals. By contrast, a political analysis of race and ARTs must, I would argue, take up issues of social and political structures and inequalities, of power relations, and of the role that notions of race have played in creating and maintaining these. I frame my discussion with a series of questions offered by Neil Postman concerning for what and for *whom* technologies are intended and the unintended consequences that may flow from their use. Using these questions, I explore the racialized construction of "infertility," the ways in which ART practices can participate in and further systems of global inequality, and the role of race in the construction and maintenance of the "natural" in and through ART use. This analysis will show that ARTs are far from racially neutral.

Building both on the above discussion of common race debates and on the use of philosophy of technology in chapter 1, in chapter 2 I suggest that we try thinking of race not simply as political but as *technological*. Using the concept of technology as a theoretical lens for thinking about race brings together the well-rehearsed but important insight that race is socially constructed with the repeatedly overlooked but necessary insight that the race idea is used to construct political and social realities. It asks us to keep always in mind that race is both produced and productive. Moreover, it leaves important room for us to acknowledge the ways that different people in different eras take up old race ideas for new purposes, some of which have to do with resistance to oppression and inequality. Though there is a great deal to be gained simply by thinking about the race idea using analogies to concrete technological artifacts, I also elaborate on more abstract Heideggerian and Foucauldian conceptions of technology and propose that they too can bring crucial insights to our analysis of race.

In chapter 3, I consider the possible relationship between contemporary ARTs and the highly racialized eugenics movements of the early twentieth century, arguing that thinking about the history of race technologically points to deeply rooted connections between the two. I thus offer an alternative approach to the history of race that highlights its technological elements, including (1) the recognition by many theorists of race both that race was a conceptual category imposed by people onto nature and that racial purity was a human goal rather than a natural reality; (2) the deeply explanatory role race was thought to play in human history, such that management of race would be necessary for shaping the future of nations and peoples; and (3) repeated analogies to animal breeding that suggest that the development of the scientific race concept was always deeply influenced by discourses of human improvement and perfectibility through reproduction. Here, Heidegger's insights about how the modern worldview is essentially technological and how modern science is always already enframed by a human drive to master nature prove particularly provocative and instructive.

In chapter 4, I continue my history of race in the American context. I show how the use of race as a political technology in the United States has operated through the notion of kinship, such that race has, for some time, been able to serve as a proxy for kinship. In this role as a proxy for kinship, race itself can be considered as a more personal and intimate technology operating alongside other technologies in the fertility clinic and other reproductive contexts. Thus the persistence of race as an important category in ART practices (as described in chap. 1) is more than merely a troubling continuation of the false biological conceptions of race that have created and maintained the American system of racial hierarchy. It also serves a productive or, as I argue, a *technological* function within those practices. It is a constitutive feature of ARTs that they enlist people, instruments, and techniques (and often genetic material) outside of or beyond the intended parent(s) in the process of reproduction. In this context of uncertainty, I will argue, race, ethnicity, and culture appear as resources available to fertility patients in their construction of naturalizing narratives, which help to disambiguate various contributors to the child's birth and to name particular people as the child's "true" parents. The various metaphors and analogies that have emerged in the history of the race idea, I claim, allow racial categorizations and identifications to serve as a proxy for kinship in the world of reproductive technology. This personal use of the political technology of race is not without consequences.

Finally, in chapter 5, I use the Foucauldian concept of *technologies of the self* to argue that notions of race are being transformed and put to new purposes in the era of (neo)liberal eugenics. As neoliberal technologies of the self, practices of racial matching in ART contexts serve to individualize, privatize, and therefore depoliticize race itself, turning it into just another biological feature to be chosen in keeping with one's identity. At the same time that race is construed as just another choice, however, I contend that it has also been portrayed in ART practices as a nonchoice, serving as a limit to liberal notions of reproductive freedom, as a means of justifying and maintaining current racial inequalities, and as a way to separate current efforts to master reproduction from past ones.

It is my hope that these chapters, taken together, will lead the reader to think about both race and assisted reproduction (and the two together) in new and nuanced ways. Perhaps this particular investigation of ARTs will expand the reader's notion of which topics ought to be considered in the realm of bioethics and of how such consideration might take place. Perhaps thinking of race technologically will begin to illuminate for the reader the construction and function of race in an entirely different context. At the very least, I hope the reader encounters and is intrigued by a few histories and contemporary practices of which she was not previously aware.

Notes

1. Taylor, *Race*, 9.
2. See, for example, Roberts, *Fatal Invention*; or Weiss and Fullerton, "Racing Around, Getting Nowhere."
3. Ikemoto, "In/Fertile, Too Fertile, Dysfertile," 1013.
4. Bernasconi, "Critical Philosophy of Race," 551.
5. Crenshaw et al., *Critical Race Theory*, viii.
6. Ibid.
7. Ibid., xiii.
8. Ibid., xiv.
9. Ibid., xxxii.
10. Taylor, *Race*, 15.
11. Mills, review of *Ethics along the Color Line*, 190.
12. Taylor, *Race*, 13.
13. Ibid., 38.

14. Ibid., 47–48.
15. Ibid., 23.
16. Ibid., 49.
17. Ibid., 50.
18. Ibid., 51.
19. Hoffman, "Science of Race," 4.
20. Appiah and Gutmann, *Color Conscious*, 81.
21. Outlaw, *On Race and Philosophy*, 5.
22. Ibid., 7.
23. Ibid., 8.
24. Stubblefield, *Ethics along the Color Line*, 72.
25. Ibid., 73.
26. Ibid., 71.
27. Ibid., 12.
28. Young, *Intersecting Voices*, 17.
29. Mills, *Racial Contract*, 125–26.
30. Bernasconi, "Critical Philosophy of Race," 555; Sartre, *Critique of Dialectical Reason*, 171.
31. Mills, *Racial Contract*, 125.
32. Bernasconi, "Nature, Culture, and Race," 1, my emphasis.
33. Ibid.
34. Montagu, *Man's Most Dangerous Myth*, 20.
35. UNESCO, "Statement of 1950," 497.
36. Bernasconi, "Nature, Culture, and Race," 3.
37. Ibid., 6, 21.
38. Voegelin, "Growth of the Race Idea," 283–84, my emphasis.
39. Ibid., 284.
40. Voegelin, *Race and State*, 8.
41. Voegelin, "Growth of the Race Idea," 285–86.
42. Voegelin, *Race and State*, 8.
43. Mamdani, "Race and Ethnicity as Political Identities in the African Context," 7.
44. Ibid., 4.
45. Ibid., 7.
46. Ibid., 16.
47. Ibid., 9.
48. Taylor, *Race*, 52.

1 Reproductive Technologies Are Not "Post-Racial"

ANDREA CANNING (Voiceover) Michael and Tracey admit having this Indian woman potentially give birth to their child is a strange concept. But the couples who come here are color-blind. They just want a baby.

—*ABC News Transcript,* Good Morning America, *September 28, 2007*

I‍т was the above line in a *Good Morning America* news story that first sparked my interest in the role of race in assisted reproductive technologies (ARTs). The piece introduced the so-called outsourcing of surrogacy to India (also known as reproductive tourism), portraying it as a sort of strange but practical last resort and citing a fertility clinic in India where "women are lining up to carry babies for American couples at a fraction of the cost."[1] The whole notion was new and fascinating to me at the time, but I was also struck by the story's use of the term *color-blind*. As a popular American ideal, *color blindness* (in the figurative sense that concerns whether or not one "sees" race) is dubious at best. The idea is that those who are color-blind will treat everyone equally regardless of race, color, or creed, but many would argue not only that most people cannot help "seeing" and reacting to race, even if only on an unconscious level, but also that treating people appropriately involves taking respectful account of their difference rather than denying it all together. More to the point, however, it is not at all clear what *work* the color-blind ideal is supposed to be doing in this surrogacy story. If to say that someone is figuratively color-blind is supposed to indicate that that person does not see (or pay attention to) the skin color (or race or ethnicity) of the people with whom she interacts, then the fact that Michael and Tracy "admit" that their surrogate's ethnicity makes her role as their surrogate into a "strange concept" would seem to be a contradiction. Indeed, this sort of contradiction and the reluctance to speak openly about racial preferences it reflects lie at the heart of my work in this chapter. Michael and Tracy are both using race in the creation of their family and denying that very use—a denial that is critical to the success of the use itself.

Of course, it may be that to be color-blind simply means that the person in question, while *noting* another person's color/race/ethnicity, chooses not to take it as a relevant factor with regard to whether or how one should interact with that other person. If this is the case, we might be able to say that Michael and Tracy and the other non-Indian couples who have gone to India as reproductive tourists are color-blind in the sense that they did not intend to let the fact that these surrogates were Indian stand in the way of their quests for babies. But even then we must note that the circumstances offered significant financial incentives to such couples to ignore the skin color of their surrogates. Further, we ought to acknowledge that from Michael and Tracy's perspective, the most important skin color to be concerned with was likely that of their child, to whom the Indian surrogate would not be genetically related. Were they expecting (and perfectly content) to receive a child who would be visually identified as part Indian— that is, if gestation were thought to impart ethnic or racial characteristics or identity—then the color-blind label might be more appropriate (especially if they were paying full price).

A few days after seeing the story on television, I looked up it up on the ABC website; but while the story I found was very familiar, the reference to color blindness was nowhere to be seen.[2] In fact, when I finally retrieved from Lexis-Nexis the transcript of what I had heard and compared it to the online story, that reference seemed to be the only significant detail to have been removed. While someone apparently thought better of that particular piece of copy, I believe its odd placement in the original story marks the often implicit yet critical importance of race in ART practices. Indeed, as we shall see, race seems always to be lurking just below the surface when it comes to assisted reproduction.

In what follows, I will make explicit the often implicit operations of race in ART practices. This explicit and detailed highlighting of race is a novel move, not only within mainstream bioethics and the philosophy of technology but even with respect to critical feminist approaches. For the purposes of the forthcoming discussion, assisted reproductive technologies should be understood, following Charis Thompson, as "the means that are used in noncoital, technically assisted reproduction where gametes are manipulated or embryos are created outside the body."[3] These include techniques and practices like in vitro fertilization, artificial insemination, and surrogacy. Feminists working on ARTs have uncovered a number of limitations of certain bioethical frameworks for thinking about ARTs, including an overemphasis on individual rights, and concomitant failures to attend to social and political contexts and inequalities. Nevertheless, it has been difficult for many feminist analyses to look at both race and gender at the same time.

In an effort to foreground the issue of race (and push beyond individualistic or autonomy-based frameworks), I adopt and model one possible use of philosophy of technology to interrogate the relationship between race and ARTs. Race, in these contexts, tends to be treated by ART users and practitioners as a property that resides within human gametes (sperm or eggs) and that can be known by identifying the race of the person whence the gamete came. In other words, it seems to hold a sort of *pseudogenetic* status. Yet because, for reasons discussed in the introduction, we are more concerned here with what race *does* than what it *is*, I believe a more precise definition of race would only hinder the forthcoming analysis. Ultimately, by leaving open the definition of race and focusing instead on the variety of ways the concept can be put to work in ARTs, we will arrive at a much richer and more nuanced understanding of how race undergirds our contemporary notions of reproduction and family formation.

I begin now by introducing both some feminist critiques of traditional bioethical approaches to ARTs and some alternative considerations that animate feminist work on the subject. I then touch briefly on the question of intersectionality as it pertains to my analysis. Next, I introduce a set of questions that Neil Postman uses in his philosophy of technology, arguing that they serve as a useful lens for bypassing bioethical approaches and examining more critically the role of race in ART practices. The largest and remaining portion of the chapter is then spent working through this lens, wherein I suggest that norms of whiteness have shaped the social construction of fertility and infertility, that ART practices are enmeshed with local and global systems of inequality, and that the idea of race is used to police the "natural" in ART practices.

Beyond the Bioethical Approach

Typically, philosophers have addressed questions to do with reproduction and reproductive technologies in terms of ethics or bioethics. Exemplary of bioethical approaches in general are Beauchamp and Childress's famous four principles of biomedical ethics: autonomy, beneficence, nonmaleficence, and justice (conceived in terms of fair distribution of goods and services). For Beauchamp and Childress, ethical practice is achieved when these four principles, which may come into conflict in any given biomedical situation, are weighed and balanced to the best of one's ability.[4]

While philosophers utilizing this and similar approaches have opened up a variety of important points for discussion and debate, the work of feminist philosophers on ARTs has revealed how traditional bioethical frameworks can suffer certain limitations. Take, for example, Heather Deitrich's discussion of her experience on the Australian National Bioethics Consultative Committee in 1988, in which she argues that bioethics as a framework for discussions of reproductive technologies often stands in tension with feminists' concerns and goals. "In bioethics, as in economics," she writes, "an emphasis on liberal individual rights is a conservative ideology. It neither recognizes nor includes the differentials of power between people in the society to which it is applied."[5] She argues that because a clear separation between abstract intellectual principles and "moral, emotional desires or liking" was established in the deliberations, despite the committee's gender-equal membership, "arguments that began 'surrogacy does not seem or feel right' could not hold their own against propositions based on intellectual principles attributed to prominent philosophers and steeped in historical references." Furthermore, "lost between the head and the heart poles was the notion of the 'social'—the social context and social construction of the surrogacy arrangements being considered."[6] In the end, Deitrich reports, "The ethical considerations, which the report took to be its main concern, excluded any consideration of class, gender, or race. Equity was not interpreted in the current socioeconomic context, but it was taken to mean individual rights and how to promote them."[7]

Note that while Deitrich and her fellow feminist dissenters on the committee were very much concerned with justice, they did not frame it in terms of the distribution of goods or services. Rather, they were concerned with what I might label the *political*—that is, social responsibility, collective life, and the dynamics of social orders. When a bioethical approach seeks primarily to justify or condemn particular uses of particular reproductive technologies by particular individuals, such an attempt risks creating a separation between the ethical and the political. The ethical, where it is centered on autonomy conceived in terms of personal freedom, comes to be concerned only with what is permissible in ART practices in terms of individually conceived ethical rights, duties, obligations, or prohibitions. With ethical rules in place, reproductive decision-making is taken to be a private matter, with little relevance to politics or (nondistributive) social justice.

By contrast, explicitly feminist approaches to ARTs have been guided by a core set of feminist concerns that urge us to think beyond this type of ethical framework. In most feminist work on ARTs, one can find appeals to one or more of the following broad, overlapping feminist principles: (1) the promotion of women's autonomy and empowerment, including women's control over their own bodies; (2) a commitment to identifying and altering structures that create or uphold women's oppression; (3) the promotion of women's well-being—physical, mental, and economic; (4) a commitment to valuing both women's experience and forms of work traditionally performed by women; (5) an attempt to recognize and valorize the diversity of women's experiences; and (6) a recognition of and commitment to addressing the intersecting forms of oppression and privilege experienced by women on the basis not only of gender but of class, race, sexuality, nationality, ability, and other intersectional statuses. (Arguably, while the first four principles have long been at the core of feminism, the last two emerged and became particularly important through and following a series of criticisms leveled against white, middle-class bias in second-wave feminism.) Not only do these principles themselves insist on attention to social context and sociopolitical inequality, but attempts to apply the principles call into question any aim of ultimately justifying or condemning most ART practices.

Indeed, evaluation of the feminist literature on ARTs reveals that these principles can generally be used to argue for *or* against the use of ARTs. Not only is it difficult to find a single feminist principle that can offer a clear answer about whether ARTs are laudable or deplorable, but making almost any argument based on one principle seems to risk contradicting another. For example, if one argues that ARTs increase autonomy for all women, one risks ignoring intersectionality and the way that different ART practices affect different women in different ways. If one argues that commercial surrogacy practices should be banned because they risk exploiting poor or nonwhite women, one risks implying that poor or nonwhite women are incapable of appropriately exercising their agency and cannot be trusted to avoid that which is not in their best interests. If one argues that reproductive technologies alienate women from their reproductive experience by downplaying or disregarding the feelings of connectedness inherent in gestation and childbirth, one risks portraying as unnatural those women who experience pregnancy differently or those who have no desire to experience pregnancy at all and would prefer an experience of reproduction that more closely matches that of men. If one argues that the desire for biological children is socially constructed and contributes to systems of gender oppression, one risks unfairly dismissing the suffering of infertile women who do experience the desire for biological children. As Jennifer Parks describes, while feminists have been thinking and talking about ARTs for decades, "it is still an open question whether ART will eventually bring about radical change or whether radical change is required before ART can be liberating." She argues that the length of the debate, along with the fact that both society and the technologies are in constant flux, suggests that an "either/or," "good/bad" approach to the effects of ARTs is neither realistic nor desirable.[8]

Given this complexity, my work here does not take sides on feminist debates about ARTs. Instead, I will use these feminist debates to affirm three major ideological or methodological commitments already suggested by the earlier discussion of *Critical Philosophy of Race*: (1) the need for close attention to social context in order to avoid uncritically reifying assumptions that support current social and political inequalities, (2) the challenging of any stance's claim to political neutrality and the acknowledgment of one's own partiality and founding assumptions, and (3) a willingness to engage in and to remain engaged in continual criticism and self-reflection. Therefore, in contrast to ethical approaches that are based on individual rights, autonomy, and decision-making and that focus on offering prescriptions for action, I argue that a *political* analysis of race and reproductive technologies must take up issues of social and political structures and inequalities, of power relations, and of the role that notions of race have played in creating and maintaining these. It must consider how reproductive technologies evolve from, participate in, reinforce, and even shift these structures and relations. Rather than placing limits on what is ethically permissible only where we can identify specific harms to the personal freedom of other individuals, we must give attention to historical context, social values, and often intangible harms to socially defined groups.

One way to achieve this broader perspective is through questions and insights brought forward in philosophy of technology. According to Langdon Winner, "The basic task for a philosophy of technology is to examine critically the nature and significance of artificial aids to human activity."[9] I therefore aim to examine critically both (1) the nature and significance of assisted reproductive technologies to American ideas and practices surrounding race and (2) the nature and significance of race ideas to assisted reproductive technology practices. I do so using a series of questions offered by Neil Postman concerning for what and for *whom* technologies are intended and the unintended consequences that may flow from their use. Using these questions I explore the racialized construction of infertility, the ways in which ART practices can participate in and further systems of global inequality, and the role of race in the construction and maintenance of the "natural" in and through ART use. This analysis shows that ARTs are far from racially neutral.

First, however, a brief note on the issue of intersectionality (that is, concern for the effects of multiple forms of social disadvantage) in ART contexts. As I implied above, women of color have criticized some white feminists for failing to take race into account in their gender-based analyses of ARTs. These critics have also offered their own analyses of ARTs, which have centered on the (previously marginalized) reproductive experiences of women of color. Grounding one's work in the lived experiences of members of marginalized communities— as Dorothy Roberts does in *Killing the Black Body*, to offer just one example—is a hallmark of one intersectional approach to scholarship.[10] However, while this intersectional method, with its focus on overlapping and interacting forms of marginalization and oppression, is an extremely important one, it is not the approach taken in this work. Instead of focusing primarily on the experiences that raced individuals may have or have had with ARTs, I have focused on how concepts of race operate within and are reinforced by ART practices. Given this focus on operations of race (rather than the experience of raced individuals), I suggest that in order to think productively about the role of various social positions and identities (like race, gender, sexuality, class, and disability) in the analyses of ART practices that follow, it may help to think of the relationship between these social positions and identities as analogous to that between (shifting) foreground and background.

In offering this suggestion, I draw on Ellen Feder's work on the relationship between race and gender in academic analysis. In Feder's account we find an image that "captures the confounding inability to regard simultaneously the operation of race and gender in what are sometimes called 'reversible figure-ground' drawings, popularized by Gestalt psychologists." One well known example of such a drawing—typically rendered in black and white—is seen as depicting either a vase or two faces in profile. Which image one sees—vase or faces—depends on whether the white or the black is considered the background. Moreover, we cannot see both at once: "Despite the fact that the contours of the vase define the faces and vice versa, each image becomes visible only when the other image is forced to the ground; only one is visible at a time."[11]

Trying to see the operation of both race and gender can be much like trying to see both the vase and the faces. The one often forms the background against which the operation of the other becomes visible. This particular contrast between race and gender may be particularly salient when it comes to issues of family and reproduction because, while the (heterosexual) family is seen as a site of gender *difference*, it is simultaneously expected (as we shall see) to be a site of racial *sameness*. Work that focuses on gender dynamics in assisted reproduction may thus take the reproduction of race in these contexts for granted. Similarly, my efforts to uncover racial dimensions of ART practices may leave certain gendered assumptions (along with assumptions about sexuality, class, ability, etc.) undertheorized.

The Gestalt drawings are a simplified representation of our analytical processes; they are rendered in two colors. When talking about complex, real-world situations, however, the background for the focus of our analysis will necessarily be made up of a variety of suppressed assumptions. Where possible, I will make reference to the more salient background assumptions for a particular issue, but there will be a great deal left unsaid. For example, when I argue that ARTs as infertility treatment target the infertility issues at a certain intersection of race and class, I note (but do not discuss) the fact that the problem of delayed child-bearing among middle-class white women is a function of gendered divisions of labor. Similarly, when I speak about racial matching, even among same-sex couples, I do not interrogate the importance given to matching a donor to the intended parent and the relationship of that practice to gendered historical notions of kinship and legitimacy. And later (in chapter 5), when I argue that the idea of racial selection is used as a boundary that marks when a new eugenic project will have gone too far, I do not discuss the demonization of disability that underlies many of those new eugenic projects and is rarely questioned. In short, while in the following discussions (and the rest of the book) I have intentionally focused on race, this should not be taken to mean that gender, sexuality, class, and ableism are not in operation. Rather, these analytical dimensions have been pushed to the back, where they form the background against which the function of race is made visible.

Whose Progress?

Philosopher of technology Neil Postman argues that in the twentieth century, "the idea that progress is real, humane, and inevitable died," leaving us with the burden of believing that "*we* must make our own future, bend history to our own will." According to Postman: "Perhaps because of such a psychic burden, we have held on to the idea of progress but in a form that no eighteenth-century philosopher or early-nineteenth-century heir of the Enlightenment would have embraced—could possibly have embraced: the idea that technological innovation is *synonymous* with moral, social and psychic progress."[12] Though Postman believes we are *capable* of adapting to a good many new technologies, whether or not such adaptation would actually represent moral, social, or psychic progress is very a different matter. He suggests we consider whether any given technology represents progress by asking a series of six questions:

1. What is the problem to which this technology is the solution?
2. Whose problem is it?
3. Which people and what institutions might be most seriously harmed by a technological solution?
4. What new problems might be created because we have solved this problem?
5. What sort of people and institutions might acquire special economic and political power because of technological change?
6. What changes in language are being enforced by new technologies, and what is being gained and lost by such changes?[13]

Each of these questions can, and indeed should, be considered in reference to assisted reproductive technologies, racial identities, and the institutions of race and racism.

The "Problem" of Infertility

What is the problem to which ARTs are the solution, and whose problem is it? It makes sense to take the first two questions together since, as will become apparent, they are constitutively linked. According to Ikemoto, as the fertility industry has formed and developed, ART use, initially cast as "infertility treatment," was recast first as "assisted reproduction" and more recently in terms of "family formation" (with the latter focusing on the end product—parents and children—rather than on the initial issue or the means used to address that issue).[14] Nevertheless, a typical understanding of ARTs still sees them as tools for helping a person or couple to conceive a child where such conception cannot be achieved through simple sexual intercourse. Thus, if one thinks in terms of the problem to be addressed with technologies at a fertility clinic, that problem is still understood as *infertility* (a term that has the heterosexual couple as its background assumption). This "problem," however, is not a given natural fact that simply presents itself in its objective significance during the course of our human experience. Quite the contrary, as Ikemoto argues, "human procreation, and in/fertility in particular, is a culturally significant site upon which political contests play out." This means, among other things, that "the dominant understandings of infertility and the infertile are shaped with respect to our understanding of fertility and the fertile."[15] These understandings, we shall see, are thoroughly raced.

Though we tend to think of *reproductive technologies* as those technologies that *facilitate* reproduction, as Janice Raymond and many other feminists have pointed out, there are two sides to the technological reproduction coin. On one side, "In the industrialized countries of the West and the North, it is *infertility* that is of concern to the reproductive experts who tell us that infertility rates are skyrocketing," thereby justifying "invasive medical intervention, drugs, and surgery on women 'for our own good.'" On the other side, "In the East and in the developing South, it is *fertility* that is of concern to the reproductive experts. . . . This perception of unrestrained female fertility justifies invasive medical intervention—contraceptives, sterilization, and, most recently, sex predetermination used on women in developing countries."[16]

Of course, another way to describe these two opposing parts of the world would be *white* and *nonwhite*. The imagined hyperfertility of nonwhite people has appeared as a "problem" in a variety of historical contexts. Anglo-European colonists, particularly in large, permanent settlements like that of South Africa, were given to the fear of their cities being "swamped" by the already majority, and seemingly more fertile, native populations.[17] In the United States in the early twentieth century, nonwhite immigrants seemed to pose a similar threat, providing one of the arguments against making voluntary birth control available to the white middle and upper classes. Poor, rural whites were also thought not only to reproduce in excess quantity but to produce children of inferior quality, thereby threatening the deterioration of the white race.[18] Since the postcolonial period, the danger posed by "excessive" fertility in the so-called Third World or Global South has been expressed in terms of global overpopulation. Similarly, in the United States in the second half of the twentieth century, poor, urban blacks are often criticized for perpetuating their own poverty and draining state resources by bearing too many (illegitimate) children.[19] In other words the understanding of when, where, and why *in*fertility is considered a problem is connected to the same longtime assumptions and anxieties that have historically fueled various eugenics movements—assumptions and anxieties about how those populations seen as most fit might be overrun by those seen as least fit.

"The major paradox of infertility," writes Marcia Inhorn, "is that its prevalence is often greatest in those areas of the world where fertility is the highest."[20]

Were we to assume that, as a "solution" to the problem of "infertility," we would find the highest use of ARTs where infertility rates were highest, we would be sorely misled. Both within the United States and globally, "Poor women have greater rates of infertility than do middle-class women, but they receive less infertility treatment and are exposed to more childbearing-related risks than more privileged women."[21] This is not simply because in the United States and in many places across the globe ARTs are rarely publicly funded and thus require significant private resources. It is important to look beyond disparity in individual economic means to the broader causes of infertility in order to evaluate ARTs *as a solution.*

A major cause of infertility among poor women (and disproportionately minorities) is untreated sexually transmitted infection or poor medical treatment during an earlier birth—the social and political product of what Shanley and Asch describe as "overlapping and linked racial and economic factors."[22] Were we interested in helping these women, relatively affordable preventative measures (that would be good for health in general as well as fertility) would seem to make much more sense than expensive ex post facto interventions. By contrast, infertility among industrial and agricultural hourly wageworkers is often the result of workplace and environmental toxins. ARTs also seem an ill-fitting solution for this population.[23] Indeed, the only systemic infertility problem for which ARTs may seem like the best solution is that of delayed childbearing—which disproportionately affects professional and white-collar workers—since infertility that results from a woman's advanced age cannot be prevented in the way the other causes can. (Though certainly the gendered social structures that often force women in their twenties to choose between laying the foundations for professional success or starting families *could* be altered, rendering medical-technological solutions unnecessary).

In any case, we begin to see that far from being an ideal solution for infertility at large, ARTs have arisen and developed with the concerns of a certain population in mind and bear many traces of that particular standpoint. Ikemoto and others argue that ideological divisions between white and nonwhite, the infertile and the too fertile, not only unconsciously guide ART thinking and policy in the United States but are also reinforced by it. Roberts, for example, cites "some evidence that fertility doctors and clinics deliberately steer Black patients away from reproductive technologies," arguing that physicians cannot help but "import their own social views into the clinical setting" and that some practitioners "may feel that fertility treatment is inappropriate for Black women who they think are unable to care for their children."[24] Because fertility clinics and practitioners are necessary for high-tech fertility interventions, their explicit policies and less explicit standard operating procedures serve as gatekeeping mechanisms, determining which women (within which family structures) are "deemed not only infertile, but also fit for use."[25]

At the same time, as I will discuss below, in cases where people besides the intended parents are involved, the courts serve as the ultimate arbiter of which people should be the parents—or, in the most publicized cases, of which *woman* counts as the *real* mother. According to Ikemoto, "The answers to the questions, who *should be* the parents [decided by the courts] and which women *should be* mothers [decided by practitioners] converge at this point where race (white) and economic privilege meet." At this point of convergence, where "should be" lies, the ideals of "woman" and "mother" conflate. "That is, whiteness, middle class status, and a particular permutation of gendered woman form the right side of the line, while a raceless, classless, denatured woman forms on the other side of the line." In other words, it is white, middle class, married, heterosexual women who are meant to be mothers and who, if so unlucky as to be infertile or to be married to men who are infertile, deserve the aid of the medical establishment. And, in the case that such women should selfishly delay parenthood until it is almost "too late," ARTs lie in wait to usher those women back into their natural place. In stories of successful "treatment" of white, middle-class, married women over thirty, "the infertile were always mothers; they were the only ones who did not realize that. It was their exercise of choice and control that denatured them. And it is the use of technology that can restore them to nature."[26]

The image of the infertile white career woman as selfish in exercising too much will by not accepting her natural role as mother, then, stands in contrast to the image of the too fertile woman of color who bears children too young, too often, and out of wedlock due to her inherent *weakness* of will—her selfish inability to control her sexual appetites, which, though welfare payments, will soon prove a drain on society. The mutually constitutive nature of these images is demonstrated in the following comment from the *Chicago Tribune* defending a fifty-nine-year-old British woman who, in 1993, was able to give birth to twins by means of egg donation and in vitro fertilization:

> What has the woman done that merits such ethical concern and public criticism? She isn't an unmarried, 15-year-old high school dropout whose unplanned baby will put her on welfare, perhaps for decades. She isn't 21 and having her fourth baby by four men, none of whom will actively father their children.
>
> She hasn't been using crack or other illegal drugs during pregnancy, condemning her unborn infant to neurological problems of unpredictable severity. She's not passing along the AIDS virus or forcing fetal alcohol syndrome on her child by drinking. She's not risking her baby's health by skipping prenatal care. Her twins aren't the unintended and unwanted consequences of careless sex.[27]

These highly racialized images, which refer very clearly if not explicitly to poor black women and girls in the American racial imaginary, are thus used to mark out which women are deserving of motherhood and thus of technological assistance in achieving motherhood and which women are not deserving of motherhood and not only should not be helped but should in fact be prevented from becoming mothers.

Referring back to Postman's first two questions, then, we might say that ARTs are intended to solve the problem of infertility and that infertility, by relatively implicit cultural understanding, is the problem of heterosexual, middle-class, married white women who have delayed childbirth in favor of careers. Where ARTs are (consciously or unconsciously) understood in this way, whether in the United States or globally, they may simply not be offered or made available to certain populations who are seen as "too fertile." Thus, Maura Ryan points out, even when "the prevalence of infertility in resource-poor countries is acknowledged, it is often with the unstated assumption that social investments in overcoming infertility are inappropriate, either because infertility is regarded as a natural antidote to population pressures . . . or because the low priority of infertility services in underfunded and heavily burdened healthcare economies is obvious." Under this assumption, little recognition is made of the fact that social factors in these countries may in fact *increase* the priority of infertility services. For example, "in some parts of the global South, especially in high-fertility, pronatalist societies, an infertile woman is at high risk for domestic violence (either at the hands of a partner or her extended family), abandonment and/or divorce, and infidelity."[28]

The social construction of categories of fertility and infertility does not complete my answer to Postman's questions, however. We must also consider the views of potential ART users themselves, which, in the case of nonwhite users, are often shaped by histories in which reproduction and reproductive technologies were used *against* their communities. Though in later articles (2005 and 2009) Roberts will note an increase both in the marketing of ARTs to nonwhite women and couples and in the utilization by nonwhites of such services, in her *Killing the Black Body* (1997) she does speculate on the effects the experiences and perceptions of potential black fertility "patients" might have on their desire to utilize such technologies. Assuming that infertile couples' reliance on advanced technologies "reflects a confidence in medical science to solve life's predicaments," and given the fact that "where new reproductive technologies have been directed towards Blacks, they have been used to restrict procreative freedom, not increase it," Roberts suggests that "many Blacks harbor a well-founded distrust of technological interference with their bodies and genetic material at the hands of white physicians."[29] Similarly, Ryan notes that feminists may be ambivalent about encouraging ARTs as a solution to infertility in the Global South given that many areas have a "history of externally or hierarchically imposed family planning programs; under such conditions, the contradictory possibilities of ART as means of healing and vehicle of control are especially visible." She adds: "Concern among women's rights advocates that ART will further subject women to the control of the state are underscored by the evidence in some areas (e.g., India) that IVF has been offered precisely to encourage the acceptance of sterilization."[30]

In some cases, those women or couples who classify themselves as "infertile" and are seeking a solution that will allow them to raise children have other options to choose from—most obviously adoption. As Roberts points out, ARTs have "far more to do with enabling people to have children who are genetically related to them than with helping infertile people to have children." Roberts thus suggests that, as opposed to white couples, black couples may be less concerned with genetic ties and more likely to turn to adoption first, especially as a means to help out black children in need. "Blacks have understandably resisted defining personal identity in biological terms," she writes. "In America, whites have historically valued genetic linkages and controlled their official meaning. As the powerful class, they are the guardians of the privileges accorded to biology and they have a greater stake in maintaining the importance of genetics." Given this history, she argues, blacks "tend to see group membership as a political and cultural affiliation" rather than a biological one and that black "family ties have traditionally reached beyond the bounds of the nuclear family to include extended kin and non-kin relationships."[31] As we will see in chapter 5, Roberts's more recent work (2011) is critical of new trends toward seeing racial minority membership in genetic terms.

Of course, some white couples' use of ARTs rather than adoption may have a different though still race-based reason. In the late 1970s, during the same period that the first "test-tube baby" was born (Louise Brown in 1978), there was a great deal of discussion about a "shortage" of healthy white babies available for adoption. Birth control, abortion, and the greater willingness of unwed mothers to keep their children were cited as some of the social changes responsible for this "shortage," though the "nonmarket, agency system of allocating children for adoption" was also criticized for contributing to "long queues for distributing healthy white babies."[32] This so-called shortage has not disappeared, and (white) race, (young) age, and (good) health continue to determine which children are adopted and which remain within the child welfare system. Thus, insofar as it is important to an infertile white couple to obtain a healthy white infant, ARTs may appear not simply as the most appealing but indeed as the *only* feasible solution.

Reproducing Inequalities

We now turn to the next two questions: *Which people and what institutions might be most seriously harmed by a technological solution? And what new problems might be created because we have solved this problem?* Here it would certainly be right to speak of the harm done to women of color by the perpetuation in ART discourses of images that portray their sexuality as inherently deviant and poisonous to society. As Patricia Hill Collins and other black feminist thinkers have amply demonstrated, the harm perpetrated by such controlling images is not merely ideological; the portrayal of women of color as "too fertile" can have real material effects—for example, on the type and level reproductive care women of color receive from individual practitioners or on state and national welfare policy.[33] If we are looking, however, for emergence of *new* problems due to advances in ARTs—problems whose effects are not racially neutral—we need look no further than the growing popularity of gestational (or IVF) surrogacy.

Surrogacy today can be traditional, where the child is genetically related to the surrogate, or gestational, where the surrogate carries a fetus not genetically related to her, its embryo having been implanted in her following IVF; it can also be altruistic (typically a private, familial affair) or commercial (in which a surrogacy contract is often made between the intended parents and a woman who was previously a stranger to them through a clinic or agency). While an "altruistic," traditional surrogacy is actually mentioned in the Bible—when Sarah encourages Abraham to impregnate her servant, Hagar—the first commercial surrogacy seems not to have taken place until 1980.[34] Following not long after, the first gestational surrogacy was successfully attempted in 1986. According to Heléna Ragoné, when she began her research in 1988, gestational surrogacy, due to its high-tech costs and low success rates, was not terribly popular and accounted for fewer than 5 percent of all surrogate arrangements. By 1994, however, that percentage had increased to 50, and by 2003 gestational surrogacy was thought to account for 95 percent of all surrogacies.[35]

Though using a surrogate of a difference race would have been *physically* or *logistically* possible with traditional surrogacy, it has only become socially possible and, indeed, desirable with gestational surrogacy. Of course, there are and have been individuals and couples who opt for interracial and often transnational adoption, whether for reasons of infertility or otherwise. As far as the use of ARTs is concerned, however, the expectation has always been that a child *created* will "match" the intended parents racially or ethnically. This, as I will discuss in more detail below with regards to the last two of Postman's questions, is considered "natural." As Ikemoto points out, though in reference to a different reproductive technology, "to the extent we assume that those using artificial insemination choose donors of the same race as themselves, we do not think of racial selection."[36] To create a baby of one's own race, with or without technological assistance, is considered so natural as not to even constitute a choice. We can imagine, then, that it would not even occur to white couples seeking *traditional* surrogates to look for a woman who was anything other than white.

That gestational surrogacy would change this racial "necessity" cannot even be said to be an unpredicted consequence of the new technology. Eerily enough, even before its successful execution in 1986, the new possibilities for gestational surrogacy were laid out by John Stehura of the Bionetics Foundation, Inc., an organization that arranged traditional commercial surrogacies. The prediction, as Gena Corea documents in her 1985 book, *The Mother Machine*, was that "once it is possible to have what Stehura calls an 'authentic' surrogate—a woman into whom an embryo is transferred and who herself contributes none of the child's genes—clients will find the breeder's IQ and skin color immaterial" and that at this time "the surrogate industry could look for breeders—not only in poverty-stricken parts of the United States, but in the Third World as well." Stehura also speculated (with what turns out to be disturbing accuracy) that in these cases "perhaps one tenth the current fee could be paid women."[37]

Today, both of Stehura's possibilities have become realities. Women of color in the United States and abroad have served as surrogates for white Western couples. Regarding the US domestic case, Deborah Grayson (among others) argues that:

> Gestational surrogacy invites the singling out of black women for exploitation not only because a disproportionate number of black women are poor and might possibly turn to leasing their wombs as a means of income, but also because it is incorrectly assumed that black women's skin color can be read as a visual sign of their lack of genetic relation to the children they would bear for the white couples who seek to hire them.[38]

The well-publicized case of *Johnson v. Calvert* seems to bear out that intuition. In that case, Anna Johnson, a single black woman, fought Mark and Crispina Calvert, a white man and a Filipina woman, for the rights to a child who was genetically theirs but whom Johnson had carried and delivered. As Valerie Hartouni describes, racial ideas and images were deployed in the case to discredit Johnson and her connection to the child while shoring up the Calverts' claim. For example, the fact that Johnson was black and had once been on welfare, which was brought up in court, "signified, among other things, moral depravity, lack of veracity, and capacity for deception. It marked her as someone capable of deceiving the Calverts and exploiting their procreative yearnings in a coldly calculating fashion, for gain—indeed as someone who lied rather than simply changed her mind." Meanwhile, Crispina Calvert "asserted repeatedly in court and to the press, 'He looks just like us.'"[39] Thus while gestational surrogacy is already perceived to be more secure for intended parents because the courts are likely to recognize the genetic connection as making the child *theirs*, the racial *difference* between the surrogate and the child gestated becomes an extra resource for establishing that child as *not hers*. There is some sense of extra (legal) safety achieved by contracting with a surrogate that "anyone can see" is not the "true" mother of the child in question.

This sense of security is perhaps only magnified in the case of transnational commercial surrogacy, a type of *reproductive tourism*. Reproductive tourism is most often described and discussed as a growing trend in which wealthy and middle-class couples from North America, the Middle East, Europe, New Zealand, and Australia travel to fertility clinics in India, Malaysia, Thailand, South Africa, Guatemala, Russia, and the Ukraine where services are significantly less expensive. (As Ikemoto points out, however, differences in laws, social rules, costs, or availability, along with concerns for privacy, often make Western nations reproductive tourism *destinations* as well, rather than merely points of departure.)

The exemplary case of transnational commercial surrogacy (or at least the one that has received the most media coverage) is that of India, which became a leading service provider for surrogacy "seemingly overnight" and continued in this role until its government outlawed surrogacy for foreigners in 2015. Between 2006 and 2008, India saw a 150 percent rise in surrogacy cases, and an oft-repeated estimate from 2008 described the surrogacy industry as an almost $445 million business in India, with the Indian Council for Medical Research expecting profits to reach $6 billion in the coming years. Though the exact savings are difficult to pin down, many estimates suggest that foreign couples paid two to ten times less for surrogacy in India than they would have in their home countries (and they often got tourist packages in India to boot). As Alison Bailey described: "India is well-positioned to lead the world in making commercial gestational surrogacy a viable industry: labor is cheap, doctors are highly qualified, English is spoken, adoptions are closed, and the government has aggressively worked to establish an infrastructure for medical tourism." Moreover, no laws restricted the industry before 2015, aside from a 2013 decision by the Indian government to stop issuing medical tourist visas to same-sex couples; with respect to regulation there were only government guidelines, which the estimated three thousand fertility clinics operating in India could choose to follow or not to follow. Indeed, these guidelines were criticized by Indian feminists for their focus on facilitating the growth of the industry and protecting the rights of foreign consumers rather than protecting the health of the surrogates, ensuring their rights, or guarding against their exploitation.[40]

"Until now," wrote Amrita Banerjee, "most of the philosophical literature on commercial surrogacy has been concentrated in ethics, and the dominant analyses have been through the lens of ethical paradigms such as reproductive liberalism versus the exploitation model." In arguments from (or marketing based on) reproductive liberalism, transnational surrogacy is often "projected as creating new opportunities/conditions for the surrogate to exercise greater autonomy than she could before." In most Indian cases, the surrogate was, after all, making the equivalent of nearly five years of total family income. Of course, the fact that the sum was so great relative to the surrogate's other earning opportunities lends support to the opposing exploitation arguments, which point to "the oppressive socio-political conditions (both local and global) in which she takes up or lives out her identity and sense of agency as a surrogate." But while the reproductive liberalism argument carries the danger of "normalizing or naturalizing power imbalances and the exploitation of the less powerful by the more powerful players of globalization," the "language of 'use' and 'control' at the heart of [the exploitation] paradigm can end up projecting individuals purely as passive victims who are always at the mercy of superior forces external to them."[41] Susan Markens finds the same "two competing frames: exploitation/inequality vs. opportunity/choice" in her analysis of US media framings and public discourses about transnational surrogacy.[42]

Keeping in mind the dangers of the exploitation model, I still think it is important to examine in general the global economic context in which transnational surrogacy arrangements take place and to consider in particular the roles that race or skin color and racialized inequalities played in this context. One way of doing this is to look at transnational commercial surrogacy as a form of labor within a globalized reproductive market and to consider the racialized nature of such a market. Simply put: "Surrogacy, like the kidney trade in India, brings together desperate but wealthy buyers with very poor sellers under conditions which almost always suit the former."[43] The inequalities of such exchanges, however, are not limited to the financial resources held by each party; the biological resources of the parties are also valued differently. As Sarojini, Marwah, and Shenoi point out, not only do "the physical, social and cultural attributes of the donor affect the price of the reproductive material," but "the movement of reproductive material and processes follows along 'modern routes of capital' flow—from 'South to North, from third world to first world, from poor to rich bodies, from black and brown to white bodies, from young to old bodies, from productive to less productive . . . bodies.'" They argue that it is "these processes and structures, which trade in reproductive material operates within and through, that raise significant questions for theory, praxis and policy."[44] Or, in Kalindi Vora's words: "Race and gender also operate in the global political economy to make some bodies more economically useful as biological entities than as the source of labor, and to render some subjects seemingly more appropriate for reorganization as biological laborers than others."[45] As a poor woman in the developing world, the Indian surrogate was offered more for her biological labor than she could ever earn through any other form of wage labor. At the same time, the color of her skin, read as symbolic of cultural deficiencies and socially disadvantageous for the desired child, rendered any genetic contribution on her part largely worthless.

Yet even as the surrogate's biological labor was being purchased, it was also devalued. Vora concluded:

> Articulating surrogacy as a form of work and identifying the value transmitted by the biological and affective commodities it produces—commodities that are invested directly by the work of care and nurture into an individual or community's life—enables us to view human lives as a site of the accumulation of the value produced by surrogates as workers. In the context of transnational surrogacy, this value is Indian surrogacy and commodified vital energy transmitted from lower resource communities to higher resource communities through the devaluing of this work as a result of its racialization and gendering.[46]

Race, then, plays a crucial part in the deep structural inequalities that characterize not only global markets in general but global reproductive markets in particular, with the contributions of nonwhite reproductive laborers being both necessary and necessarily erased. The result is described by Banerjee as a "transnational reproductive caste system," marked (1) by the stratification of women's reproductive labor within the global economy along racial and other lines, (2) by the physical, psychological, and structural violence of the transnational surrogacy industry, and (3) by an "unfair distribution of benefits, burdens, and opportunities across social hierarchies."[47]

Ultimately, it is white or lighter skin as a physical characteristic that is valued and actively produced, since such skin confers social advantage on the end products of reproductive markets: babies. Examples of the greater value conferred to lighter skin in the global reproductive market abound. Oddly, Bailey was one of few writers on the subject of transnational commercial surrogacy to give significant emphasis to this fact, aggregating examples from various sources. In one, a *Times of India* article noted: "Traits such as Fair skin, Lighter hair, Blue/green or light eyes and High IQ levels are greatly in demand by the Indian couples coming to fertility clinics." Sarojini, Marwah, and Shenoi even pointed to a form of "reverse tourism" seen in egg donation whereby companies bring in first world women to donate their eggs as well as travel in India. Florida-based Proactive Family Solutions (PFS) was one such subsidiary that recruited intended parents and egg donors. PFS provided intended parents with a pool of potential egg donors based on the client's criteria, which typically included hair and eye color and education level. Similarly, according to the president of Planet Hospital, client demand for ova from fair-skinned women was so high that donors were flown in from the former Soviet republic of Georgia to Indian clinics, and the company charged clients more for surrogacy packages that included those ova ($37,500 compared to $32,500 for one with Indian donor ova).[48]

Perhaps more surprising, however, is Bailey's highlighting of the fact that color and caste also played a central role in a surrogacy worker's negotiating power. For example, one clinician admitted: "Brahmans get paid more than so-called 'untouchables' or lower castes. A fair-skinned, educated middle-class Brahman who speaks English will fetch that much more." Similarly, another source claimed many foreign couples were interested in women from northern India because "they are healthy and whitish in color" while a surrogate agent explained how he could not find work for a south Indian woman because she was too dark. Bailey also pointed to a "Criteria for Selection of Surrogate" that Dr. Rama's Fertility Institute provided its customers so that they knew that "planned children are in good wombs":

> [T]he surrogate mother should be no smaller than 1.60 meters (5'3") and should weigh between 50 and 60 kilograms (110 and 132 pounds). She should be married, have her own children and a regular period, be free of sexually transmitted and hereditary diseases, be tested for ovarian problems and chromosomal analyses, be emotionally stable. . . . The skin color should not be too dark, and the appearance should be "pleasant."[49]

Ultimately, an analysis of thirty-three surrogacy-related advertisements conducted by Sama Resource Group for Women and Health, an Indian women's health resource group, revealed that about 40 percent of those ads specified that intended parents were looking for surrogates that were "fair, good-looking, and beautiful."[50] Since these were surrogates who would not be genetically related to the fetuses, Bailey speculated that "worries about skin color are most likely code for deeper worries about the surrogate's moral character," with "the racial markers that have historically marked lightskinned women as good mothers and dark-skinned women bad mothers [having] been extended to mark 'good' and 'bad' wombs."[51]

In an effort to mitigate against any discomfort by potential clients regarding the surrogate's health or moral character, some clinics operated surrogate dormitories or hostels where the surrogates were "literally kept under constant surveillance during their pregnancy—their food, medicines and daily activities . . . monitored by the medical staff."[52] Thus, contracting mother Julie, an American, reported hiring an Indian surrogate because "that kind of control would just not be possible in the United States." In the United States, Julie said, "you have no idea if your surrogate mother is smoking, drinking alcohol, [or] doing drugs. You have no idea what she's doing. You have a third-party agency as a mediator between the two of you, but there's no one policing her in the sense that you don't know what's going on."[53] This ability to have the surrogacy mediated by an agency focused on the intended parents/consumers was part of a set of "differences in class, race, etc." that seemed to "guarantee more power-over to [a contracting mother] in the relationship to begin with, in a way that might have been missing if she were to avail of the services of a woman in a better financial position, or of the same race, or one located in a different situation in the 'First World,' or all of these together."[54] Awareness of this power-over was reflected in British contracting mother Susan Morrison's comments in an interview with the *London Evening Standard*:

> I had considered the problem of any surrogate mother carrying my babies becoming attached to them before I met Vimla but I never thought about it again afterwards. In a way I wanted her to become attached because I wanted her to care for them during the pregnancy.
>
> But it would not have been in her interest to keep the babies because she could not afford to—and in any case they were going to be white kids and it would have looked a bit funny.[55]

Yet from a very different social position, a similar comment was made by surrogate Najima Vohra. In reporting that she was mentally prepared to hand over the baby, she said: "It won't even have the same skin color as me, so it won't be hard to think of it as Jessica's."[56] It seems this sort of thinking is not uncommon in surrogates. As I will discuss later, where race serves as a proxy for kinship, it can become a tool for various parties to a reproductive procedure in naming the "correct" person or people as the true parent or parents of a child produced.

As a major factor in assisted reproduction, then, race served at one time to limit the pool of women available to serve as surrogate mothers to infertile couples. With the advent and improvement of the technologies that make possible *gestational* surrogacy, a much wider pool of women became available, which resulted in the creation of a surrogacy industry predicated on structural inequality. Within that industry, race and color became significant market factors and served key ideological functions as well. Markens even suspected that "a certain U.S. cultural fascination" with the transracial aspects of these gestational and kinship relationships might account for the US media focus on India as a "reproductive outsourcing" location rather than countries like Poland, Georgia, and Ukraine, which also provided such services. "[I]n many of the other countries where the surrogacy industry is growing, the (poor) women who become surrogates are 'white,'" she wrote. "In contrast, the dark-skin of Indian surrogates, visually displayed in the pictures accompanying several of the stories, helps mark them as a racialized 'other' by which transnational surrogacy can be both exoticized and justified."[57] Both Dorothy Roberts and Angela Davis point to a connection between these contemporary surrogates and slave women during American chattel slavery. "Slave women were *birth mothers* or *genetic mothers*—to employ terms rendered possible by the new reproductive technologies—but they possessed no legal rights as mothers of any kind," Davis writes. "Considering the commodification of their children—and indeed, of their own persons—their status was similar to that the contemporary *surrogate mother.*"[58] Davis also points to a more contemporary connection between poor and nonwhite women as surrogates and those same women as nannies and domestic workers. Though the position of today's surrogates and domestic workers is certainly more voluntary than that of the slave woman, all are founded on structures of social inequality and help to maintain and reproduce that inequality. Thus, by creating a market for gestational surrogates, the solving of the problem of white infertility continued a long historical pattern of structural inequality and created new possibilities for the economic exploitation and ideological devaluation of women of color.

Race and the "Natural"

Finally, we turn to Postman's last two questions: *What sort of people and institutions might acquire special economic and political power because of technological change? And what changes in language are being enforced by new technologies, and what is being gained and lost by such changes?* In trying to answer these questions in terms of race and ARTs, it is helpful to think in terms the "natural." As Bruno Latour and others have shown, contrary to what the term itself represents, the "natural," as a concept and within any given context, is socially constructed. So too are the "facts" that seem to follow from it; rather than being simply "discovered," "facts," like the "natural," are constructed as part of a collective process.

The idea of the natural is a particularly important one for discussions of ARTs. Consider the following two characterizations of reproductive technology from Ikemoto and Ferrell. Ikemoto writes:

> We understand technology to be something that humans invent. Procreative technology use blurs the line implicit in that understanding of technology—the line between human and technology. We . . . take for granted that we have technology to better the world and to improve nature, whether nature be human, environmental, or other. At the same time, we use the concept of the "unnatural" to signal when technology has gone too far.[59]

Relatedly, Robyn Ferrell points out that although ARTs can be seen to "adapt themselves" to "traditional family life,"

> the point of the reproductive technologies would seem to be *not* to assist nature "to do what she cannot do for herself," but instead to instruct us in desires that are *impossible* in nature. . . . The technological versus the sexual is a particular example of the opposition of the cultural and the natural, and indeed the possibility of a *reproductive technology* signals its collapse.[60]

Reproductive technologies are attempts to correct or improve on nature, ways of pushing past natural limits to fulfill human projects and desires. However, because reproductive technologies are interventions in that which is seen as most natural in human life, they inevitably provoke anxieties about shifting boundaries of the "natural" and "unnatural," which, by definition, are supposed to be fixed. These boundaries must then be renegotiated, typically in a way that will uphold the status quo of inequality but, most importantly, in a way that conceals the contested and contestable quality of the negotiation process itself. One way, then, to address Postman's last two questions is by asking: (1) What sorts of racially inflected desires are reflected and naturalized in the uses of and rhetoric surrounding ARTs? And (2) how is the category of race itself renaturalized in this process?

Assisted reproductive technologies, as they have been developed and practiced in the United States, take the nuclear family as the appropriate site of reproduction and aim at facilitating reproduction in that context. As Ikemoto argues, the fact that procreative technology has been "characterized first and foremost as infertility treatment" is a contingent one—it does not represent the only thing procreative technology *could* be. Indeed, the advent of ARTs *could have* called the entire structure of family life and what it means to be human into question; limiting its characterization to fertility treatment was a means of privileging and protecting the nuclear family model.[61] Since, as discussed earlier, infertility is taken to be a problem facing white, middle-class, heterosexual married women, procreative technology *as* infertility treatment has been specifically aimed at producing children within that context. The nuclear family model, though not a reality for all middle-class white people, serves both as an ideal for that group and as a standard against which nonwhite people are often found lacking—as, for example, in the condemnation of single motherhood in black communities. Davis argues that historically, "family relationships within the Black community have rarely coincided with the traditional nuclear model."[62] This fact, she shows, has led to different ways of dealing with childlessness, including foster motherhood, adoptive motherhood, or play motherhood. Play motherhood, she writes "is deeply rooted in the Black community tradition of extended families and relationships based both on biological kinship—though not necessarily biological motherhood—and on personal history, which is often as binding as biological kinship."[63] An emphasis on ARTs as a solution to infertility is thus an emphasis on a particular form of family life that discourages other possible responses to childlessness and defines proper womanhood in general according to a particular raced model. To the extent that certain women of color emulate that particular model of womanhood, they may avoid the stigmas attached to other members of their group, but women of color as a whole are unlikely ever to be seen as true women in this sense.

The privileging of genetic links above other kinds of links, reflected in ARTs, is also both a cultural artifact and a racially inflected one. "The legal meaning of the genetic tie offers telling insight into its indeterminacy," Roberts reminds us.

For example, the institution of slavery made the genetic tie to a slave mother critical in determining a child's social status, yet legally insignificant in the relationship between male slaveowners and their mulatto children. Although today we generally assume that genetic connection creates an enduring bond between parents and their children, the law often disregards it in the cases of surrogate mothers, sperm donors, and unwed fathers. The importance of genetic connection, then, is determined by social convention, not biological edict.[64]

Crucially, the social conventions around genetic connection in the United States have been shaped by their use in helping to "maintain a racial caste system that preserved white supremacy through a rule of racial purity."[65] As Seline Quiroga puts it: "In the United States, the racial hierarchy relies on the idea that intrinsic to whiteness are so-called superior traits that are linked to success. Implicit in this reasoning is that whiteness itself is heritable."[66] Thus it is that in this society, "perhaps the most significant genetic trait passed from parent to child is race."[67]

All of which helps to shed light on the fact, mentioned earlier, that when individuals or couples use ARTs to create racially matching children, no racial selection is seen as taking place. The choice is so natural as not to be a choice at all. This phenomenon is well demonstrated by the "findings" of an article on the eugenic implications of donor insemination (DI) by F. Allan Hanson. Hanson conducted a study in which all respondents were white, middle aged, well educated, and affluent (though their relationship statuses and sexual orientations varied), and all were "actively involved" in the choices of their sperm donors.[68] He then tried to determine whether the respondents participated in DI with "eugenic intentions," ultimately concluding from his data that "very few women who reproduce by DI aim to endow their children with outstanding qualities for the purpose of giving them a competitive edge." This conclusion involves Hanson explaining away the importance placed by his respondents on the donor's intelligence as something that the respondents wanted for their children primarily because they felt it was one of their *own* distinguishing qualities. Tellingly, however, Hanson does not even feel the *need* to account for the fact that almost 90 percent of his sample rated the donor's ethnicity as "very important" or "quite important."[69] Concerns over ethnicity in ART are not considered "eugenic" but rather perfectly natural. This is because, as Ikemoto puts it: "Despite common knowledge of basic genetics and despite our apparent embrace of colorblindness as a legal standard and social norm, we still see race as immutable."[70]

It is only in the *violation* of this rule of racial matching that the rule itself is made manifest. The anxiety produced by the crossing of the color line in ARTs became visible in a series of stories from early 1994 reacting to the fact that a black woman had chosen to be implanted with white ova. According to Ikemoto, this women's "racial transgression" was held up in the stories as an example of science going too far, with "the immutability of race mark[ing] the desirable line between the natural and the unnatural." The anxieties arise, on Ikemoto's account, because the "image of a black woman claiming authority over a white child inverts the racially-based rules of status and ownership" while the "use of transracial egg donation to change the conclusion that blackness begets blackness challenges the assumption that black mothers create the traits deemed inferior by white supremacy."[71] Those who would see the black woman's choice of a white egg as "unnatural" do not seem inclined to interrogate the supposed "naturalness" of the social and legal definitions of race and racial descent that have given us the very standards the woman is thought to have transgressed. (Nor do their objections appear when a black woman serves as the surrogate rather than the intended mother.) The idea of the transmission of race through lines of descent, even where such descent is not immediately visible, has been well established by the laws and conventions that have been used to establish and maintain racial inequality. By contrast, since ARTs are relatively new, the contests over how the "natural" should be understood in ART practices are still being settled. As Latour shows us, contestation is the norm rather than the exception during the development of any technoscience. While those in technoscience tend to claim that "nature" will serve as the ultimate arbiter of disputes, the reality is that while various opposing parties may believe "nature" is on their side, it is ultimately other, *social* factors that decide the winners. It is only after the dispute is settled that the winners can claim that they "always had nature on their side."[72] Precisely because our ideas about race have become quite visceral, those ideas can be deployed to help settle disputes over the "natural." Moreover, by being used in this way, those ideas about race are reified.

The upshot of the fact that it is considered "natural" to desire that a child created with the help of ARTs be of one's own race is the renaturalization of our current concepts of race. This renaturalization occurs in spite of the fact that contemporary genetics cannot give us *scientifically* the "races" whose existence has been assumed, constructed, and reified *sociohistorically*. The persistence in ARTs of constructed racial categories is demonstrated by the fact that donor semen is categorized racially and that "sperm banks rely on donor self-identification and physiognomy to assess the validity of a donor's claim to whiteness."[73] According to Dov Fox, "twenty-three of the twenty-eight sperm banks operating in the United States provide aspiring parents with information about donor skin color, and the largest banks organize sperm donor directories into discrete sections on the basis of race."[74] As Fox describes, the catalog of the world's leading sperm bank, California Cryobank, Inc., is prominently organized according to race, with separate sections devoted to "Caucasian Donors," "Black/African American Donors," "Asian Donors," "Jewish Donors," and "Other Ancestries Donors." A message appears in bold font at the top of each catalog page identifying the racial identity of the donors listed on that page. The company's website also provides a "Quick Search" drop-down menu that prompts users to sort available donors according to three characteristics featured on the main search page: hair color, eye color, and ethnic origin. Until very recently, semen samples from each donor were stored and shipped in vials that are color-coded according to race:

- A white cap and white cane indicate a *Caucasian* donor.
- A black cap and black cane indicate a *Black/African American* donor.
- A yellow cap and yellow cane indicate an *Asian* donor.
- A red cap and red cane indicate donors of *Unique* or *Mixed ancestry*.[75]

This color coding was in fact a measure designed to ease fears of "racial mix-ups," which, when they have occurred, have garnered significant media attention—as in the 1990 case where a white couple sought artificial insemination with what was supposed to be the husband's sperm and ended up with a child described as black. The woman sued not simply because she had been inseminated with the wrong sperm but later at the point when "the racial taunting of her child became unbearable."[76]

Quiroga has also described how doctors have used their own views of race, sometimes in conflict with those of their patients, to determine which donated sperm is appropriate to which patient. In these sperm bank practices, categories that most scientists and anthropologists have acknowledged are "real" only in the sociohistorical sense are given genetic (or at least pseudogenetic) status. And in the reaction to "racial mix-ups," their social meaning and importance of racial categories is also reaffirmed. Thus, in answer to Postman's final two questions, we find that the special economic and political power of whiteness and the language that describes race as natural are reflected in and reinforced through the use of ARTs.

Conclusion

Using Postman's approach to new technologies as my guide, I have argued that ARTs in the United States fail to be racially neutral in three ways: first, the understanding of infertility in the practice of ARTs is shaped by racist assumptions, and thus ARTs have primarily been aimed toward solving the fertility problems of white, middle-class married couples; second, ART practices both reinforce existing inequalities in local and global labor markets and open the way for new forms of exploitation; and third, ART practices reinforce the privileging of whiteness and the naturalization of racial categories. In this analysis, in vitro fertilization, artificial insemination, and gestational surrogacy were the technologies in question; now, with these points in mind, I would like to consider what we might gain by analyzing race *itself* as technology.

Notes

1. "Rent a Womb? Extreme Measure to Get Pregnant."
2. "Cheaper Overseas."
3. Thompson, *Making Parents,* 1.
4. Beauchamp and Childress, *Principles of Biomedical Ethics,* 417.
5. Deitrich, "Social Control of Surrogacy in Australia," 372.
6. Ibid., 373.
7. Ibid., 379.
8. Parks, "Rethinking Radical Politics," 23.
9. Winner, *The Whale and the Reactor,* 4.
10. Berger, "Discussion with GAI Reading Group."
11. Feder, *Family Bonds,* 90.
12. Postman, *Building a Bridge to the 18th Century,* 40–41.
13. Ibid., 41–53.
14. Ikemoto, "Eggs as Capital," 767–68.
15. Ikemoto, "In/Fertile, Too Fertile, Dysfertile," 1008.
16. Raymond, *Women as Wombs,* 1.
17. Dubow, *Scientific Racism in Modern South Africa,* 276; Klausen, *Race, Maternity, and the Politics of Birth Control,* 13–14.
18. McCann, *Birth Control Politics in the United States,* 100.
19. Roberts, *Killing the Black Body,* chapter 5.
20. Inhorn, "Globalization of New Reproductive Technologies," 1840–41.
21. Shanley and Asch, "Involuntary Childlessness, Reproductive Technology, and Social Justice," 857.
22. Ibid., 855
23. Ibid., 852.
24. Roberts, *Killing the Black Body,* 254–55.
25. Ikemoto, "In/Fertile, Too Fertile, Dysfertile," 1037.
26. Ibid., 1037–44.
27. Beack, "Far Worse Things a Parent Can Be Than Old."
28. Ryan, "ART in the 'Developing World,'" 808–10.
29. Roberts, *Killing the Black Body,* 256–60.
30. Ryan, "ART in the 'Developing World,'" 808.
31. Roberts, *Killing the Black Body,* 252–53, 261.
32. Robertson, "Surrogate Motherhood," 47.
33. See Collins, *Black Feminist Thought,* chapter 4.
34. Farquhar, *The Other Machine,* 149.
35. Ragoné, "Of Likeness and Difference," 56–57; Hamilton, "She's Having Our Baby."
36. Ikemoto, "In/Fertile, Too Fertile, Dysfertile," 1016.

37. Corea, *The Mother Machine*, 215.

38. Grayson, "Mediating Intimacy," 540.

39. Hartouni, *Cultural Conceptions*, 95–96.

40. Bailey, "Reconceiving Surrogacy," 716–17; Ikemoto, "Reproductive Tourism," 278; Sehgal, "Reproductive Tourism Soars in India"; "Cheaper Overseas"; Unnithan, "Infertility and ARTs in a Globalising India," 13.

41. Banerjee, "Reorienting the Ethics of Transnational Surrogacy," 107–10; Pande, "Transnational Commercial Surrogacy in India," 620.

42. Markens, "Global Reproductive Health Market," 1748.

43. Unnithan, "Infertility and ARTs in a Globalising India," 11.

44. Sarojini, Marwah, and Shenoi, "Globalisation of Birth Markets," 2.

45. Vora, "Indian Transnational Surrogacy and the Commodification of Vital Energy," 267.

46. Ibid., 275–76.

47. Banerjee, "Race and a Transnational Reproductive Caste System," 114.

48. Bailey, "Reconceiving Surrogacy," 719–20; quoted in Sama Resource Group for Women and Health, *ARTs and Women*, 6; Sarojini, Marwah, and Shenoi, "Globalisation of Birth Markets," 7; Cohen, "A Search for a Surrogate Leads to India."

49. Schultz, "The Life Factory," 3.

50. Sama Resource Group, *ARTs and Women*, 74.

51. Bailey, "Reconceiving Surrogacy," 720.

52. Pande, "Transnational Commercial Surrogacy in India," 620.

53. Thakur, "'Wombs for Rent' Grows in India."

54. Banerjee, "Reorienting the Ethics of Transnational Surrogacy," 118.

55. Bhatia, "Mumbai Clinic Sends Couple Email."

56. Haworth, "Surrogate Mothers."

57. Markens, "Global Reproductive Health Market," 1751.

58. Angela Davis, "Outcast Mothers and Surrogates," 357.

59. Ikemoto, "In/Fertile, Too Fertile, Dysfertile," 1013–14.

60. Ferrell, *Copula*, 33.

61. Ikemoto, "In/Fertile, Too Fertile, Dysfertile," 1021.

62. Angela Davis, "Outcast Mothers and Surrogates," 361.

63. Ibid., 359.

64. Roberts, *Killing the Black Body*, 267.

65. Ibid.

66. Quiroga, "Blood Is Thicker Than Water," 145.

67. Roberts, *Killing the Black Body*, 267.

68. Hanson, "Donor Insemination," 292.

69. Ibid., 288–89.

70. Ikemoto, "In/Fertile, Too Fertile, Dysfertile," 1016.

71. Ibid., 1017.

72. Latour, *Science in Action*, 97–99.

73. Quiroga, "Blood Is Thicker Than Water," 150.

74. Fox, "Racial Classification in Assisted Reproduction," 1846.

75. Ibid., 1853–54.

76. Williams, *Alchemy of Race and Rights*, 186.

2 Race Isn't Just Made; It's Used

> *Race, gender, and capital require a cyborg theory of wholes and parts. There is no drive in cyborgs to produce total theory, but there is an intimate experience of boundaries, their construction and deconstruction. There is a myth system waiting to become a political language to ground one way of looking at science and technology and challenging the informatics of domination—in order to act potently.*
>
> —Donna Haraway, "A Manifesto for Cyborgs"

Stubblefield has suggested that our real question should not be "What *is* race?" but rather "How should we think about race?" In other words, we should develop and argue for those ways of thinking about race that we believe best illuminate its operations within given contexts, and always with an eye toward fighting racism and racial injustice. Our context here is the development, uses, and understandings of assisted reproductive technologies. In the previous chapter, I showed how questions from the philosophy of technology could be used to focus on the social and political effects of notions of race on ART practices and, reciprocally, of ART practices on notions of race. Now, I would like to take the philosophy of technology framework a step further and propose that we think about race *itself* as technology.

The use of technology as a theoretical lens opens up a variety of insights about the nature and function of race—both in general and, in particular, with respect to the relationship between race and ARTs. For the duration of this work, I will be exploring several different but overlapping ways in which we can investigate the technological dimensions of race. Where I describe race as *a* technology or refer to *the* technology of race, I do not intend to imply that race was constructed or has operated in a single, unified way throughout its history. I do, however, wish to bring our focus to the particular ways in which race has been constructed and has operated in particular contexts—in other words, to focus on *how* race has been made and what race *does*.

Of course, it will not do for these purposes to take a naïve stance on technology. Rather, I propose applying critical insights from the philosophy of technology to the Critical Philosophy of Race. As we have already begun to see, those writers and works that can be gathered together under the designation *philosophy of technology* typically challenge at least one of two broad and popularly held assumptions about the relationship between human life and technology. First is the belief that technological innovation always brings about, represents, or is necessary for social progress. Second is the belief that, while their use by human agents can be judged, technological objects themselves are mere tools and, as such, are morally or politically neutral. By contrast, Winner writes: "If the experience of modern society shows us anything . . . it is that technologies are not merely aids to human activity, but also powerful forces acting to reshape that activity and its meaning."[1] In other words, the technologies that we use can affect our intentionality with respect to our world, our sense of what is possible, desirable, and useful. Think, for example, of changes in communication technologies and their effects on our sense of time. How long might you be willing to wait to receive a response to a query sent in letter? What about an email? Or a text? These technological shifts change our expectations of others, of ourselves, of our working lives and our personal ones. They change how we talk to each other and how we listen.

Technologies can also come to serve as frameworks for our worldviews, reorganizing our senses of "nature," of the "normal," and of what constitutes "evolution" or "progress." For example, it is not simply growing scientific knowledge of genetics that changes the way we think about human characteristics, human populations, and human health. It is also the technologies that make possible and follow after this knowledge that alter our understandings of the world. The coding of populations into databases both reifies those populations and provides new criteria for who can be included in or excluded from those populations. The use of DNA testing in criminal justice systems alters standards of evidence and leads some to believe criminality might be found in one's DNA itself. The possibility of decoding and manipulating the human genomes both emerges from and strengthens the imperative to eliminate disease and perfect health care. To explore technology critically, then, we must employ a "theory of technological politics [that] draws attention to the momentum of large-scale sociotechnological systems, to the response of modern societies to certain technological imperatives, and to the ways human ends are powerfully transformed as they are adapted to technical means."[2]

In this chapter, then, I will lay the theoretical groundwork for such a critical exploration of race in terms of technology. First, I will describe some general benefits of thinking about race through the idea of technology. This will involve drawing comparisons between race and those material artifacts we think of under the banner of technology. In other words, I will frame race as analogous to technology in a number of ways. In the latter parts of the chapter, however, I lay out two approaches to *technology* that take the term less literally: those of Heidegger and Foucault. Heidegger attempts to get at the *essence* of technology, which he argues lies not in technological artifacts themselves but in the way people approach the world. Foucault focuses not simply on material technologies but on social and political techniques as the means through which power is produced and operates within social contexts. Both these very specific approaches to technology can, as I will demonstrate in chapters 3 and 5 respectively, be used to help us understand race in relation to ARTs.

Race as Technology

Critical approaches to technology have revealed several different features of technology that resonate with the critical understanding of race and can thus, I argue, serve to illuminate and deepen that understanding. In this section, I offer analogies between the nature and operations of race and those of material technologies. I emphasize the way that race is both made and used and the fact that this creation and deployment occur within particular sociohistorical and political circumstances. I point to the fact that, once created, race can be used in ways it was not originally intended, including as a means of resistance. At the same time, as we become accustomed to the role of race in our lives, much of our thinking about it will fade into the background, shaping our views in ways we may fail to recognize. I describe how this technological understanding of race aligns with a historical understanding of race, which saw races as something people could and should actively shape. Finally, in keeping with the discussion of the introduction, I will urge us to see histories of race as histories of practices rather than merely ideas.

At the most obvious level, technologies are defined in terms of their instrumentality. We recognize that technologies are human-made—they are produced. Though they are developed or built from pieces or processes found in nature, it is human intention and activity that imbue technologies with the purpose or meaning that makes them technological. Furthermore, having been produced, technologies are also necessarily produc*tive*; they are used as instruments or tools to carry out certain purposes. On a more complex level, philosophers of technology have pointed out that particular technologies emerge within particular social contexts, epistemes, and sets of power relations. They do not simply appear as a natural step in some sort of predestined journey of human technological progress; their appearances are much more conditioned and contingent. Though contingent, however, they are not random. Technologies are conceived of, pursued, developed, and spread based on the needs and desires of people and groups in particular historical times and places, and based on the relative power and ability of those people and groups to pursue their needs and desires.

Eli Whitney's infamous cotton gin, for example, responded both to other technological improvements in the English cotton textile industry (which cheapened the manufacture of cotton goods and thereby increased demand for them) and to the desire of planters in the US South to find a new cash crop to replace tobacco. Given the plantation system already in place, an invention that made the work of seeding cotton much easier and more efficient did not improve the lives of those seeding cotton (enslaved blacks) but rather made their lives worse by increasing the demand for slave labor in growing cotton and thereby breathing renewed life into the chattel slavery system.[3] A technology that worked out very well for large plantation owners (with their financial and political power) worked out quite poorly for enslaved blacks and for small-scale white farmers in the South (who had little to no control within the system). Technological determinism, then, gets it wrong at least insofar as it fails to recognize that we determine technologies at least as much as they determine us—not in the sense that they are neutral tools awaiting our good or evil use but in the sense that their very existence is already shaped by the context in which they are brought forth.

Given these features of technology, if we think of race as a technology in any given context, we find that it is both produced and productive, constructed and constructive. Though human phenotypical variation is a natural reality, the meanings assigned to those variations are contingent. Race is not *discovered* but rather *built*. Interpretations of race and racial difference have emerged within particular historical contexts and epistemes and have served particular political purposes. Collins, for example, outlines different stages of antiblack racism in America, which are tied to different social, political, and economic structures. In the period of chattel slavery, she argues, race was used to dehumanize black people, allowing for their objectification, commodification, and exploitation. By contrast, during the period of legal racial segregation in the US South, a focus on racial classification, racial difference, and the dangers of black sexuality and interracial sexual contact justified the separation of blacks and whites in all spheres of social interaction. In race (and racism), as with technology, different historical conditions lead to different primary concerns, which are addressed through different mechanisms and yield different results.

It is far from revolutionary to argue that race is socially constructed, but as I pointed out in the introduction, simply acknowledging or even proving this fact is unlikely to do all the antiracist work we are seeking. Aside from the risk that the social construction argument will be taken up as a call for a naïve eliminativism or color blindness, there is also a risk of focusing too heavily on race as a disembodied discourse. The race idea is very much a product (and an essential coconspirator) of a variety of discourses from the modern era to the present. Donna Haraway, for example, names four "major discursive streams" that "poured into the cauldron in which racial discourse simmered" in the late nineteenth and early twentieth centuries in Europe and the United States— the ethnological, Lamarkian, polygenist, and evolutionist traditions. Yet she emphasizes that race was "real, fundamental, and bloody," arguing that race is "the place to look" for an example of "the inextricable weave of historically specific, discursive, scientific, and physical reality" and that the discursive "has never been lived with any greater vitality than in the always undead corpus of race and sex."[4] If thinking about race technologically is to serve our purposes, it must do so not merely as another counterdiscursive turn of phrase but also as a reminder of the very *material* nature of race. Understanding race as technology must go beyond seeing race *as constructed* to involve examining the things race is *used to construct* and how this is accomplished.

Thinking in terms of technology, we are also reminded that the social construction of race should not be seen as the end goal, as if the entire project of world racism has been carried out as a sort of conspiracy with the express purpose of lowering the quality of certain lives. Rather, we should think of race as a tool, as a means by which other sorts of ends—for example, social cohesion, economic prosperity, or political mastery—are achieved. In her description of race as a technology, for example, Falguni Sheth describes race as "a vehicle to draw and redraw the boundaries by which select populations are assured the protection of the law," arguing that, historically, race does not simply distinguish populations from each other but rather divides, separates, and hypostatizes them into "self-cohering wholes who are to be despised, vilified, and if not cast outside the gates of the city, then at least subordinated and exploited, if not physically or psychically managed."[5] That race can be used in this way creates a sense of vulnerability even among the populations that the law protects and thus ensures their compliance and collusion with systems of power (lest they be cast out as well). The goal, then, is not the harm done to members of those populations not protected by the law (though a great deal of such harm is indeed done); the goal is the maintenance of a particular social order and the benefits that accrue to certain people within that order.

At the same time, while technologies may be intended, consciously or unconsciously, to serve and reinforce the desires and interests of certain people or groups within a particular historical context, they may also engender shifts in those desires and interests and may enable or facilitate the emergence of new social possibilities. For example, it was research teams working for the Defense Advanced Research Projects Agency (DARPA) under the US Department of Defense that developed the precursor to today's internet. While governments and militaries still make use of internet technologies, of course, so too do a variety of individuals and groups whom governments and militaries consider highly dangerous. The infamous Wikileaks is just one example of information and communication technologies put in the service of opposing or breaking down military and government secrecy. Once introduced, the development of a technology cannot be fully controlled and may lead to projects never intended by those who first conceived or assembled it. Technologies develop in practice in ways that exceed their theories. Conversely, theories surrounding a particular technology may be developed after the fact, providing explanations of that technology that reflect the current practices surrounding it rather than its historical trajectory.

Technologies may possess transformative possibilities and offer various means of resistance to structures of domination. Those transformations may also come to be thwarted or end up serving existing power structures in new and unexpected ways. Moreover, teasing out the causes and effects, uses and trajectories of any given technology may prove exceptionally difficult because of the way that technologies have a tendency to disappear from view when one has become used to them and so long as they are working well. (You don't think about your contact lenses until one of them gets an eyelash stuck underneath it. The air-conditioning system in your office goes largely unconsidered until the hot summer day on which it breaks down.) As Haraway points out, technologies are so integrated into our lives that it makes little sense to try to separate that which is "natural" from that which is "technological," especially where that attempt is made in pursuit of a position of moral, political, or epistemological purity or innocence. Instead, as I elaborate below, she argues that we should understand ourselves as cyborgs—beings whose daily existences are infused with technology and whose very identities are at least as constructed and externally imposed as they are "natural" or "discovered."

Thus, thinking of race as a technology also allows us to recognize and explore how concepts of race have, in many ways, taken on lives of their own and have often been employed in the service of resistance to systems of domination and oppression. We can recognize the potentially socially transformative roles that positively construed or oppositional racial identities may play (as I suggested was important in the discussion of Outlaw's definition of race in the introduction). Eduardo Mendieta, for example, describes the label "Latinos" as something that Latin Americans in the United States have "learned to identify and be identified as" not only "because the mainstream society lumped us together under a bureaucratic label created for the purposes of the Census" but also because the label "localizes the history and geography of the Latin American experience that is the background against which we must make sense of the Latino experience in the United States" and can serve as a political and cultural tool rather than a mere ethnic designator.[6] We can also see how the aforementioned UNESCO account that portrayed the problems of race and racism as based in mistaken beliefs about the correlation of behavior and biology (itself a theory about the technology of race) developed as a response to the post–World War II context, even though that account did not reflect the actual historical trajectory of the race technology. Moreover, we can acknowledge that old racial concepts can be taken up anew or adjusted for new eras and political contexts. This may occur for good or for ill or, perhaps most likely, for something neither wholly positive nor negative but at the same time both.

One significant benefit of framing race as technology is its power to explain the way that much of our thinking about race has faded into the background, shaping our view of the world without our being fully conscious of it. It is when something goes "wrong" with race—when there is a social outcome in which race plays an unexpected role or fails to play an expected role—that race comes into question for us and demands a response. One chilling example of this phenomenon is the times when a raced body appears in what is presumed to be a white (or nonraced) space and is met with a response of violence, as in the shooting of Trayvon Martin, to name just one prominent instance. Another example is captured in a 2016 documentary on O. J. Simpson. Describing the infamous slow-motion police chase following which Simpson was arrested, a news helicopter pilot tells us: "If O.J. Simpson were black, that shit wouldn't have happened. He'd be on the ground getting clubbed."[7] In other words, Simpson's blackness failed to play its expected role during the pursuit and arrest, leading the pilot to the conclusion that Simpson could not rightfully be considered black at all. On this interpretation, it is not Simpson's phenotype but the way police treated him that best defines his racial status. In any case, the helicopter pilot's surprise at the humane treatment Simpson received suggests that race is, under normal circumstances, a very effective technology for justifying inhumane levels of police violence against certain populations. Simpson, here, is the exception that leads the helicopter pilot to articulate the rule—to name one typical function of race.

Another benefit of thinking of race technologically comes through reflection on Haraway's notion of the cyborg, which asks us to resist seeking a neat separation of the natural and the constructed in the race concept. Literally speaking, a cyborg is "a hybrid of machine and organism, a creature of social reality as well as a creature of fiction." It is a man-made combination of that which is natural or biological and that which is artificial or technological. For Haraway's purposes, the cyborg becomes a helpful, critical figure intended to represent the way in which "the difference between natural and artificial, mind and body, self-developing and externally designed" in human existence has become (or perhaps has always been) thoroughly ambiguous.[8] We are all cyborgs on Haraway's account, both because our everyday practices have become entwined with and dependent on a wide variety of technological artifacts (both large and small) and, more to this point, because our very identities are not simply natural, internal, individual realties but rather constructed, interpersonal, and sociopolitical ones. Having recognized that racial and ethnic identities are constructed identities, however, Haraway argues against any attempt to "rediscover," recover, or revert to something "pure." The so-called natural, the "culturally given," and the legally or politically constructed are so deeply entwined in our irretrievably cyborg identities (and in our self-reflection on those identities) that we cannot find a place of innocence from which to take a stance. This does not mean that we should not engage in self-reflection and social theorizing about racial and ethnic identities, however, or that we should never take any stance. It means only that we must do so with the recognition that cyborg identities are neither neatly divisible nor permanently fixed.

The concept of race as technology can also help to affect two important shifts in our thinking about the history of race. First, as I will elaborate in chapter 3, when we think of races not as (falsely) discovered but as deliberately made, we bring our understanding into line with the explicit understanding of race in much of the modern period. As Bernasconi notes, "until recently races were not regarded as natural but as produced, so that racial purity was not something to be maintained but, to the extent that it was possible at all, something to be produced by breeding programs."[9] In certain strands of European intellectual history, racial essences and the particular modes of civilization that were thought to be innate in different races were seen as driving history. With the development of modern science, racial health and purity came to be considered as scientific-biological means of promoting and securing cultural and political aims. Thinking of race as technology—as a tool to achieve certain ends—keeps this history present in our considerations and helps us to resist the temptation to see race as a naturally occurring phenomenon that has simply been misused.

Second, if we take up Marx's observation that technological practice often precedes rather than follows from theory or ideology, we are encouraged to think of the history of race as a history of practices as much as it is one of ideas. Indeed, Taylor undertakes his attempt to clarify ideas about race precisely because "common knowledge" with respect to race is "overwhelmingly practical rather than theoretical: we know how to categorize people and, often enough, to react to them or how race-thinking says we should react to them, but our grasp of the principles and definitions behind these practices, such as they are, is unclear at best."[10] Yet uniform beliefs and ideologies are not required for shared practices; we can know *how* to do something without necessarily knowing *why* it is done. Furthermore, the maintenance of systems of social inequality can be accomplished by holding certain practices (many of which go largely unexamined) in place while changing the theory or ideology behind them so that it better accords with the intellectual and moral sentiments of the day. Genealogical methods like those of Nietzsche or Foucault aim to uncover precisely these sorts of historical shifts wherein a relatively permanent or enduring custom or procedure is assigned a variety of meanings, expectations, or purposes over time. In the case of punishment practices, for example, their purpose has been understood at different times as preventative, retributive, compensatory, deterrent, or even festive (and often many of these meanings are in play simultaneously).[11] If we limit our historical and current inquiries into race to the question of what we think or have thought race *is*, we risk extensively mapping the tip of the iceberg without looking below the surface of the water. By shifting our framing of race to technology, we shift our attention to uncovering and examining the often unremarked practices through which race is continually reconstructed and maintained.

As Taylor, Collins, Foucault, and others have shown, it is new sets of techniques that often signal the emergence of a new period.[12] For example, Taylor argues that, while colonization and the rise of chattel slavery "certainly presupposed and encouraged forms of racist domination," the high modern era, particularly after 1870, was marked by "the emergence of newly comprehensive forms of racist political domination."

> After the emergence of mass politics and the attendant need to manage public opinion, after the fermenting of nationalist aspirations to self-determination, and after industrialization and capitalist expansion began to occasion labor migrations and other social upheavals, states needed ways to unify, mobilize, and mollify their increasingly literate and politically active populations, especially in the face of economic distress, cultural disruption, and potential class conflict. At the same time, individuals and communities needed ways to understand and cope with the changes going on around them. Newly hardened forms of racism spoke to these needs, often using new or newly proliferating media, like journals, newspapers, scientific societies, film, and public exhibitions, to do so.[13]

The rise of the Nazi Party in Germany serves as another classic (if well-trodden) example. In these cases, the technology of race interacts with other technologies and various movements within social and political life. We see clearly how, like other technologies, it is both conditioned by its context and conditioning of the context itself. It responds to particular social and political needs and desires and helps to shape new needs and desires, new ideas of science and nature. As Taylor puts it: "Once we say that race-thinking shapes social life, we can say that it is *constructive*—not in the sense of being positive or useful necessarily, but in the sense that it creates new conditions and states of affairs."[14]

Thus far I have argued (by analogy to the operations of material technologies) that is it useful to think of race as a technology because it puts the focus squarely on human activity, emphasizing the instrumental nature of race ideas and allowing us to see the social construction of race not as an end in itself but as a means to other social and political ends. I have also claimed that it allows us to recognize the ways different people in different eras take up old race ideas for new purposes, some of which have to do with resistance to oppression and inequality. Furthermore, I contend that seeing race technologically matches with how it has been developed historically, where races were not something to be simply discovered but something to be actively produced. I have suggested that histories of race must be not only histories of ideas but also histories of practices. I now turn first to Heidegger and then to Foucault to explore their understandings of and insights with respect to technology and to consider how their less literal approaches might also illuminate our thinking on race.

Heidegger's Essence of Technology

At the beginning of his 1953 essay, "The Question Concerning Technology," Martin Heidegger writes:

> [T]he essence of technology is by no means anything technological. Thus we shall never experience our relationship to the essence of technology so long as we merely conceive and push forward the technological, put up with it, or evade it. Everywhere we remain unfree and chained to technology, whether we passionately affirm or deny it. But we are delivered over to it in the worst possible way when we regard it as something neutral; for this conception of it, to which today we particularly like to do homage, makes us utterly blind to the essence of technology.[15]

Heidegger argues that we must establish a free relationship to technology, which can be done only by opening ourselves to its essence; to relate freely to technology, we must know *what it is*. This is not a trivial question for Heidegger or within the philosophy of technology in general; the ability to prescribe general rules for our behaviors regarding technology rests on the ability to give a satisfactory description of what technology, as a general phenomenon, is. As Heidegger rightly points out, however, the essence of technology must not be confused with anything in technological artifacts themselves since a wide range of technological artifacts exist, and, materially speaking, many have almost nothing in common with each other. What, for example, does a hammer have in common with a printing press? Or a printing press with a cell phone? Or in vitro fertilization with any of the above?

Heidegger acknowledges that the most promising answers would seem to be related to purpose, in the most general sense of the word, or to origin. We might say, for example, that they are all tools of some sort ("Technology is a means to an end"), or that they are all man-made ("Technology is a human activity").[16] In other words, we might say, as I suggested above, that technology is essentially instrumental. For Heidegger, both these features of technology are a part of the answer—and truly do seem to cover the entire historical range of technology—and yet are too neutral, too superficial to account for the complexity of our relationship to technology. To see technology as instrumental is, in Heidegger's words, "merely correct" but "not yet true."[17]

There is something much more fundamental to which Heidegger wishes to draw our attention. He wants to ask about instrumentality itself—that way of being in the world to which the concepts of *means* and *end* belong. The realm of instrumentality is one of causality. People, seen as the type of beings capable of envisioning ends and pursuing those ends by initiating a causal chain of means in the world, are thought of as efficient causes. Efficient cause, says Heidegger, has come to set the standard for all causality. He believes, however, that this represents a perversion of the original Greek sense of causality as that to which something is indebted, and that this perversion leads to a misunderstanding of our relationship to technology. Where people are understood as efficient causes in the sense of producers or envisioners of technology, we can only understand technology as a set of neutrally instrumental products of human invention. Thus, when we begin to feel that technology is getting out of hand, the response is to try to regain mastery of those products, to bring them *back* under control. This, I will argue in the next chapter, is very much the view of technology adopted by those who see the problems with eugenics as stemming *not* from the aim of social improvement through reproductive or genetic intervention but rather from the poor science on which it was based, the racial and class biases through which it pursued its aims, and the fact that its application was frequently coercive or involuntary. Thus, their attempt to determine whether contemporary reprogenetic technologies can be justly and ethically pursued ultimately rests on a shallow and dangerous (mis)understanding of technology—one that fails to question its essence. The problem and solution are thought to be in how we use the technological instrument and in the level of control we do or do not exert over that use.

In the old Greek definition of causality, Heidegger finds a meaning of responsibility for a thing that goes beyond the idea of human beings as envisioners and producers of material products. What Heidegger describes as the process of *bringing-forth* things in the world includes not only the work of the craftsman or technologist but also the work of nature—for example, the blossom that the plant brings forth as it grows. Even more than that, however, in the human realm, *bringing-forth* includes the giving of meaning to a thing. The giving of meaning to a thing is often seen as the *discovery* of an inherent meaning—the uncovering of the thing's "truth"—when, in fact, it is done (though not consciously) by people. *Bringing-forth* in this sense is described by Heidegger as the *revealing* of things. Such revealing is neither objective nor neutral.[18]

It is here that we find the deeper essence of technology that Heidegger has been seeking. In a key passage, he explains how we arrive at this understanding:

> Instrumentality is considered to be the fundamental characteristic of technology. If we inquire, step by step, into what technology, represented as means, actually is, then we shall arrive at revealing. The possibility of all productive manufacturing lies in revealing.
>
> Technology is therefore no mere means. Technology is a way of revealing. If we give heed to this, then another whole realm for the essence of technology will open itself up to us. It is the realm of revealing, i.e., of truth.[19]

Thus, we move from our superficial understanding of technology as instrumental—as means—to a questioning of the notion that lies beneath instrumentality: causality. In this investigation, we discover that the causes of things in the world are not simply twofold—that is, nature (in the case of living things) and people or craftsmen as efficient causes (in the case of technological artifacts). Rather, the "possibility of all productive manufacturing" lies in between these two causes, in the way that human beings *reveal* the natural world—that is, in the meaning given to things in the world by human beings. A thing is revealed or known in a technological way when its aspect and matter are gathered together in advance "with a view to the finished thing envisaged as completed."[20] It is this view that underlies technology. The essence of technology, then, is as a *way* of revealing—that is, technology's essence is found in how an orientation toward technology leads us to relate to things in the world. This way of understanding the world—the meaning that things have for us in this world—will be experienced not as one possible interpretation of things but rather as the "truth" of those things. A free relationship with technology would thus require first understanding the way that technology frames our truth and then questioning that framework.

When we turn back to the idea of *race* as technology, this much is already very suggestive. On a Heideggerian account of technology, the essence of race comes to be understood as a way of revealing or of knowing the "truth" of *people*. Conceptually prior to, or more fundamental than, the actual delineation of racial categories (or any efforts to prove scientifically either the existence of those categories or the correlation between physical, mental, and moral traits within those categories) would be the identification—or revealing—of the people in the world (with their natural human variations) as the types of beings that can be divided up into groups (based on certain of those variations). Within the revealing of race, people are beings that are *naturally* divided, classified, and ranked for the purpose of understanding nature, explaining history, and organizing society.

The connections between Heidegger's understanding of technology and the concept of race become even more interesting, however, when we recall that the development of the race concept belongs essentially to the modern period—a period which, on Heidegger's account, is marked by an intensification of the technological worldview he describes. With respect to the modern period, Heidegger calls into question our typical understanding of the relationship between technology and science. He notes that modern technology is not simply based on modern science. Rather, there is a mutual relationship between technology and science grounded in the fact that experimental sciences not only provide the theoretical basis for modern technologies but also rely on modern technologies for their experiments and the gathering of data. The modern period saw the invention of scientific tools like the microscope (1590) and the telescope (1608), for example, which were not simply outgrowths of scientific discovery but also shapers of the way scientific experiments came to be conducted and the type of information that such experiments could gather. But while Heidegger believes establishing the mutuality of this relationship is correct, he finds a more decisive question: "Of what essence is modern technology that it thinks of putting exact science to use?"[21] Though *modern* technology, like all technology, is a revealing, on Heidegger's account, there is also something new in it. These particular characteristics of modern technology are essential, as I will show in the next chapter, not only for understanding race as technology and as a fundamentally modern phenomenon but also for recognizing the inexorable links between race, heredity, and eugenics.

"Reckoned chronologically," Heidegger admits that modern technology "got under way only when it could be supported by exact physical science." Thought of "historically," however, this relation "does not hit upon the truth" for Heidegger. Prior to both the actual manufacture of technological artifacts *and* the science that enables them is the identification—or revealing—of the things around us in nature as materials for the production of those artifacts. This is what Heidegger sees as a technological *enframing*. "Modern science's way of representing pursues and entraps nature as a calculable coherence of forces," writes Heidegger, and, as such, it "will never be able to renounce this one thing: that nature report itself in some way or other that is identifiable through calculation and that it remain orderable as a system of information."[22] This becomes clear when one thinks about the modern tendency to describe nature in terms of technological metaphors—as when one speaks of nature's purposes, mechanisms, economy, or efficiency.

For Heidegger, one of the fundamental characteristics of modern technology (as opposed to prior technology) is an intensification of that revealing into a *challenging*, which "puts to nature the unreasonable demand that it supply energy that can be extracted and stored as such." Nature is not simply harnessed as in the case of the windmill or set in order as in the cultivation and maintenance of fields in old-time farming. In challenging, nature is *set upon*: "Agriculture is now the mechanized food industry. Air is now set upon to yield nitrogen, the earth to yield ore, ore to yield uranium." The Rhine is dammed up to provide hydroelectric power. There is a drive toward "the maximum yield at the minimum cost."[23] Furthermore, there is a storing up. One takes from nature not simply what one needs now but what one will need in the future. Within the revealing of modern technology, the energy concealed in nature is to be unlocked, transformed, stored, distributed, and switched about, ultimately ordered into interlocking systems to be regulated and secured. Heidegger's general term for things thought of in this way is *standing-reserve*. When things come to be seen as standing-reserve, they cease to be seen as objects standing apart from us. They are simply resources for us, with no meaning of their own beyond their usefulness to come.[24] The essence of modern technology, then, lies in *enframing*. Enframing, for Heidegger, is that which "challenges [man] forth, to reveal the real, in the mode of ordering, as standing-reserve."[25] In other words, enframing calls on man to see nature in purely instrumental terms as that which is ready to be used by him. Enframing is not technological activity itself (the creation of technological artifacts that is done by man) but rather that to which man responds in taking up technological activity. Enframing is thus deeply fundamental to human experience.

These technological insights are particularly useful in our thinking about race because, as I will show in the next chapter, they offer an alternative framework within which to understand the history of race. Heidegger's description of the relation between technology and science in the modern era helps us to think critically about the relation between race science and the technological practices of eugenics because it suggests that the two are more fundamentally related than some scholars would like to believe. Rather than seeing eugenics as the political misapplication of a conceptually prior and flawed racial science, Heidegger's view invites us to see an essential human drive to master nature (a technological or eugenic enframing of the world) as that which underlies the racial worldview itself, along with the conceptually subsequent attempts to support that view scientifically. Voegelin makes a similar point about this conceptual relationship between (race) science and technology when he writes "Modern race theories give the impression of an aggressive optimism because, like technology, they are eager to put to use the lawful course of nature in order to arrive at a specific objective they consider desirable."[26] In Heideggerian terms, when race comes to be seen as a *force* or *cause* in nature, it too becomes part of nature's concealed energy and thus becomes something unlocked and transformed—something to be mastered for optimal societal efficiency and yield.

Foucault's Focus on Technologies

As Jim Gerrie notes, while Michel Foucault is not often taken to be a "philosopher of technology," his work is full of "technological terminology and metaphor," and his reflections on power "uniquely parallel a position accepted by a significant segment of philosophers of technology, that is that technology is not simply an ethically neutral set of artifacts by which we exercise power over nature, but also always a set of structured forms of action by which we also inevitably exercise power over ourselves."[27] Indeed, it is precisely through notions of *technologies, techniques* and *practices* understood in this way that Foucault carries out his genealogies and critiques of power, of subject formation, and of the variety of ideas and institutions through which power can be exercised. Foucault is interested in uncovering and elaborating what he calls *regimes of truth* and in showing how those regimes of truth evolve, shift, appear, and disappear over time—in other words, how truth is neither ahistorical nor transcultural but rather both embedded in and characteristic of particular contexts. The goal of Foucault's project is not to prove any one regime of truth to be more truthful than any other, nor is it to paint any contemporary regime of truth as either a triumph of objective reason over past error or as fundamentally misguided with respect to some deeper truth forgotten or yet to be discovered. Rather, he aims to expose not only the ideas and assumptions that characterize a particular regime of truth but also the concrete means, instruments, rules, and practices through which that regime of truth emerges, is instantiated, and is maintained.

In his well-known *History of Sexuality*, for example, Foucault challenges the regime of truth represented by the "repressive hypothesis" of sexuality—the belief that social forces attempt to silence or prohibit all expressions of sexuality outside the marital, reproductive context. Performing a genealogy of sexuality and discourse on sex, Foucault demonstrates how an understanding of society and its history as sexually repressive serves to mask the productive nature of contemporary power and the true mechanisms of its operation within contemporary society. He describes *confession* as a mechanism by which subjects who are compelled to speak "the truth" about themselves are, in fact, constructing those selves together with those who hear, interrupt, and judge their confessions. He identifies the mechanism of *population* (conceived of primarily in statistical terms and involving the analysis of things like birth rate, age of marriage, legitimate and illegitimate births, and the precocity and frequency of sexual relations among groups) as a new type of target for intervention that both makes possible and justifies new forms of intervention on the part not only of governments but of doctors, educators, and other social institutions. He also points to certain sexual *figures*—the hysterical woman, the masturbating child, the Malthusian couple, and the perverse adult—as mechanisms of a new form of control that operates through the creation and proliferation of medically or socially pathological types. By challenging the repressive hypothesis and uncovering these mechanisms, Foucault seeks to reveal a shift from what he describes as juridico-discursive power to a new form of power he labels *biopower*.[28]

In his own words, in his 1978–79 lectures entitled *The Birth of Biopolitics*, Foucault tells us that in his explorations of madness, disease, delinquency, and sexuality:

> it was not a question of showing how these objects were for a long time hidden before finally being discovered, nor of showing how all these objects are only wicked illusions or ideological products to be dispelled in the light of reason finally having reached its zenith. It was a matter of showing by what conjunctions a whole set of practices—from the moment they become coordinated with a regime of truth—was able to make what does not exist (madness,

disease, delinquency, sexuality, etcetera), nonetheless become something, something however that continues not to exist. . . . It is not an illusion since it is precisely a set of practices, real practices, which established it and thus imperiously marks it out as reality.[29]

It should not be difficult at this point to see *race* as just this sort of nonexistent and yet very much real object, established and continually reestablished through a set of practices, emerging from and upholding particular regimes of truth, and serving particular political functions that are nevertheless disguised by the ways in which rules and practices surrounding race act as if it exists.

According to Foucault, the circulation of power within any truth regime occurs through four major types of technologies, "each a matrix of practical reason," and each of which, though possessing a specific nature, operates in constant interaction with the others:

(1) technologies of production, which permit us to produce, transform, or manipulate things; (2) technologies of sign systems, which permit us to use signs, meanings, symbols, or signification; (3) technologies of power, which determine the conduct of individuals and submit them to certain ends or domination, an objectivizing of the subject; (4) technologies of the self, which permit individuals to effect by their own means or with the help of others a certain number of operations on their own bodies and souls, thoughts, conduct, and way of being, so as to transform themselves in order to attain a certain state of happiness, purity, wisdom, perfection and immortality.[30]

To work within this Foucauldian understanding of technologies, rather than speak of *race as technology*, we might speak of *technologies of race* in two different but overlapping and co-constituting senses, which map onto my earlier description of race as both produced and productive: (1) we can speak of the technologies or practices through which concepts of race are created, reinforced, and given important social reality (the technologies that produce race); and (2) we can speak of the ways in which concepts of race are deployed in the service of political ends (the means by which race becomes productive). With respect to ARTs, then, rather than simply asking whether the notions of race employed and reproduced by ARTs are false or oppressive, we are urged to ask *how notions of race are being taken up, deployed, and transformed in and through ARTs* and *what sorts of diverse and multifaceted power relations are being supported, resisted, and reproduced in the process*. While I believe Foucault's concept of and approach to technologies resonates with and could illuminate almost all aspects of my overall project on race and ARTs, it will serve specifically as the theoretical grounding for chapter 5. There, I will draw on Foucault's observations about neoliberalism to argue that race is being both deployed and transformed in contemporary ART contexts as a technology of the self.

Conclusion

In this chapter, I have proposed that we further our investigation of the relationship between race and assisted reproductive technologies by thinking about race itself in terms of technology. I have offered several justifications for using the theoretical lens of technology to critically examine race, both in terms of philosophy of technology in general and in terms of Heidegger's and Foucault's insights in particular. In the remaining three chapters, I will carry out a series of overlapping analyses designed both to demonstrate the technological aspects of race and to shed light on the complex connections between race and ART practices.

Notes

1. Winner, *Whale and the Reactor*, 6.
2. Ibid., 21.
3. Franklin, *From Slavery to Freedom*, 98–100.
4. Haraway, "Race: Universal Donors in a Vampire Culture," 251–52.
5. Sheth, *Toward a Political Philosophy of Race*, 38–39.
6. Mendieta, "Migrant, Migra, Mongrel," 152–53.
7. Edelman, *O.J.: Made in America*, "Part 3."
8. Haraway, "Manifesto for Cyborgs," 8–11.
9. Bernasconi, "Critical Philosophy of Race," 13.
10. Taylor, *Race*, 6–7.
11. Nietzsche, *On the Genealogy of Morality*, 52–54.
12. See, for example, my argument comparing Collins and Foucault in "Black American Sexuality and the Repressive Hypothesis."
13. Taylor, *Race*, 44–45.
14. Ibid., 95, my emphasis.
15. Heidegger, "The Question Concerning Technology," 311–12.
16. Ibid., 312.
17. Ibid., 313.
18. In his effort to render *un*familiar what is most familiar (foundational or taken for granted) in our thinking or modes of existence, Heidegger often invents new, philosophically technical terms by altering existing vocabulary. Though these terms are interesting and the subject of significant study, I skip over several of them in my analysis in hopes of finding a balance between complexity and clarity. I find *bringing-forth*, *revealing* and *enframing* useful in my current context but have chosen to pass over terms like *lying ready*, *occasioning*, and *presencing*.
19. Heidegger, "The Question Concerning Technology," 318.
20. Ibid., 318–19.
21. Ibid., 320.
22. Ibid., 326–28.
23. Ibid., 320–21.

24. There is an argument to be made, though I do not make it here, for thinking about donated, banked, and stored gametes and embryos as a sort of reproductive *standing-reserve*. Such an argument might be able to examine the ethically troublesome intensification of reproductive technologies in a different way than the more typical language of commodification. Iain Brassington, for example, considers the question of whether biotechnologies, including ARTs, might render the field of medicine one in which human beings are enframed as standing-reserve. Ultimately, however, he concludes that, in spite of its use of modern technology, medicine (as a technology) is not "modern" in Heidegger's sense. See Brassington, "On Heidegger, medicine, and the modernity of modern medical technology."

25. Heidegger, "The Question Concerning Technology," 329.

26. Voegelin, *Race and State*, 177f14.

27. Gerrie, "Was Foucault a Philosopher of Technology?," 66.

28. Foucault, *History of Sexuality*, vol. 1.

29. Foucault, *Birth of Biopolitics*, 19.

30. Foucault, *Technologies of the Self*, 18.

3 A Technological History of Race

The fact that the word race does not occur in the description of nature (but instead, in its place, the word variety*) cannot keep an observer of nature from finding it necessary from the viewpoint of natural history.*

—Immanuel Kant, *"On the Use of Teleological Principles"*

IN THE 2011 movie *The Adjustment Bureau*, aspiring politician David Norris (played by Matt Damon) discovers that his life is being tampered with by a mysterious group of men in suits, dark coats, and hats, known simply as the Adjustment Bureau. These men (not quite human, all men, the most senior of whom are white) are known simply by their unremarkable last names. They are "the people who make sure that things happen according to plan." This constantly shifting plan, created by the godlike "Chairman," is written and rewritten in black notebooks that the bureau members carry with them at all times. In this screen adaptation of a short story by Philip K. Dick (which does not contain the historical soliloquy quoted below), we are meant to experience the triumph of free will as David fights for the right to choose his own life path and be with the woman he loves (played by Emily Blunt).

In one thematically climactic scene, a senior member of the bureau attempts to explain the importance of the Chairman's plan by giving a brief "history" lesson:

DAVID NORRIS: Whatever happened to free will?

THOMPSON: We actually tried free will before. After taking you from hunting and gathering to the height of the Roman Empire, we stepped back, to see how you'd do on your own. You gave us the dark ages for five centuries, until finally we decided we should come back in. The Chairman thought maybe we just needed to do a better job of teaching you to ride a bike before taking the training wheels off again. So we gave you the Renaissance, the Enlightenment, the Scientific Revolution. For six hundred years we taught you to control your impulses with reason. Then in 1910, we stepped back again. Within fifty years, you'd brought us World War I, the Depression, Fascism, the Holocaust, and capped it off by bringing the entire planet to the brink of destruction in the Cuban Missile Crisis. At that point a decision was taken to step back in before you did something that even we couldn't fix. You don't have free will, David; you have the appearance of free will.[1]

In this highly abbreviated and decidedly Western history, the Enlightenment, defined by the dominance of reason over impulse, is contrasted not only with the Dark Ages before it but with the violence, economic instability, and genocide of the twentieth century. We are meant to see the Enlightenment as a time of learning and human prosperity, as largely just and nonviolent, and as essentially unconnected to the events of the twentieth century, including Hitler's eugenic program. The Hollywood movie industry may not be known for its historical accuracy, but the fact that such a scene can be written, directed, produced, and distributed in this day and age—that its sentiments do not instantly appear to everyone as patently absurd—does seem to say something about the degree to which popular history has been written by the winners. It goes almost without saying that a great deal is left out of the above timeline, even if it is taken to be an exclusively Western one. After all, the same countries who are credited with the Enlightenment also colonized much of the rest of the world, draining it of its resources for Anglo-European gain. These same countries created the transatlantic slave trade.

One way to describe this phenomenon is through Charles Mills's notion of the *Racial Contract*—a metaphorical social contract with political, moral, and epistemological dimensions in which members of the dominant group (typically whites) agree to see the world and its history in a particular (and ultimately false) way. I quote Mills here at some length:

> *Globally*, the Racial Contract effects a final paradoxical norming and racing of space, a *writing out* of the polity of certain spaces as conceptually and historically irrelevant to European and Euro-world development, so that these raced spaces are categorized as disjoined from the path of civilization (i.e., the European project). . . . By the social contract's decision to remain in the space of the European nation-state, the connection between the development of this space's industry, culture, civilization, and the material and cultural contributions of Afro-Asia and the Americas is denied, so it seems as if this space and its denizens are peculiarly rational and industrious, differentially endowed with qualities that have enabled them to dominate the world. One speaks of the "European miracle" in a way that conceives this once marginal region as sui generis, conceptually severing it from the web of spatial connections that made its development possible. *This* space actually comes to have the character it does because of the pumping exploitative causality established between it and those *other* conceptually invisible spaces. But by remaining within the boundaries of the European space of the abstract contract, it is valorized as unique, inimitable, autonomous.[2]

In this passage, Mills marks the consistent erasure not only of a history of atrocities committed against non-Anglo-Europeans but also of a causal link between the aforementioned era of prosperity and development on the one hand and the atrocities of the twentieth century on the other. In other words, Mills might argue that what *The Adjustment Bureau* explains as a dramatic shift in the balance of good and evil brought about by the sudden absence of divine guidance should in fact be seen as part of the continuous development and refinement of a political system of white supremacy.

In what follows, I suggest that one way of thinking through the historical relationship between race and reproductive technologies is by tracing the interconnected history of race and eugenics, the ultimate villain of reproductive technologies. By offering a history that emphasizes this interconnection, I aim to challenge a popular contemporary distinction between rac*ism* and eugenics. As described in the introduction, the reduction of race to a form of scientific categorization (which we can now argue is false) has served an ideological function in allowing governments or entities like UNESCO to denounce racist beliefs without questioning the extent to which both racialized knowledge and a long history of racist practices permeate and structure the contemporary world. Similarly, the understanding of reproductive or eugenic technologies as essentially neutral tools that can be put to good or bad use by human agents serves the ideological function of distancing present efforts to solve social problems through control of reproduction from the much-denounced eugenic programs of the first half of the twentieth century. In short (to be expounded below), proponents of contemporary eugenics argue that by ensuring that current efforts are not backed by false race science and are not conducted by racists, such efforts can reasonably be seen as free from the discredited race project of which eugenics was originally a part.

Yet, in the previous chapter, I described how, for Heidegger, the essence of technology is found in a human drive to mastery that shapes the very terms on which "nature" is subsequently "discovered" and investigated by science (making technology both conceptually prior and deeply linked to science).[3] Thus, this history of race and eugenics seeks to demonstrate how the concept of race participates in this essence of technology by organizing people in the world into explanatorily powerful and technologically manipulable groups. Moreover, as a concept that was made "scientific" on the basis of rules of reproduction, race, we shall see, is not so easily banished from a larger desire and subsequent technological attempts to control human reproduction.

I will begin with a brief discussion of whether or how current and future reproductive and reprogenetic technologies should be seen as connected to the eugenics movements of the early twentieth century, focusing on a typical argument for the moral and political distinctness of the two. It is *against* this argument for distinctness that I offer an interpretation of the history of race that highlights its *technological* elements, including (1) the recognition by many theorists of race both that race was a conceptual category imposed by people onto nature and that racial purity was a human goal rather than a natural reality, (2) the deeply explanatory role race was thought to play in human history such that management of race would be necessary for shaping the future of nations and peoples, and (3) the repeated analogies to animal breeding that suggest that the development of the scientific race concept was always deeply influenced by discourses of human improvement and perfectibility through reproduction. These elements suggest that it is not the false concept of race that led eugenic efforts astray but rather eugenic desires that framed the invention of the race concept and put it to the work we now repudiate. In other words, the deep-seated human drive to mastery that Heidegger identifies and critiques underlies not only past and contemporary eugenic projects but also the very concept of race itself. Finally, I will present a brief argument for the idea that Heidegger himself saw racial breeding as a quintessential example of the technological worldview he sought to uncover and critique. I hope that this rendering of the history of race and eugenics provides an argument for their deep interconnection that is neither facile nor reactionary but rather nuanced and convincing.

Back Door to Eugenics?

Today's genetics proceeds under the shadow of eugenics. Nowhere is this shadow more obvious than in the case of reproductive and reprogenetic technologies. Those who argue for the necessity of ethical considerations in the development and execution of reprogenetic practice frequently warn of a return to eugenics. Such a return, they point out, will not be obvious or easily avoided. "To put it metaphorically," Troy Duster writes, "when eugenics reincarnates this time, it will not come through the front door, as with Hitler's *Lebensborn* project. Instead it will come by the back door of screens, treatments, and therapies."[4]

The term *eugenics* was coined by Englishman Francis Galton in his 1883 work, *Inquiries into Human Faculty and Its Development*, where it replaced the French word *viriculture*. Galton, a cousin, contemporary, and admirer of Charles Darwin, defined eugenics there as the "science of improving stock—not only by judicious mating, but whatever tends to give the more suitable races or strains of blood a better chance of prevailing over the less suitable than they otherwise would have had."[5] When Galton speaks of "races or strains," he is not concerned merely with something like the five human races (Caucasian, Mongolian, Malayan, Ethiopian, and American) that Blumenbach identified a century earlier. Rather, he is particularly concerned with the health of the *English* race and the risk of degeneration posed to it both by high fertility rates among the lower classes and by intermarriage between the fit and unfit.

Of course, the historical manifestation of eugenics that casts the greatest shadow is not Galton's concern for the vitality of the English race; it is that of Nazi Germany, with its euthanasia and forced sterilizations (first practiced against unfit "Aryans"), exterminations, and medical experimentation. However, we ought not to let this single most shocking and oft-discussed case prevent us from recognizing and taking into account the existence of diverse eugenics movements around the globe, often with different goals, beliefs, and proposed policies.[6] Indeed, according to Leila Zenderland, "a wide variety of eugenic ideas proved influential in at least thirty countries during the first four decades of the twentieth century." Far from being a unified movement with a single objective, she argues, eugenics before the First World War must be understood as a broad coalition of persons or groups promoting overlapping yet diverse scientific, social, or political agendas, including, in America alone, scientists, socialists, sexual reformers, immigrant radicals, physicians, agriculturalists, and popularizers.[7] Among the differences to be found between various proponents of eugenics were: (1) whether a eugenicist favored *positive eugenics* (encouraging the most fit to marry among themselves and have larger families) or *negative eugenics* (curbing the fertility of those judged least fit); (2) the extent to which eugenic interests were combined with a focus on race; (3) the specific policies that were recommended; and (4) political orientation.[8] Of course, the fact of this diversity also points to the ubiquity of eugenic thinking at the time.

In their ambitious, jointly written work on questions of ethics and justice in the application of new genetic technologies to human beings, bioethicists Allen Buchanan, Dan W. Brock, Norman Daniels, and Daniel Wikler identify three core tenets shared by most eugenicists of the early twentieth century. The first was a concern about degeneration, understood either as a consequence of modern social processes interfering with natural selection by rescuing and nurturing the unfit or as the result of race mixing, the offspring of which were thought to be inferior to either "pure" race from which they came. The second was a belief in the heritability of a variety of not merely physical but *behavioral* traits, like talents, temperaments, proclivities, and dispositions. Therefore, third, was the belief "that social problems had both a biological basis and, to some degree, a potential biological remedy" such that "reproduction was seen by all eugenicists as an act with social consequences rather than a private matter." Buchanan et al. go on to argue that "concern for human betterment through selection" or "taking measures to ensure that the humans who do come into existence will be capable of enjoying better lives and of contributing to the betterment of lives of others" is "an unexceptionable aim" and conclude that "much of the bad reputation of eugenics is traceable to attributes that, at least in theory, might be avoidable in a future eugenic program."[9]

One such attribute is the "pseudoscience" on which the old eugenics was based, which was infused with bigotry, racism, and class prejudices. On their account, the eugenics movement was, in this, simply "a creature of its time": "Racism, class snobbery, and other forms of bias were openly expressed even by learned scholars; these sentiments, so obviously objectionable today, were invisible then, because, of course, they were so widely shared."[10] Buchanan et al.

then consider and reject a number of theses about the wrong of eugenics. They defend the right—and indeed the duty—of parents to avoid bringing into the world children with severe disabilities. They argue that most of the values pursued by eugenicists, like intelligence and self-control, are widely shared by the population. They find—making no reference to the rather recent use of welfare policies to discourage or penalize reproduction among poor black women—that "reproductive freedoms are sufficiently well-established that we need not entertain serious fears about the return of coercive eugenics in the wake of the Human Genome Project."[11] They reject the idea that it is state participation in eugenics that poses the greatest risk to vulnerable populations and argue that the state might in fact provide protections to such populations. Having thus addressed major critiques of eugenics that might be thought necessarily to persist in any genetic program, Buchanan et al. are left with only two problems: poor science and unjust applications. With respect to the first, they write: "The eugenicists were ahead of their time—which was probably a good thing. Since they lacked the means to detect recessive genes in the population, even with full compliance their proposals would hardly make a dent in the distribution of the genes they imagined to be of social importance. . . . There is no reason to think that the eugenicists 'improved' the gene pool to any appreciable degree, nor could they have."[12] By contrast, they claim: "Our powers are much more impressive, and humankind's future abilities to rewrite our genetic code are apparently limitless."[13]

Working from the assumption that we now have the scientific and technological means to make a real difference in people's genetic lives, their question becomes how to do so justly: "Thus construed, the central moral problem of eugenics is akin to the perennial ethical quandary of public health, which seeks to benefit the public but in some cases exacts a penalty, such as quarantine or involuntary vaccination, on some individuals."[14] In other words, we must seek a just balance between public welfare and private freedoms. Such a balance is to be struck through careful attention to the effects of the new genetics on reproductive freedoms, by ensuring the "distribution" of self-respect to all members of the population despite differences in ability and performance that may arise from genetic intervention, and by ensuring that genetic difference does not result in a ghettoizing of those seen to carry higher genetic health risks. If we can do this work and remain vigilant with respect to the return of past abuses of eugenics, the argument goes, then there is no need to avoid pursuing its benefits. Thus, Buchanan et al. argue for a conceptual and ethical distinction between racist ideology and the idea of improving the health of a population through eugenic measures. They believe there are ways to use genetic science and technologies to pursue both private and public goods without bringing about the coercion and abuse that the term *eugenics* now connotes.

Such arguments can be very compelling and seem to be based in solid reasoning. They operate, however, only on the surface of the issue, failing to utilize key insights from the philosophy of technology or science and technology studies. They ascribe to science and technologies an essential neutrality prior to their use by human agents, and in so doing they necessarily call for people to control and regulate their uses of science and technology. Science and technology must be mastered and put to good and just use. If there is a "back door to eugenics," then, we must simply close it and keep a vigilant eye on it going forward to make sure it stays shut.

By contrast, Duster, in his much less optimistic approach, appeals to the sociology of knowledge to understand the history and future of eugenics. Rather than profess faith in our rational ability to choose to act justly, he expresses concern that we have come to see the world through a "prism of heritability."[15] If it is this prism that poses the *true* danger, how are we to take a vigilant stance with respect to the very ordering of our understanding? And what exactly does race have to do with it? These, I would argue, are the deeper questions; they bear serious investigation. When we look at race not simply as (bad) science, its role is harder to dismiss. Seen as technological, particularly in a Heideggerian sense, race can be recognized as a fundamental part of the prism of heritability that shapes our view of the world.

The Technological Science of Race

What follows is simply one of many possible narratives that could be offered about the history of race—more particularly, about the development of what we understand as the scientific concept of race (or what Voegelin calls *race theory*). The scientific race concept first reached a sort of coherence or maturity in the nineteenth century, which is to say that most people by that time believed race existed and was important, even if its exact workings and what ought to be done with it remained in passionate dispute. The development of the concept, however, was far from simple or linear. Rather, as Hannah Augstein describes, it emerged through the combination of previously rather distinct traditions: "a liberal, lay, anti-monarchical political outlook; the rise of the nation-state; biological and zoological investigations; phrenological and physiognomical fortune-telling; a political interest in finding a scientific justification for slavery; and the philological investigation of languages as a mirror of national character."[16] This diversity of influences and the diversity of views it spawned make the construction of a single, all-encompassing narrative about the scientific race concept exceptionally challenging, if not impossible.

It also suggests that we must avoid the temptation to frame the history of the concept entirely in terms of racist political motivations. Aside from the transatlantic slave trade (as just one example of an established practice in which phenotypical difference marked out certain people as exploitable), innovations in methods of world travel, the proliferation and popularity of travel logs, and the transplantation of both people and animals to climates different from their places of origin all contributed to the formulation of new questions about humanity that required new explanations. Indeed, Bernasconi and Lott warn that "the development of a rigorous scientific concept of race in Europe in the late eighteenth century was motivated more by the obsession with classification and an obsession with the causes of black skin rather than by the need to justify slavery."[17] To say that race theory did not develop simply in order to justify slavery and other similar practices that targeted specific groups, however, is not to say that such practices were not *racist*. It is simply to point out that: "It was possible for the Spanish or the English to exploit Jews, Native Americans, and Africans, as Jews, Native Americans, and Africans, without having the concept or race, let alone being able to appeal to a rigorous system of racial classification."[18] In other words, race theory is not required for racist practices (though it may certainly be used to justify them after the fact). Nevertheless, we should not imagine race theory as a purely scientific endeavor without political purpose. For example, in Kant's theory of race (to which I will turn next as arguably the first scientific concept of race), it is clear that Kant is concerned with providing a theory that accounts both for the unity of humankind (monogenesis) and for significant and permanent differences between various branches of humanity. As Sarah Figal argues, such theories were not merely explanatory but rather served an important function as a countermovement against the (potentially radical) concept of universal biological brotherhood implied by other defenses of biblical monogenesis.[19]

In any case, my chief aim here is not to clarify the senses in which race theories were or were not political in terms of their relation to practices like slavery, as others have already done. Rather, the less common story I want to tell is about how race theories should be understood not as simply or purely scientific but rather as importantly technological. Kant will serve as a (nonchronological) starting point and organizing example in this endeavor. I will explain how his was the first properly scientific elaboration of the race concept and how his explicit acknowledgment that race is something human beings *use to organize nature*—rather than something *discovered* in nature—makes this elaboration technological in a Heideggerian sense. I then discuss how race came increasingly to be seen as a driving force in history. Eventually, I argue, the race idea had so enframed modern science that new scientific theories, like Darwin's, had to be adapted to race rather than providing any perspective from which to challenge its existence. From this point, I demonstrate, eugenics are not so much a misstep as an already predetermined endpoint.

Kant's Scientific Concept of Race

Francois Bernier's essay, "A new division of the earth according to the different species or races of men," published anonymously in 1684, is commonly identified as the first use of the term *race* in something approaching its modern meaning, where humanity is divided into a few different groups characterized according to hereditary physical traits. In the essay, Bernier suggests that rather than dividing the earth according to countries or regions, geographers ought to consider dividing it by races. He suggests four to five such races or species: the first encompasses Europe, the northern coasts of Africa and parts of Asia and the Middle East; the second is constituted by the rest of Africa; the third is the rest of Asia; the Lapps (much maligned in race theory) are the fourth; and the (Native) Americans are a possible fifth. Bernier then goes on to muse about the beauty of the women of different races. He concludes that beauty "arises not only from the water, the diet, the soil, and the air, but also *from the seed which must be peculiar* to certain races and species."[20] While Bernier attributes human difference at least in part to internal components, however, his recommendation is limited to a new classification system. He does not speculate on the emergence of the different races or their relation to the human species as a whole, nor does he offer a clear distinction between the concepts of "race" and "species."

It was not until Immanuel Kant's 1775 essay "Of the Different Human Races" that someone gave the concept of race "sufficient definition for subsequent users to believe that they were addressing something whose scientific status could at least be debated."[21] In an expanded 1777 version of the essay (referenced below), Kant makes a clear distinction between race and species that was not found in other writings on race up to that point. He also defends monogenesis, incorporating climate theory to explain the development of different races while arguing for the internally determined permanence of racial types. At the same time, he articulates new criteria for natural science.

At the opening of the essay, Kant distinguishes between natural and artificial divisions of animals, in a rejection of Linnaean taxonomy. He writes: "An artificial division is based upon classes and divides things up according to similarities, but a natural division is based upon identifying distinct lines of descent that divide according to reproductive relations. The first of these creates an artificial system for memorization, the second a natural system for the understanding. The first has only the intent of bringing creatures under headings; the second has the intent of bringing them under laws."[22] This search for laws, understood in terms of causality and predictive power, was to become definitive of a new era of natural history or natural *science*. In a footnote later in the essay, Kant elaborates on this distinction, which he claims is novel:

We commonly make no distinction between the expressions "the description of nature" and "natural history." However, it is obvious that knowledge of the things of nature as they now are will always leave us wishing for knowledge of how they once were and by what series of changes they went through to come to their present place and condition. . . . Natural history would presumably lead us back from the great number of seemingly different species to races of the same genus and transform the presently overly detailed artificial system for the description of nature into a physical system for the understanding.[23]

In this footnote, we see that finding an explanation for the enduring human differences that would come to be conceived in terms of "races" was considered crucial to the study of mankind and of nature as a whole in the modern scientific era. Far from simply misguided and peripheral to the emerging biological sciences, the concept of race was foundational.

Kant continues his essay by offering a definition of races as "deviations that are constantly preserved over many generations and come about as a consequence of migration (dislocation to other regions) or through interbreeding with other deviations of the same line of descent, which always produces half-breed offspring."[24] Racial difference is thus distinguished from other forms of variety, like hair color in the white race, in terms of the possibilities of reproduction, as a brunette mother can still produce blond children. Kant identifies four races—the white race, the Negro race, the Hun race, and the Hindu race—and argues that "it is possible to derive all of the other hereditary characters of peoples from these four races either as mixed races or as races that originate from them," the latter case occurring "when a people has not yet lived long enough in a specific climate to take on fully the character of the race peculiar to that climate."[25] Kant's belief in the development of races over time and through mixtures also leads him to remark that: "The reason for assuming that Negroes and whites are the base races is self-evident."[26] This sense of black and white as being at opposite ends of the racial spectrum was also an enduring one.

Finally, in the last two sections of the essay, Kant sets himself to identifying "the immediate causes of the origin" and "the occasional causes of the establishment" of different races. In keeping with the understanding of heredity that was to prevail, Kant argues that features transmitted through reproduction cannot have external causes. Instead: "Any possible change with the potential for replicating itself must instead have already been present in the reproductive power so that chance development appropriate to the circumstances might take place according to a previously determined plan." Kant reasons that human beings, having been "created in such a way that they might live in every climate and endure each and every condition of the land," must have within them "numerous seeds and natural dispositions" that "lie ready . . . either to be developed or held back in such a way that we might become fitted to a particular place in the world."[27] The development of these seeds and dispositions in different directions is thus attributed to early human migration to different environments. It is, however, only "the original lineal formation" of the human being that possesses this full potential for environment adaptation; "in those regions where a race has become deeply rooted and stifled the other seeds, it resists further transformation, because the character of the race has become predominant in the reproductive power."[28] Thus, Kant provides an account of human natural history such that all of humanity stems from one original act of creation, further human adaption is due to environmental factors, and races, once developed, are permanent and cut off from those potentialities developed by other races. This account therefore accords with Christianity but does not imply ultimate human equality across races.[29]

Kant's account holds a strong claim to being the first scientific concept of race, then, because: (1) it provides a clear definition of the term, distinguishing *race* (as a set features that persist in reproduction) from *species* (as consisting of members capable of producing fertile offspring) and *varieties* (as features not guaranteed to persist in reproduction); (2) it offers an explanation for how racial difference emerged within the human species (in terms of climates and seeds); and (3) it describes the status of races (as permanent once sufficiently formed). Perhaps most importantly, as Kant himself emphasizes, the account is *scientific* in a sense similar to how we understand the term today because (4) it privileges internal causes as providing natural laws and therefore as being the most essential to human understanding. Now, if Kant's view is (newly) scientific for these reasons, in what senses can it be understood as technological? The answer is found in Heidegger's notion of technology as *revealing* and *enframing* nature. As described in the previous chapter and reiterated below, technology for Heidegger is a worldview in which human beings necessarily see the "truth" of nature through the lens of their own existing projects and concepts.

Race as Envisioned and Purposive

When Kant defends his concept of race in his 1788 essay, "On the Use of Teleological Principles in Philosophy," he states clearly something that we tend to think past holders of scientific conceptions of race would not believe: that the concept of race is something human beings *impose* upon nature. "What is a *race*?" Kant asks. He answers:

> The word itself certainly does not belong in a systematic description of nature, so presumably the thing itself is nowhere to be found in nature. However, the *concept* which this expression designates is nevertheless well established in the reason of every observer of nature who supposes a conjunction of causes placed originally in the line of descent of the genus itself in order to account for a self-transmitted peculiarity that appears in different interbreeding animals but which does not lie in the concept of their genus. The fact that the word race does not occur in the description of nature (but instead, in its place, the word *variety*) cannot keep an observer of nature from finding it necessary from the viewpoint of natural history.[30]

In short, Kant is arguing here that race is not something found in nature but rather a way for human beings to understand nature. This way of understanding nature is necessary because natural history demands not simply that we describe nature but that we grasp it teleologically—that is, in terms of its development according to causes and final purposes. On a Heideggerian account of the essence of technology, Kant's teleological framework for nature is explicitly technological since it *reveals* nature to human beings as purposive and *reveals* race as an essential explanatory device for understanding nature's purposes. Kant's view does not quite accord with Heidegger's description of the essence of *modern* technology, however, insofar as Kant does not portray nature's purposes as something that human beings are challenged to make more efficient. Indeed, as I will describe later, Kant explicitly takes up and rejects an early framing of a eugenic approach to reproduction.

Kant's theory of race also points to the absence at that time of the sort of disciplinary distinctions that we are often tempted to read back into the history of race thinking. In Kant's account of race, there are no neat separations between explanations that deal with the course of human natural development (what we might see as the biological), the course of human cultural development (the anthropological), the course of human events (the historical), and questions of underlying purpose (the philosophical). As already mentioned, it is important to recognize this lack of distinctions in the history of race so that we know better than to try to banish racism simply by disproving the biological reality of race. For my purposes here, however, recognizing the lack of disciplinary distinctions also helps to shed light on another technological aspect in the history of race theory—the fact that race came increasingly to be seen as a (or even *the*) driving force in human history. Thus, Robert Knox could write in 1850: "Race is everything: literature, science, art—in a word, civilization, depends on it"[31]; Benjamin Disraeli could say in 1852: "All is race. In the structure, the decay, and the development of the various families of man, the vicissitudes of history find their main solution."[32] Indeed, according to Eric Voegelin: "Since the history of national cultures in all periods is *also* a history of wars, of external and internal struggles, victories, and defeats, all its phases in principle can be interpreted in terms of race theory."[33]

G. W. F. Hegel's philosophy of history, on which he lectured regularly from 1822 until his death in 1831, provides an early example of this type of totalizing race-based interpretation of human events, typically constructed through rather selective use of travelogues. As Bernasconi describes, though the earliest travelers both to America and to Africa recognized differences between the various nations found on those continents, ultimately "the homogenizing discourse of race supplanted those differentiations," leaving the impression that only the Caucasians were sufficiently sophisticated to merit careful ethnic and national divisions, and "Hegel expressly accepts this differentiation between the races that divide into peoples and those that do not when he introduces the notion of a 'people.'"[34] Thus, while it is *peoples* rather than races that participate in history for Hegel, world history proper only begins, on his account, with the Caucasians.[35]

Later developers of these ideas would not hesitate to posit race itself as the principle engine of human history, linking physical differences with various typologies or drives thought to fuel the development of civilization and progress. One such figure was Gustav Klemm, a German anthropologist and librarian who published his ten-volume *Allgemeine Kulturgeschichte der Menschheit* (*General Cultural History of Mankind*) between 1843 and 1852. On Klemm's account, active races (like Caucasians) were smaller in number but multiplied more vigorously and were characterized by a striving for dominance, independence, and freedom. Passive (colored) races were psychologically akin to women in that they developed quickly but soon stagnated; they were also intellectually lazy and possessed only practical knowledge, rather than philosophy or science.[36] In Klemm's description of the active and passive races, we can note a number of important racial themes; naïve ethnocentrism is revealing its more sinister undertones. (Undertones that are far from new at this stage, being already clear in John Locke's *Two Treatises of Government*, published in 1689.) The passive races are described as numerous but seen as largely unproductive, contributing to a colonialist rationale that sees lands held by passive races as being wasted and as in need of the industry of the active races. Conquest is given a positive moral character, seen as both natural and productive. Finally, the active and passive races are distinguished by the former's capacity for reason and, specifically, its scientific worldview. Science, made synonymous with progress, thus comes to be seen as the exclusive property of the active, Caucasian races.

Klemm's understanding of race as driving history through race mixing was further developed by Joseph Arthur Comte de Gobineau, with whom the idea came to be most associated and whose work was taken up in his own time and later in Germany as justification for policies aimed at preserving racial purity. Ironically, Gobineau's *Essay on the Inequality of the Human Races* (1853–55) does not actually oppose race mixing. His view, though quite similar to Klemm's, brings a fundamental pessimism to the process, which undoubtedly appealed to those who wished to paint a picture of impending doom for which the only solution would be strong racial politics. Gobineau argued that man's time on earth would span a total of twelve to fourteen thousand years and could be divided into two periods: "the first, which has passed, will have seen and possessed the youth, vigour and intellectual greatness of humanity; the other, which has already begun, will see its waning and inevitable decline."[37] In other words, the human race (through race mixing) had reached a peak and (also through race mixing) had begun a long, slow decline into mediocrity. This conclusion was, for

Gobineau, a scientific fact and not one to be moralized. Society simply existed, carrying with it no morality, and the idea of continual, perpetual progress was a foolish illusion.[38]

As Voegelin points out, these ideas are based "implicitly in Klemm, explicitly in Gobineau—on the premise that the polar opposites of the race types, whose contacts serve as explanation of world events, remain constant throughout known history."[39] At the same time, however, the *mixing* of races is the crucial element of the process, making racial purity (as the source of race type) more important as an *ideal* than as something one would actually expect to discover in the modern world. By making racial type an abstract ideal, physical anthropologists like Paul Topinard could defend the important of race even in the complete absence of any of the empirical evidence they hoped to gather on the human races using their increasingly sophisticated methods of measurement. He wrote of races in 1883: "we cannot deny them, our intelligence comprehends them, our mind sees them, our labor separates them out; if in thought we suppress the intermixtures of people, their inter-breedings, in a flash we see them stand forth—simple, inevitable, a necessary consequence of collective heredity."[40] In other words, races are real because we can see them so clearly in our imagination and our ordering of the world.

Such was the importance of the role of race in understanding human natural and cultural history by the mid-nineteenth century that even a paradigm-shifting framework like Darwin's theory of evolution would adapt itself and be adapted to many of the key elements of race theory, rather than challenging them. In November of 1859, Charles Darwin published his groundbreaking work, whose full title was *On the Origin of Species by Means of Natural Selection, or the Preservation of Favoured Races in the Struggle for Life*. While Darwin used the word *race* in the title simply as a synonym for *variety* and deliberately confined his discussion to the rest of the animal kingdom, leaving the controversial question of *human* origin and evolution out of things, his readers were eager to think about Darwin's new theory in terms of humanity. Though the theory of evolution clearly points to a single origin for all of humanity and had gained wide acceptance by 1870, as with earlier theories of monogenesis (like Kant's), Darwin's work did not function to establish a universal brotherhood of all humankind. Rather, evolutionary theory could be made to accord with the view that race was the most crucial mechanism of human development and history through arguments like that presented by Alfred Russell Wallace in 1864. Wallace claimed that the common ancestors of all humankind lived long ago and that by the time the human species developed the intellectual capacities that made it truly human, the various human races had already been differentiated by natural selection, after which point natural selection ceased to affect racial development, and those races remained static as far as their physical structure was concerned.[41] This allowed Wallace to claim both original unity and current difference for mankind and to prioritize difference.[42] Besides explaining racial physical types as distinct and permanent, Wallace's 1864 paper argued for how moral and intellectual differences between the human races could serve as the basis for a racial struggle for survival. According to Wallace, the less morally and intellectually able of the races perished in that struggle while the more able survived to spread themselves across the globe.[43] Darwin was much pleased by Wallace's paper, though, much to Darwin's dismay, Wallace's views were to change significantly by the time Darwin put similar thought to paper in *The Descent of Man, and Selection in Relation to Sex*, published in 1871.

Because Darwin is figured by many as a hero in the narrative of scientific progress, he has many apologists who insist that Darwin not be seen as responsible for the racialist uses to which his theory (or what they might argue were perversions of his theory) were put. They point to the facts that he was a monogenist and an abolitionist—both true. Yet we need not label Darwin a "racist" to acknowledge that, as Stepan argues: "In essence, Darwin himself carried out the task of accommodating the new evolutionary science to the old racial science."[44] Darwin's annotations of various contemporaneous books on humankind indicate not only that "he took to his readings a commitment to the idea of human races as discrete, biological units with distinct mental and moral traits" but also that he "searched the available literature on man for evidence that all the elements of his evolutionary scheme—variation, struggle, migration and extinction—were found at the human, racial level."[45] In his early notebooks, Darwin wrote: "When two races of men meet, they act precisely like two species of animals. . . . they fight, eat each other, bring diseases to each other, etc., but then comes the more deadly struggle, namely which have the best fitted organisation, or instinct (i.e., intellect in man) to gain the day?" And, indeed, this early idea is repeated in *Descent*, where "Darwin took the view that natural selection worked on individual and racial variations to select, during racial struggle, the most fit races and to raise them up in the scale of civilization."[46]

In the first part of *The Descent of Man*, reliance on existing views of race, racial difference, and racial hierarchy (which differences and hierarchies were taken to be obvious)[47] also helped Darwin to answer what he saw as a principle objection to the application of his principles of evolution to human beings: the "great break in the organic chain between man and his nearest allies, which cannot be bridged over by any extinct or living species."[48] In his efforts to highlight the anatomical, mental, and moral continuity between various animals and mankind, Darwin divided mankind into "civilized races" and various "savage" or "lower" ones. He then argued for both the similarities between "savages" and animals on the one hand and for a developmental hierarchy along which "lower races" and "civilized" ones could be placed on the other. Thus the "lower races" and "savages" were used to fill part of the perceived mental and physical gap between Darwin's European readers and the rest of the animal kingdom. As for the remaining distance between even the "lowest savage" and the most advanced primate, Darwin argues that

> these breaks depend merely on the number of related forms which have become extinct. At some future period, not very distant as measured by centuries, the civilised races of man will almost certainly exterminate, and replace, the savage races throughout the world. At the same time the anthropomorphous apes . . . will no doubt be exterminated. The break between man and his nearest allies will then be wider, for it will intervene between man in a more civilised state, as we may hope, even than the Caucasian, and some ape as low as a baboon, instead of now between the negro or Australian and the gorilla.[49]

In this clear summary of Darwin's answer to those who viewed mankind as too superior to have evolved from other forms of life, Darwin both reiterates existing racial hierarchies and justifies the extermination of "savage races" as natural and, indeed, inevitable.

Thus, any serious challenge to race theory posed by the idea of evolution as continual change was subverted, demonstrating how tight a grip the idea of race not only as *type* but as *cause* had on the scientific community.[50] Multiple theories of *polygenist evolution* sprung up, intent on proving the insurmountable *dissimilarity* between the human races, whether by pushing their emergence from a common human ancestor way back in evolutionary history or by arguing that the different races evolved into humanity from different primate ancestors. As the most visible and politically charged sign of human diversity, the notion of race was foundational to nearly all theories of human heredity at that time, and evolutionism simply "provided a new, emotionally charged, yet ostensibly scientific language with which to express old prejudices."[51] New science was adapted to old ideas, rather than the other way around, as narratives of science as progress would have it.

This preponderance of race theories that took race to be a key mechanism in human history (whether the theorists recognized that race is an imposed category—as did Kant and Topinard—or not) points to the role of race as *enframing* modern science and, therefore, as essentially technological in Heidegger's sense. Race became a conceptual framework for nature and the lens through which to understand humanity. Kant's call for a shift from the "description of nature" to what he called "natural history" called for the classification of living things not in terms of exhaustive lists or so-called arbitrary traits but rather in terms of systems and laws. It would no longer be enough to simply describe human and animal diversity and to assume that the reasons for it were known by God. Indeed, all external causes, like God and climate, would be called into question in favor of internal (and unchanging) causes, which though not directly observable, were to be understood through the power of reason.

In the development of science, human beings were eager to see nature not as mysterious but as predictable, as operating with purposes analogous to human goals. It was no longer enough for human diversity to have an explanation; ultimately it needed to have a function. If, after all, racial difference is so apparent to us, it must have been important to human cultural and biological history. This, as Voegelin described, was the race *idea*, and it was that *idea* (or technological worldview or prism of heredity) that was to fuel and guide race *science* (not the other way around). Race science would not "discover" race but would instead be called upon to explain that which, to paraphrase Topinard, our mind already sees and our intelligence already comprehends. As Heidegger would suggest, by this point, this comprehension and a demand for an explanation of race cannot now— and, indeed, never could have been—neatly separated from the drive to control it.

Race as Producible and Produced

Given the importance race and race mixing came to have as explanatory devices with respect to (what we would describe today as) both the natural and social sciences, it is not at all surprising that attention would turn to taking control of these processes for the advancement of humanity and human civilization. After all, for Heidegger, what characterizes the *modern* essence of technology is not simply the view of nature as offering the material for human projects but, more-over, the challenge nature seems to pose to humanity to harness and store up its powers. What is particularly important here in thinking about the relationship between race (as science) and eugenics (as technology), however, is Heidegger's assertion that technology does not simply follow after science but rather offers the conceptual framework within which science is produced in the first place. Here, then, I seek to show how animal breeding as a technology provided the conceptual framework within which the scientific race concept emerged and developed, making eugenic thinking much more essential to the race concept itself than is typically recognized.

According to Enrique Ucelay Da Cal, an "intense and somewhat blind 'humano-centrism'" has shaped the study of racism, with most investigators of racism evincing "no particular curiosity in animals as a historical subject with relevance to their research."[52] By contrast, he argues for the importance of human—animal parallels as well as botanical models in the historical under-standing of the natural world, reminding us that Linnaeus was a botanist by training, that much of the Enlightenment interest in taxonomy was botanical, and that preoccupations in raising both the value of property and its productivity through botanical manipulation were easily translated to English animal hus-bandry in the eighteenth century.[53]

Returning to Kant's essay on race as the first articulation of a scientific race concept, we should recall that his definitions of species, race, and variety all rest on rules for reproduction. Two animals belong to the same species if they can meet "Buffon's rule" by mating and producing fertile offspring. Racial deviations between two animals of the same species are those deviations that are consistently preserved in reproduction through many generations. Two animals of the same species belong to different races if, when they mate, they produce half-breed offspring (that is, the enduring racial deviations belonging to the two parents are mixed in the offspring). Deviations belonging to mere varieties are those that may or may not be preserved in reproduction. These rules of reproduction, which shape the first scientific concept of race, and which remain important in accounts of race mixing as driving history (as in Klemm and Gobineau), have clear origins in the study of mating and breeding possibilities in nonhuman animals, which study, I would argue, is based in the *technology* of animal breeding.

Indeed, one account of the origin of the term *race* (in its current use as a way of describing human groups or lineages) traces its first emergence to the Spanish language, where *raza* was extended to human beings from a more primary definition referring to the "caste or quality of authentic horses." While the human application was a secondary definition of *raza* in the earliest Spanish dictionary in 1611, Audrey Smedley argues that by 1737, "the caste of quality of origin or lineage" in reference to human beings had become *raza*'s first and primary meaning.[54] This emergence of the term *race* in the Spanish language took place in the context of the Spanish Inquisition (established in 1478 and not abolished until 1834), which was "designed to weed out recalcitrant converts or 'secret' Jews by investigating personal behavior and genealogies for the taint of Jewishness."[55] This "identification of race with a breeding line or stock of animals carries with it certain implications for how Europeans came to view human groups," argues Smedley, since "unlike other terms for classifying people (e.g., 'nation,' 'people,' 'variety,' 'kind,' etc.), the term 'race' places emphasis on innateness, on the inbred nature of whatever is being judged."[56] Whereas conversion, a "voluntary" human action, was once sufficient to alter one's social status, now one's lineage gained major significance. Human lineage, like that of a horse, could be documented but in theory could not be changed.

In the French context, Buffon, of whom Kant made use in his attempts to divide animals according to laws, also relied in the development of his theories on the drawing of parallels between human and animal physiology—what was called the "analogical method." Buffon's highly influential *Histoire naturelle* was published in forty-four volumes between 1749 and 1804. From Buffon's viewpoint, "one of the most salient distinctions between human tribes was that between civilization and the savage state." Comparing this directly to the difference between domesticated and wild animals, Buffon concluded that "all the insights of professional livestock breeders could be exploited to explain mankind."[57] The analogical method was useful because the *practice* or *technology* of animal (and plant) breeding operated successfully well in advance of any scientific theories that could effectively explain breeders' results, with breeders establishing practice-based axioms and breeding rules that yielded significant power to "mold" organisms for specific features from the mid-eighteenth century on.[58] Indeed, Müller-Wille and Rheinberger point to the erosion in the early nineteenth century of institutional barriers like those between naturalists and breeders as paving the way for the discourse of heredity. This, as we shall see, is clearly visible in the work of Charles Darwin, and even earlier in that of his grandfather, Erasmus Darwin (who was also the grandfather of Francis Galton). In some cases, like that of Pierre-Louis Moreau de Maupertuis (writing before Buffon in the first half of the eighteenth century), no erosion of barriers was necessary. Maupertuis both bred his own pets looking for hereditary patterns and recorded the genealogy of a human family in Berlin, some members of which were born with extra fingers and toes (polydactyly).[59] Buffon also conducted his own breeding experiments.

Analogies to animal breeding were also popular among a number of physicians in the mid- to late eighteenth century. Scottish philosopher and professor of medicine John Gregory, in the aptly titled *A Comparative View of the State and Faculties of Man with Those of the Animal World*, speculated that humans possess a natural "stamp" passed through families that places a natural limit on their potential cultivation through education and training. Given this important role he posits for heredity, he argues, by analogy to animal breeding, that the question of "how a certain character or constitution of Mind" can be transmitted from parent to child should be given greater focus. "Yet we every day see very sensible people," he laments, "who are anxiously attentive to preserve or improve the breed of their Horses, tainting the blood of their Children and entailing on them not only the most loathsome diseases of Body, but Madness, Folly, and the most unworthy dispositions."[60] In this, the comparison to animal breeding points not only to the *possibility* of human improvement through control of reproductive practices but also to its *desirability* and *wisdom*. Similarly, in his *Essai sur la manière de perfectionner l'espece humaine* (*Essay on the Manner of Perfecting the Human Species*), French physician Charles Augustin Vandermonde argued that: "If chance is responsible for the degeneration of the human species, art can just as well perfect it." Nature would provide variety, but it was up to human beings to bring order to the chaos by learning to combine nature's varieties intelligently.[61]

English physician (natural philosopher, industrialist, and social reformer) Erasmus Darwin—known among his contemporaries as "Dr. Darwin"—also had a particular (though arguably historically neglected) interest in the hereditary nature of human diseases, which included not only physical ailments like gout and consumption but also alcoholism and insanity. Dr. Darwin felt about medicine much as Kant did about natural history, arguing that: "A theory founded upon nature, that should bind together the scattered facts of medical knowledge, and converge into one point of view the laws of organic life, would . . . on many accounts contribute to the interest of society."[62] Moreover, Dr. Darwin felt that such a theory should be used "to learn how best to exert power over nature" in order to overcome or prevent diseases.[63] In his efforts to promote human progress through positive control of nature, Dr. Darwin referenced the lessons learned by animal breeders. Citing breeders' knowledge that breeding animals within the same family (even if that family showed a number of good traits) always carried the risk of strengthening dangerous defects found in the family line, he attempted to convince the aristocracy, in particular, to avoid the perpetuation of hereditary diseases by marrying outside the ancestral lineage.[64] For Dr. Darwin, then, analogies to animal breeding not only served to generate theories about the heredity nature of human disease but also suggested that human progress could be pursued biologically by learning the laws of nature and then exerting power over them.

These views suggesting the possible benefits of technological control of human reproduction using analogies to animal breeding practices (which, though effective in improving livestock, could not yet be explained scientifically) form the background against which Kant attempted to elaborate a scientific race concept using rules of reproduction. And, indeed, Kant felt the need to address this technological possibility in his essay on race. Yet, in spite of a sort of naïve racism visible in the essay (as when he offhandedly describes the Negro as "lazy, indolent, and dawdling" but describes whites as having blood with a perfect mixture of "juices" and a strength in their human stock greater than that of others), when Kant takes up Maupertuis's proposal for an early eugenic project, he rejects human intervention in favor of following nature's purposive course for humanity.[65] Though Kant does not adopt a policy of human intervention in reproduction, the fact that he is aware of such proposals and addresses them in his essay is significant. It not only challenges a view of eugenics as the (immoral) technological application of an already developed racial science but also suggests that thoughts on human reproductive control understood by analogy to animal breeding framed Kant's purposive view of nature in terms of races. In other words, it offers further evidence in favor of Heidegger's claim that human projects (technology) shape the human view of nature (science), even where explicit pursuit of technological control of nature is rejected.

Further indicative of the technological context in which scientific race concepts were elaborated is the appearance in the eighteenth century of the concept of "police" or the "science of administrating a state."[66] The question of maintaining the health and productivity of the population of a state was an important one for this science, as demonstrated by the publication, beginning in 1779, of Johann Peter Frank's six-volume *System einer vollständigen medicinischen Policey* (*System for a Complete Medical Police*).[67] Convinced that the human race, in his time, as compared to earlier generations, had deteriorated in strength and dignity, Frank believed in the power of *medical police* to gradually restore it. "For why should we be less successful in experiments with the animal-like man," he asks, "than in experiments with other animals whose races we have learned to improve sometimes in a whole country by diligence and art?"[68] To this end, in the first two volumes of the work, Frank laid out a "radical proto-eugenic plan for a state-sponsored program of restricted breeding practices."[69]

Within a context of growing concern for the social consequences of reproduction and increasing confidence in the manipulability of both animal and human heredity, a flexible (though still purportedly scientific) concept of race had a number of roles to play. "For ambitious scientists eager to use emerging knowledge of heritability and biological generation to facilitate the generation of a new and better world," writes Figal, "the species as a whole functioned effectively as a rallying point toward which efforts could be focused." Yet the whole human species was far too large and abstract an entity to be the useful target for any practical plan for improvement.[70] At the same time, the idea of improving individual families seemed too small in scale and might fail to impress upon people the importance of allowing for public intervention in their intimate affairs. The idea of improving a *race*, however, was both sufficiently meaningful and seemingly manageable. Racial differences, whether they were conceived in terms of the major four or five races in the world or the local races of Europe, had sufficient and sufficiently visible reality for people to generate their concern. Visible racial difference could also stand in for the wide variety of invisible traits and diseases that were thought to be hereditary (including those involving intelligence and character), and which might pose a threat to national health or human civilization at large. In other words, as Figal argues, "part of the appeal of the broad and vague notion of race for writers of the era . . . was its function as a bridge between these two extremes, the individual reproducing unit and the species, the part and the whole."[71]

As animal breeding became increasingly elaborate and fashionable in eighteenth-century England, it came to represent and perpetuate a particular modern view of the world. The English gentlemen-farmers who sought systemically to improve breeds of cattle and sheep during this period also established new institutions for the comparison and improvement of animal types, such as the country fair. According to Da Cal, while fairs for selling animals were nothing new, "the cult of types" was. Stud services for "improving" types and "bettering" stocks not only made money but were viewed as "a patriotic service to the 'National Herd.'" Similarly, a new world of thoroughbred horses sprung up, with a simpler admiration for fine animals being overlain by systematization and official codes concerning the horses' genealogical "blood" and "temperament." From about 1791 on, "thoroughbreds" were listed by parentage in an official stud-book, "an equine equivalent of the human 'blue-blood's' family tree." By the 1850s, the obsession with animal pedigree even led to a domestic "poultry craze." "Scarcely surprising, then," writes Da Cal, "that this same period would see the highpoint of scientific and literary fascination with human types, from the physiognomic treatises of Lavater or F.X. Messerschmidt or the comparative anatomy of Negroes and apes, to the extensive Romantic literature describing 'customs' by national or social 'character.'"[72]

Charles Darwin's interest in and analogical use of animal breeding is well documented in the Transmutation Notebooks he kept while constructing his theory of natural selection between 1837 and 1839. Moreover, in March of 1839, apparently feeling the need for a greater volume of information from breeders than he could reasonably gain through personal correspondence, Darwin wrote up an eight-page pamphlet entitled "Questions about the Breeding of Animals," which he had printed privately and then distributed himself.[73] According to Millman and Smith, it is important to see the emergence in Darwin of the analogy between artificial selection and natural selection as part of a larger process of comparison and contrast within the domains of the natural (or nature) and the human (or "man"), wherein human intervention in breeding is understood as *art* (technology) in contrast to the workings of nature. Darwin's process included contrasting "domesticated species and wild species, 'civilized man' and 'savage,' reason and instinct, domesticated varieties made by humans and domesticated varieties made by nature."[74]

In 1838, after Darwin read economist and population theorist Reverend Thomas Robert Malthus, a major leap in Darwin's thinking occurred, leading to increased emphasis on competition between species and between individuals within the same species, such that "an element of intensified competition, struggle, and consequently selection was introduced into [Darwin's] picture of nature."[75] Though Darwin's initial concept of natural selection was not constructed by analogy with artificial selection, he would come to draw an analogy between the two processes in the months following his Malthusian insight. "As the contrast between the two mechanisms of artificial and natural selection eroded, Darwin turned things around: There are still differences, but they are differences in the length of time the processes have had to work and in the completeness of selection."[76] Once the relationship was recast in terms of degree or intensity (rather than polar contrast), Darwin could then solicit detailed data and observations on the process of artificial selection from breeders and bring it to bear on the process of natural selection, which, given the time period over which it acts, cannot be observed in its own right.[77]

Moreover, this analogy to artificial selection did not simply aid in Darwin's *own* conceptualization and development of the theory of natural selection. By March of 1839, "Darwin had enough confidence in his new theory of the mechanism in nature that he could sketch notes to himself about how to use the analogy in expressing his theory and in persuading others, using examples of artificially produced breeds to introduce the idea of selection as a mechanism distinct from directed adaptation and acting on accidental variation."[78] This additional use of the analogy in explicating the theory to *others* serves to multiply the influence of the analogy on the theory as a whole.

By the time of Darwin's major publications on natural selection (1859–71), breeding was very much present in the public imagination. "Mid-century brought the jump from animal husbandry to animal fancy," writes Da Cal, "that is to say that the cult of the type reached the pet, specifically the dog. . . . The first dog show was held in Newcastle in 1859, the British Kennel Club founded in 1873." Without the concern for productivity that guided animal husbandry (or even the breeding of dogs for racing or hunting), artificial selection in the realm of pets "could soar to new and extravagant typologies supported by breeding associations and their neo-aristocratic paraphernalia."[79] In dog fancying, the concept of breed "meant the codification of external characteristics, ascribing to a given combination certain moral values (a breed that is, for example, inherently 'loyal'), and finally nationalizing, since breeds have been increasing conceived of as 'national' types."[80] Note that in this context (as compared to earlier animal husbandry), *moral character* has taken on greater significance. As Paul White describes: "In Victorian discourses of breeding, natural historical and moral character were considerably intertwined" and the "power to mold character through the manipulation of conditions and the exercise of will, was in fact the operative principle in another Victorian creature: the self-made man."[81] Here, too, an analogy is drawn between the human and animal realms, this time relating the gentleman farmer or breeder himself (and his pedigree) to those animals he cultivates (and the stud book he keeps). "Much attention has been given to the intellectual (say philological) or scientific or religious sources surrounding [political] racism," Da Cal argues, "but little attention has been paid to the capacity of animal breeding—both husbandry and fancy—with its vast associative network to reach far beyond where sophisticated academic debates could be heard."[82] It is, of course, this same capacity that Darwin recognized in choosing to explain his theory of natural selection in terms of breeding practices.

Yet the effect of human technological control over animal reproduction can be seen as going far beyond simply making "natural mechanisms" broadly intelligible. Rather, innovations in the management of animal populations can be seen as paving the conceptual way for similar interventions on the human level.

Da Cal demonstrates that many sanitation, hygiene, and vaccination practices in human populations (whether seen now as progressive or repressive) have animal analogs. For example, "with the success of the Pasteur anti-rabies vaccine (1885), hydrophobia—an ancient fear which had always provoked reactions of isolation towards both animal and human victims—became *the* image of effective social prophylaxis." Similarly: "The most interesting idea surrounding the dog pound, and the one that most clearly links it to ideas of social hygiene (in fact, being formulated in criminology at the same time) is that dogs and other animals gathered up for destruction are considered dangerous because they are a *potential* hazard, not because they actually do have any disease."[83] Though Da Cal recognizes a number of other social factors and institutional backgrounds that contributed to the events of the Holocaust, he concludes, in what I see as a largely technological argument, that "the handling of animals is the only real social model, i.e. existing in industrial society, for the kind of segregation and elimination that the Nazis tried to carry out." Without attempting to make any extreme, simplifying, or totalizing claims, Da Cal simply suggests "that the animal breeding sub-culture [was] a sort of 'lower common denominator' of biological information in the late XIXth and XXth century European societies," which was "key to transmitting 'highbrow' racist ideas to 'lowbrow' audiences" in that it "created a visual vocabulary and a living representation of race theory that was equally powerful on peasant farms or urban settings."[84]

Practices of animal (and plant) breeding were, in their origins, just that—practices. Theories came after. In other words, for a long time, animal breeding was a technology rather than a science. As I argue below, this technology—more than the race *science* that emerged on its heels—should be seen as the precursor to eugenics. Having pointed to some instances of the intersections between the studies of race, heredity, and natural science on the one hand and the rules and practices of animal breeders on the other, I hope to have shown that these various ideas share a particular modern sensibility—a sensibility that Heidegger has described as technological in the way that it presents the natural world to human beings as something that challenges them to intervene in "natural" processes in the name of industry, efficiency, productivity, and ultimately perfectibility. It is also helpful to emphasize here the role of metaphor and analogy in the linkages of these concepts. With the modern period, we find science developing precisely *as* the interpretation of the natural world through technological metaphors. Nature is expected to exhibit a form of rationality and to reveal to man its essential laws. As Heidegger notes, and Kant and Darwin both demonstrate, to the extent that such laws were discovered in the physical sciences, those sciences set the standard for all science. Natural or biological scientists were therefore expected to make similar discoveries. They were tasked with uncovering the *laws, mechanisms*, and *final causes* of biological life (and indeed human history and culture), and they did so largely through race.

Race, Heredity, and Eugenics Proper

The story of what race was in the eighteenth and nineteenth centuries is much more complex than is implied either by the aforementioned UNESCO critique, which focused on race as a (misused) scientific category, or by views that take the idea of race to have developed primarily to justify chattel slavery or other widespread racist practices of modern period. It is important to recognize how an increase in global travel and trade (colonization and expedition) brought the question of human (racial) diversity to the forefront of the public and scientific imagination and how the effort to understand the causes of human diversity eventually led to the perception of human diversity itself *as* a cause for history and civilization. Because the persistence of human diversity called for a longer biological time line than previously given by the Bible, however, it was not possible to gather the sort of data and observation about human development called for in the new scientific method. Here, then, analogies to animal breeding became particularly useful because the arenas of animal and plant breeding offered relatively controlled environments, and changes made in animal populations occurred quickly enough as to be observable by humans. Indeed, breeders were having great success in prescribing rules for their practice and getting reasonably predictable results. Thus analogies were made both between humans and animals as biological beings (comparing diversity in the human species with diversity in animal species) and between humanity and nature (comparing human technological activity with the activity of nature). While in many ways productive, such analogies served, in the first instance, to obscure the role of politics, economics, and culture in the course of human biological and anthropological development and in the second instance to attribute a sort of moral authority and final cause to the course of nature. The function of these analogies, then, was to support the development of both race science and eugenics.

As Millman and Smith remind us, "analogies go in both directions, with each domain being elaborated, restructured, or both."[85] The breeding analogy served both as a generative analogy for scientific theorizing and as an interpretive analogy for the public in understanding the new science. As such, it also slipped easily between the descriptive and the prescriptive, as in the advent of *social Darwinism.* This slippage can be described as follows: First, the breeders' actions of artificial selection are seen as providing a microcosmic view of natural selection in the whole natural realm; second, natural processes are described as both inevitable and good; third, it is argued that human beings *should* follow (and indeed help along) the course of nature. The result, then, is that human beings use technology to carry out a natural "imperative," which itself stems from human technological action in the first place. Ultimately, however, recourse to nature as justification is not always necessary. Insofar as the mixing of racial types was thought to account for human cultural and biological development (whether for good or ill) and the (re)creation of pure racial types was thought to be desirable or necessary, animal breeding practices offered a model for how this could be achieved. As Da Cal reminds us, "many breeds have to be artificially maintained by killing off all that part of the litter that does not correspond to type (Dalmatians are a well-known example)."[86] The power of the "type," then, belongs not to nature itself but to human perception and the technological efforts that follow from that perception. People take the importance they see in race, originally attributed to (a purposive) nature, and then argue that something as crucial as the health and progress of humanity (or races or nations) ought not to be left to chance. Nature, if it cannot necessarily be resisted or tampered with, can certainly be improved upon or helped along.

Given the extensive role of analogy just discussed, it should come as no surprise that Francis Galton, the so-called father of eugenics, wrote in an 1865 article for *Macmillan's Magazine* that: "The power of man over animal life, in producing whatever varieties of form he pleases is enormously great. It would seem as though the physical structure of future generations was almost as plastic as clay, under the control of the breeder's will. It is my desire to show more pointedly than—so far as I am aware—has been attempted before, that mental qualities are equally under control."[87] Here an analogy between heredity in man and heredity in other animals is combined with an analogy between physical heredity and mental heredity.[88] Nor should it be surprising that, despite his personal focus on the improvement of the English racial stock, Galton turns to broader ethnology later in the article to offer further "proof" of the connection between physical and mental attributes. He writes: "The Mongolians, Jews, Negroes, Gipsies, and American Indians severally propagate their kinds; and each kind differs in character and intellect, as well as in colour and shape from the other four."[89] He also points to the supposed uniformity of character among the American Indians despite their different environments to argue that it is heredity rather than environment that accounts for this character.[90]

The concept of the "hereditary" itself has its origins in analogy. According to Carlos López-Beltrán: "The adjective 'hereditary', in the natural sciences, is an ancient borrowing from the legal and social sense, based on the straightforward analogy between handing down property or titles to descendants and transmitting physical or moral qualities to them."[91] As an adjective, the hereditary simply describes a variety of phenomena in which family members are seen sometimes to resemble each other more than other members of the population or in which members of a family may be found to be prone to the same diseases or medical concerns. "For centuries, most Aristotelian theorists of generation considered the hereditary accidental and irrelevant for their pursuits," López-Beltrán notes. "It was not until the eighteenth century brought to a head the strongest discussions on generation that the role of the hereditary began to be emphasized to defend or criticize the alternative views."[92] Indeed, the word *heredity* was introduced into the English language only between 1860 and 1870, to match the French use of the word *hérédité*, when "a *noun* was needed to refer to the maturing domain of scientific enquiry that had come to crystallize around the set of phenomena that were previously loosely clustered around the adjective 'hereditary.'"[93] A point had been reached where "the homogeneity of the genealogical groups through the generations [was] to be assumed, and all the inner (specific, group, familial) irregularity, variation and diversification [became] a surprising irregularity in need of explanation."[94] Making reference to what I have described as the modern technological mind-set, López-Beltrán argues that: "This change from adjective to noun points to a change from analogy (or metaphor) to a direct, ontological commitment to the reference of the concept . . . that implies a particular kind of independent causation (mechanism, force)."[95]

The appearance of *heredity* in the nineteenth century can be understood as the crystallization of a knowledge regime that emerged from "several, highly specific, and altogether separate domains of knowledge," many of which have already been discussed, including: (1) the classification of diseases as hereditary, (2) natural history in general, and botany in particular, (3) animal and plant breeding, and (4) anthropology, which had taken up the study of physical differences like skin color, and their origins, in an effort to account for human diversity.[96] As demonstrated by Kant's essay "Of the Different Human Races"—one of the first to be written on heredity and race—philosophy served in many ways as a privileged Enlightenment arena for bringing together the disparate elements listed above. As Müller-Wille and Rheinberger describe, though from our contemporary perspective philosophy may have "lacked control through experiment and the rigor of later theorizing in biology," this also meant it "could easily transgress boundaries between knowledge domains, between the practical knowledge of breeders and physiological speculation."[97] This, I believe, makes Heidegger's approach to the search for the *essence* of technology an appropriate one for investigating the questions I have posed here; it is through Heidegger's insights that we come to see how these various strands are united not merely in the concept of *heredity* but in a modern technological drive for mastery.

Take, for example, the views of John Harris, a contemporary bioethicist who supports what are broadly termed *enhancement technologies*, which include interventions in reproduction. Harris sees human dependence as a weakness and feels we have too long been "slaves" to such aspects of life as disability and death. It is time, he argues, for us to take control. In the introduction to his book, *Enhancing*

Evolution (2007), Harris argues that "we have reached a point in human history at which further attempts to make the world a better place *will have to include* not only changes to the world, but also changes to humanity."[98] Changes to humanity are described by Harris not simply as a possible means of progress but as a necessary one. Indeed, Harris asserts that his book "builds on work of the last twenty years which has at its center the moral responsibility of human beings to make responsible, informed choices about their own fate and the fate of the world in which we live" and that in the face of threats both to humankind and the ecosystem "this responsibility is nothing short of a clear imperative to make the world a better place."[99] For Harris, then, it seems there is nothing more we can do—or at least nothing genuinely effective—to make the world a better place *without* "enhancing evolution."

Galton makes a strikingly similar argument in a chapter on "The Comparative Worth of Different Races" in his 1869 book, *Hereditary Genius*, from which I offer an extended passage:

> It seems to me most essential to the well-being of future generations, that the average standard of ability of the present time should be raised. Civilization is a new condition imposed upon man by the course of events, just as in the history of geological changes new conditions have continually been imposed on different races of animals. They have had the effect either of modifying the nature of the races through the process of natural selection, whenever the changes were sufficiently slow and the race sufficiently pliant, or of destroying them altogether, when the changes were too abrupt or the race unyielding. . . . And we [the English] too, foremost labourers in creating this civilization, are beginning to show ourselves incapable of keeping pace with our own work. The needs of centralization, communication, and culture, call for more brains and mental stamina than the average of our race possesses. . . . Our race is overweighted, and appears likely to be drudged into degeneracy by demands that exceed its powers. . . . We can, in some degree, raise the nature of man to a level with the new conditions imposed upon his existence, and we can also, in some degree, modify the conditions to suit his nature. It is clearly right that both these powers should be exerted, with the view of bringing his nature and the conditions of his existence into as close harmony as possible.[100]

What we hear from both Harris and Galton in these passages is an insistence not merely on the *desirability* of genetic enhancement or improvement but on its *necessity* for "our" very survival. (The "our" for Harris ostensibly represents all of humanity, where, for Galton, his primary concern is the English "race.") Also essential to Harris and Galton's shared views is, I would argue, the shared assumption that mastery of evolution (both in terms of the actions to be taken and the results they will yield) is not only desirable but in fact fully possible. They seem to see natural selection as an essentially competitive process and evolution as synonymous with progress. Taking natural selection as the "survival of the fittest," Harris and Galton seek to render humankind more "fit" to ensure its survival. Greater fitness, here, is thought to require a sort of speeding up or taking control of humankind's natural evolutionary progress, taken as intrinsically good. Today's humans are better than yesterday's, and tomorrow's will (and indeed must) be better still. Evolution is not simply a *progression*, in the sense of a series of events, but *progress*, in the sense of absolute improvement.

This technological attitude, which Heidegger describes as essential to modernity, is also, as Voegelin pointed out, a hallmark of modern race theory. "As we probably are only beginning to realize today, in times when genetic screening, testing, and patenting pervade all sectors of social and economic life, and with the synthetic powers of genomics on the horizon," write Müller-Wille and Rheinberger, "the epistemic space that heredity came to constitute has reconfigured life in its entirety."[101] Both the modern race concept, the discredited version of eugenics, and contemporary reproductive technologies were developed and exist within this epistemic space, which is, I have argued, essentially technological. Thus, we oversimplify when we come to believe we need only remove the racism and coercion from the old eugenics and come up with a new, beneficent version.

A Note on Heidegger

Before concluding this chapter, allow me to suggest, perhaps provocatively, that rather than simply constituting a creative application of Heidegger's notion and critique of technology, this use of the concept of technology to critique ideas of race and practices of eugenics is in keeping with critiques of race and breeding that were put forward by Heidegger himself (though such critiques were certainly not well known or influential at the time). These critiques, according to Bernasconi, were part of an attempt, beginning in the late 1930s, "to present an account of how the Western philosophical tradition was deeply implicated in the racist policies of all the major political powers."[102] On this account, though the attempt began with an effort to reject biological reductionism through the existential analysis of *Dasein*, Heidegger "became increasingly preoccupied with the question of how the global turmoil he saw around him could be understood as a symptom of the completion of the history of Western metaphysics;" ultimately, however, "he largely gave up on that effort to highlight the connection between Western metaphysics and technology, including the technologies of racism."[103]

The critique in terms of metaphysics is visible in Heidegger's discussion of "The Overman" in his 1939 lecture on "Nietzsche's Metaphysics": "Only where the absolute subjectivity of will to power comes to be the truth of being as a whole is the *principle* of a program of racial breeding possible; possible, that is, not merely on the basis of naturally evolving races, but in terms of the self-conscious *thought* of race. That is to say, the principle is metaphysically necessary."[104] As Bernasconi is quick to warn, Heidegger's statement that a principle of racial breeding is "metaphysically necessary" should not be misunderstood as meaning "necessary" in the ordinary sense or as representing Heidegger's support for racial breeding. Rather, the concept of metaphysical necessity relates to Heidegger's belief that "there is a tendency for ideas and in particular goals to impose themselves in the specific historical periods to which they belong."[105] In this sense, then, Heidegger can be understood as arguing that the idea and goals of racial breeding emerge as a result of the establishment of a regime of truth defined by a human will or drive to mastery. Race within this context is not to be understood as a natural phenomenon but as the product of human thought. This view of race, which opposes biological or determinist ones, is supported in Heidegger's claim that: "History alone endows a people with national cohesion and distinctness of its ownmost. 'Space' and 'land,' climate and blood, never have the power to shape nor the will to cohere."[106]

As Miguel de Beistegui argues, "Heidegger's views regarding technology (*Technik*), which he began by calling 'machination' (*Machenschaft*), were shaped in the years 1936–1940."[107] During that time, racial breeding was one of the main examples Heidegger employed to illustrate technology (whereas by 1953, in "The Question Concerning Technology," his privileged example of technology is the hydroelectric plant).[108] Thus, while race is not under explicit discussion in "The Question Concerning Technology" (on which my discussion of Heidegger's concept of technology in the previous chapter was based), we should still see a critique of technologies of racial breeding as playing an important role in Heidegger's development of a larger critique of (particularly modern) technology.[109]

Conclusion

While the eugenics programs of the early twentieth century that culminated in the Holocaust have been academically dissected and broadly denounced, the future of eugenics is still very much under debate. Compelling arguments have been elaborated on both sides. Some see a version of liberal eugenics free of racism not only as possible but as essential to human development and survival. Others see contemporary eugenic technologies as subtle, often unintentional, movements in a dangerous backward direction toward a racist ideology that ought to have been thoroughly discredited. My efforts here place me in the latter group. By offering a history of race and eugenics that portrays them as thoroughly intertwined, I aim to cast serious doubt on the possibility of any eugenic program without racism. Race, racism, *and* eugenics all emerge from a technological worldview that sees human heredity as central to the development of human societies and the course of world history. This worldview cannot help but seek to master and control human heredity (and nature as a whole). Given the reality of human diversity—both in terms of bodies and values—this drive to mastery and the technoscientific power amassed by particular groups in its name will always be dangerous.

Notes

1. Nolfi, *The Adjustment Bureau*.
2. Mills, *Racial Contract*, 74, original emphasis.
3. See the section subtitled "Heidegger's Essence of Technology" in the previous chapter, especially the latter half of the section.
4. Duster, *Backdoor to Eugenics*, xiv.
5. Galton, *Inquiries into Human Faculty*, 25f1.
6. Buchanan et al., *From Chance to Choice*, 28–29.
7. Zenderland, *Measuring Minds*, 7.
8. Buchanan et al., 32–37.
9. Ibid., 41–43.
10. Ibid., 45.
11. Ibid., 50.
12. Ibid., 56.
13. Ibid.
14. Ibid., 52.
15. See Duster, *Backdoor to Eugenics*, chapter 2.
16. Augstein, *Race*, x.
17. Bernasconi and Lott, *The Idea of Race*, vii.
18. Bernasconi, "Who Invented the Concept of Race?", 11.
19. Figal, *Heredity, Race, and the Birth of the Modern*, 61.
20. Bernier, "A New Division of the Earth," 4, my emphasis.
21. Bernasconi, "Who Invented the Concept of Race?," 11. Indeed, writes Bernasconi, "Kant expended much more energy on securing the concept of race than one would ever guess from the secondary literature about him" (14). Kant not only revised and expanded his original essay on race in 1777 but went on to defend his race concept in two further essays: "Determination of the Concept of a Human Race" (November 1785) and "On the Use of Teleological Principles in Philosophy" (January and February 1788).
22. Kant, "Of the Different Human Races," 8.
23. Ibid., 13f1.
24. Ibid., 9.
25. Ibid., 11.
26. Ibid., 12.
27. Ibid., 14.
28. Ibid., 21.
29. Ibid., 19–20. Unsurprisingly, Kant also concludes that the white brunette must have been the original lineal human form, ostensibly on the basis of the white brunettes that he sees as inhabiting the world's most temperate regions.

30. Kant, "On the Use of Teleological Principles," 40.

31. Knox, *The Races of Men*, v.

32. Disraeli, *Lord George Bentinck*, 331.

33. Voegelin, *Race and State*, 173. For Voegelin, the "principal type of the political race idea" (which is the essential ground that underlies the development of various scientific race theories) can be outlined as follows:

> (1) All great historical cultures are based on a symbiosis of races; (2) there are human racial types that are clearly differentiated, either active or passive (Klemm) or strong and weak ones (Gobineau); (3) all races, or at least the active or strong ones, migrate; (4) in the course of migration, conquests occur—the conquest of the weak by the strong; (5) conquest results in a symbiosis of races, which ends with the disappearance of the strong race either interbreeding or through quantitative displacement; (6) as a result of the disappearance of the strong race from the symbiosis, the tension of domination within the community disappears, and a uniform level is formed—and opinions differ radically on its value. (167)

34. Bernasconi, "With What Must the Philosophy of World History Begin?," 187.

35. Indeed, in his *Philosophy of History*, Hegel insists that: "In the Frigid and in the Torrid zone the locality of World-historical peoples cannot be found" (80). As for Africa: "it is no historical part of the World; it has no movement or development to exhibit. Historical movements in it—that is in its northern part—belong to the Asiatic or European World .... What we properly understand by Africa, is the Unhistorical, Undeveloped Spirit, still involved in the conditions of mere nature, and which had to be presented here only as on the threshold of the World's History" (99). Though Hegel affects this dismissal using climate theory, his broad divisions are those that were already associated with human races. We also see that philosophy, geography, and history are interwoven in his account.

36. Voegelin, *Race and State*, 168.

37. Gobineau, "Racial Inequality," 175.

38. Gobineau, *The Inequality of Human Races*, 161–63. "Man has been able to learn some things, but has forgotten many others," he writes, and "in his wretchedness, has never succeeded in inventing a way of providing the whole race with clothes or in putting them beyond the reach of hunger and thirst."

39. Voegelin, *Race and State*, 171.

40. Topinard, *Elements D'anthropologie Générale*, 202; quoted in Stocking, *Race, Culture, and Evolution*, 59. Similarly, in 1876, Topinard argued, "By human type must be understood the average of characters which a human race supposed to be pure presents. In homogeneous races, if such there are, it is discovered by the simple inspection of individuals. In the generality of cases it must be segregated. It is then a physical ideal, to which the greater number of the individuals of the group more or less approach, but which is better marked in some than in others" (Topinard, *Anthropology*, 446–47).

41. Stocking, *Race, Culture, and Evolution*, 46.

42. He wrote: "If, therefore, we are of opinion that he was not really man till these higher faculties were fully developed, we may fairly assert that there were many originally distinct races of men; while, if we think that a being closely resembling us in form and structure, but with mental faculties scarcely raised above the brute, must still be considered to have been human, we are fully entitled to maintain the common origin of all mankind" (Wallace, "The Development of Human Races Under the Law of Natural Selection," 322).

43. Stepan, *The Idea of Race in Science*, 57.

44. Ibid., 52.

45. Ibid., 51.

46. Ibid., 57.

47. Charles Darwin, *The Descent of Man*. Darwin wrote, for example, that: "The variability or diversity of the mental faculties in men of the same race, not to mention the greater differences between men of distinct races, is so notorious that not a word need here be said" (45). Nevertheless, Darwin did make further mention of these hierarchical differences in moral virtue (134, 144, 148), in intellect (86), in language development (109), and in religious belief (119) throughout the work.

48. Ibid., 183.

49. Ibid., 183–84.

50. As Stepan summarizes:

> Instead of treating races as arbitrary divisions of populations in which many traits arise independently of each other as a result of selective pressures, it was easier to see human races as discrete units which were relatively unchanging, or if changing, units in which traits varied together in racial packages. Struggle, competition and survival, instead of occurring between individuals in populations, occurred between racial types, and it was this struggle that was believed to explain the eventual rise of some types of man from barbarism to civilisation. The evolution of culture was, therefore, not to be thought of as a capacity shared equally by all members of the species. Differences in actual customs and social structures were a result not of history, geography and other accidents, but of race. Racial extinction, even genocide was a result of biology, not history. Thus the essential link between biology and culture was kept in the new evolutionary era. (Stepan, *Idea of Race in Science*, 86)

51. Ibid., 83.

52. Da Cal, "Influence of Animal Breeding on Political Racism," 717.

53. Ibid., 717–18.

54. Smedley, *Race in North America*, 38.

55. Ibid., 65–66. Smedley continues: "The result was that many Spaniards, including some non-Jews, sought a certificate of 'purity' that, for a fee, would be issued by the church. It constituted a guarantee of one's genealogical purity from 'any admixture of Jew or Moor' or from condemnation by the Holy Office. These 'certificates of Limpieza de Sangre' (purity of blood) were not only a major source of revenue for the church, but were also vital requirements for social mobility, as certain occupations and activities were closed by law to the families of converts."

56. Ibid., 39.

57. Augstein, *Race*, xv.

58. Müller-Wille and Rheinberger, *Heredity Produced*, 12.

59. Terral, "Speculation and Experiment in Enlightenment Life Sciences," 255.

60. Gregory, *Comparative View of the State and Faculties of Man*, 29–30.

61. Vandermonde, *Essai Sur La Manière De Perfectionner L'espèce Humaine*, 91–92.

62. Erasmus Darwin, *Zoonomia*, 2.

63. Wilson, "Erasmus Darwin and the 'Noble' Disease (Gout)," 140.

64. See Erasmus Darwin, *The Temple of Nature*.

65. Kant, "Of the Different Human Races," 17, 19. Of the possibility of human intervention in reproduction, Kant writes:

> Maupertuis believes that we might cultivate a noble stock of human beings in any province, a stock in whom understanding, diligence, and probity were hereditary. His view rests on the possibility that an enduring family stock might eventually be established through the careful selection of the degenerate from the normal births. I think, however, that even though such a scheme is, strictly speaking, certainly practicable, nature, in its wisdom, acts to hinder it rather well. This is because major driving forces lie even within the mixing of evil with good that set the sleeping powers of humanity into play. These forces require that human beings develop all of their talents and approach the perfection of their calling. (10)

66. Lesky, "Introduction" to *A System of Complete Medical Police*, xv. The term *police* was first used in France to refer to the ordering or governing of a city and was quickly adopted in England and Prussia. In fact, at the beginning of the eighteenth century, the King of Prussia established a number of chairs for *Polizeiwissenshaft* (the science of police), where future civil servants were trained in "police." See Bernasconi, "The Policing of Race Mixing," 208.

67. Frank defines his subject as follows: "Medical Police, like all police science, is an art of defense, a model of protection of people and their animal helpers against the deleterious consequences of dwelling together in large numbers, but especially of promoting their physical well-being so that people will succumb as late as possible to their eventual fate from the many physical illnesses to which they are subject" (Frank, *System of Complete Medical Police*, 12).

68. Ibid., 23.

69. Figal, *Heredity, Race, and the Birth of the Modern*, 99.

70. Ibid., 90.

71. Ibid., 115.

72. Da Cal, "Influence of Animal Breeding on Political Racism," 718–19.

73. Vorzimmer, "Darwin's 'Questions About the Breeding of Animals,'" 272. The twenty-one numbered paragraphs of the pamphlet contained forty-eight questions, nearly all of which, as Vorzimmer describes, "are framed in such a way as to elicit specific responses which may or may not confirm an existing hypothesis" such that "the questions can be seen as very much the deductive manifestation of Darwin's own view of how the phenomena of hereditary transmission might bear upon his transmutation hypothesis."

74. Millman and Smith, "Darwin's Use of Analogical Reasoning," 164. They emphasize here Darwin's initial use of *dis*analogy in thinking about the relation between nature and the art of breeding but note also that Darwin continued to "look to domestication for clues" and to read the literature of plant and animal breeders (169).

75. Ibid., 174. At this point in his notebooks, Darwin adopts a mechanical wedging analogy: "Just as a more forcefully hit wedge will create a hole in the surface or ground and push aside other wedges competing for the same space, so Darwin envisioned the force in nature quite mechanistically pushing 'every kind of adapted structure into the gaps in the economy of Nature, or rather forming gaps by thrusting out weaker ones'" (171). Making an analogy to the final cause of Malthusian population pressure, which though operating as a natural force served to ensure the original dispersal of the human population over the earth and maintain human vigor and industry, "Darwin considered that there is a deeper purpose for the wedging-like force in nature: to sort out adapted from nonadapted structures in the

face of changing environmental conditions, thus producing adaptation and transmutation of species" (172).

76. Ibid., 176. Ultimately, by referring to the breeding of greyhounds, Darwin then linked natural selection and artificial selection using sexual selection as bridging analogy. Darwin overcame the disanalogy between natural and artificial selection (due to the fact that the former was based on adaptation to the environment while the latter involved picking those traits humans found useful or pleasing) by noting that the speed and skill in hunting that humans bred into greyhounds also have adaptive value in the wild and by relating both to sexual selection. As Millman and Smith describe: "Artificial selection is like sexual selection, in that both, by means of intervention in breeding, involve choice of characters that are not adaptations to the environment. Sexual selection in turn is like natural selection in that both are cases in which strength and vigor gets the day."

77. Ibid., 185.

78. Ibid., 178–79.

79. Da Cal, "Influence of Animal Breeding on Political Racism," 719.

80. Ibid., 720.

81. White, "Acquired Character," 376.

82. Da Cal, "Influence of Animal Breeding on Political Racism," 720.

83. Ibid., 722.

84. Ibid., 724–25.

85. Millman and Smith, "Darwin's Use of Analogical Reasoning," 184.

86. Da Cal, "Influence of Animal Breeding on Political Racism," 720.

87. Galton, "Hereditary Talent and Character," 157.

88. Cowan, "Nature and Nurture," 134.

89. Galton, "Hereditary Talent and Character," 320.

90. Cowan, "Nature and Nurture," 140.

91. López-Beltrán, "Forging Heredity," 211.

92. Ibid., 217.

93. Ibid., 211.

94. Ibid., 215.

95. Ibid., 214.

96. Müller-Wille and Rheinbeger, *Heredity Produced*, 12.

97. Ibid., 22.

98. Harris, *Enhancing Evolution*, 3, my emphasis.

99. Ibid., 4.

100. Galton, *Hereditary Genius*, 311–12.

101. Müller-Wille and Rheinberger, *Heredity Produced*, 25.

102. Bernasconi, "Race and Earth," 49.

103. Ibid., 55, 65.

104. Heidegger, *Nietzsche*, 231.

105. Bernasconi, "Race and Earth," 58.

106. Heidegger, *Mindfulness*, 145.

107. De Beistegui, *The New Heidegger*, 98.

108. Bernasconi, "Race and Earth," 56–57.

109. Although the word *race* does not appear, Bernasconi does argue that "it is significant that the term *Bestand*, which is so prominent in the 1953 essay, where it is translated as

'standing-reserve,' already played a role in his discussions of contemporary efforts to secure or increase racial stock" and that the same word was used by Heidegger "in order to characterize those who died in the death camps who, like those who die of hunger, were deprived of the opportunity—others might say the right—to die in the way proper to them" (Ibid., 57).

4 "I Just Want Children Like Me"

"The white Lackses know their kin all buried in here with ours cause they family. They know it, but they'll never admit it. They just say, 'Them Black Lackses, they ain't kin!'"

—*Cliff Garret, quoted by Rebecca Skloot in* The Immortal Life of Henrietta Lacks

I_N _THE IMMORTAL_ Life of Henrietta Lacks_, Rebecca Skloot tells the life story of Henrietta Lacks, the black woman whose cells became the immortal HeLa cell line. In the book, Skloot writes of her visit to the small adjacent towns of Clover and Lacks Town in southern Virginia, where the Lacks Plantation once stood. The land that makes up Lacks Town was bequeathed to the "colored" heirs of Albert Lacks in 1889, with additional land from the original Lacks Plantation inherited by the "colored" heirs of his older brother, Benjamin Lacks (known among the black Lackses as "old white granddaddy"), sixteen years later.[1] In 1999, when Skloot visits, the dividing line between Clover and Lacks Town is still stark, and the houses lining the single road of Lacks Town still include slave-era cabins.[2] Behind the four-room log cabin in which Henrietta Lacks grew up, known as the "home-house," stands a quarter-acre family cemetery, so full that family members started being buried on top of each other decades earlier.

While standing in this cemetery with Skloot, Henrietta's cousin, Cliff Garrett, remarks on the relationship between the black and white branches of the Lacks family:

> A few minutes later, seemingly out of nowhere, he pointed to the dirt and said, "You know, white folks and black folks all buried over top of each other in here. I guess old white granddaddy and his brothers was buried in here too. Really no tellin who in this ground now." Only thing he knew for sure, he said, was that there was something beautiful about the idea of slave-owning white Lackses being buried under their black kin.
>
> "They spending eternity in the same place," he told me, laughing. "They must've worked out their problems by now!"[3]

Yet when Skloot goes to Clover to visit the oldest white Lackses, Ruby and Carlton Lacks, she finds them much less sanguine on the matter:

> When I mentioned that Henrietta came from Lacks Town, Ruby straightened in her chair.

"Well, that was colored!" she snapped. "I don't know what you talking about. You're not talking about coloreds are you?"

I told her I wanted to learn about both the white and black Lackses.

"Well, we never did know each other," she said. "The white and the black didn't mix then, not like they do now, which I can't say I like because I don't think it's for the best." She paused and shook her head. "Mixing them like that, during school and church and everything, they end up white and black get together and marry and all . . . I just can't see the sense in it."

When I asked how she and Carlton were related to the black Lackses, they looked at each other from across the coffee table like I'd asked if they were born on Mars.

". . . Evidently they took it when they left the plantation. That's the only thing I can figure."[4]

One thing Cliff's comments—along with the defensive reaction Skloot observed in Ruby Lacks—point to is the role that race (and particularly the black-white color line) has played in American understandings of kinship. Despite clear (though not explicit) archival evidence pointing to Albert and Benjamin Lacks as the fathers of at least twelve "colored" children to whom (in the absence of any white children) they left significant portions of their land, Ruby, by denying past race mixing, uses the racial difference between the Lackses of Clover and the Lackses of Lacks Town as a visible indicator of their lack of kinship relation. Even the black Lackses, whose oral history acknowledges the ancestry they share with the white Lackses, recognize that the color line precludes any social aspect of kinship between the two sets of Lackses. The physical segregation of Clover and Lacks Town is mirrored by a symbolic one, which emerges from three hundred years of American legal and social norms governing social relationships and status on the basis of race.

In the previous chapter, I explored the history of race and eugenics—the most vilified of reproductive technologies. Working within the Anglo-European context, I highlighted the role of race in efforts to both explain and master human natural and cultural history. In this chapter, which also offers a history of race, I turn to the American context. I will examine how, since its founding as a settler colonial state, the use of race as a political technology in the United States has operated through the notion of kinship. These historical operations, intended primarily to establish and enforce a white supremacist racial hierarchy, have, for some time now, allowed race to serve as a proxy for kinship in a variety of contexts. One such context is the fertility clinic, or assisted reproduction more generally. Thus, within American ART practices, one finds a political technology being harnessed for personal (and indeed *intimate*) use. While not always malicious, such use, I will argue, carries historical baggage. This movement from the political to more personal uses of race also foreshadows my work in the next and final chapter, where I argue that race can be understood as a Foucauldian *technology of the self*, with its use in ARTs serving to both personalize and depoliticize the race concept itself.

As I demonstrated in chapter 1, race remains a crucial category in most ART practices and continues to be given a sort of natural, pseudogenetic status by intended parents and fertility practitioners alike. Yet the persistence of race as an important category in ART practices is not merely a troubling continuation of various notions (discussed below) that have created and maintained the American system of racial hierarchy. In the first section of this chapter, I will argue that race also serves a productive or *technological* function within those practices. The ascription to donor gametes of a "race," the tracking of donor gametes in terms of their "race," and the selection and policing in terms of "race" of who can or should use which donor gametes (performed by both patients and practitioners, and further discussed in chapter 5) amounts to the literal production of race or raced bodies. In the context of uncertainty inherent to ART practices, race, ethnicity, and culture appear as resources available to fertility patients in their construction of naturalizing narratives, which help to disambiguate various contributors to the child's birth and to name particular people as the child's "true" parents.

In the next four sections of the chapter, I aim to demonstrate how race has come to be available as such a resource. I will describe American notions of kinship and the role that race (and particularly the black-white binary) has played in their social and legal elaboration. Taking each in turn, I will show how blood metaphors, polygenist discourse, and laws and conventions of segregation have all played a role in establishing race as a proxy for kinship (and racial difference as a visible sign of the absence of kinship) in the United States. Finally, in the last section of the chapter, I will return to the present to consider why we might be concerned with these rather personal uses of the once (and still) political race concept—even where such uses might be seen as fully consensual and relatively benign.

Putting Race to Work

In chapter 1 I suggested that the importance of racial classification in ART practices might be seen as paradoxical. On the one hand, ARTs are ostensibly concerned with a "genetic" concept of reproduction and have, as their ideal result, the creation of genetically related child (or the closest possible approximation thereof). On the other hand, while current work in genetics can use genetic variation to mark out populations in terms of patterns of migration, ancestry, and descent, this work cannot give us *scientifically* the "races" whose existence has been assumed, constructed, and reified *sociohistorically*. In other words, while those phenotypic traits popularly used (typically idiosyncratically) to "discern" a person's so-called race (e.g., eye shape, hair texture, stature, and skin color) are, in fact, heritable, their distributions among world populations do not allow for any genuinely scientific demarcation of the groups any given culture considers to be "racial." What, then, are we to make of the persistent use of racial classification in artificial reproduction? While in chapter 1 I offered a number of reasons to find the social and institutional policing of race in ART troubling, here I want to focus on how race might be thought to serve a productive, *technological* function within ART practices.

Though the *product* of reproductive technologies is often taken to be a healthy child for an infertile couple (sometimes referred to as a "take-home baby"), Charis Thompson has suggested that we look at ARTs in a slightly different way: as biotechnological innovations that make not only children but *parents*.[5] It is a constitutive feature of ARTs that they enlist people, instruments, and techniques—and often genetic material—outside of or beyond the intended parent(s) in the process of reproduction. As Thompson points out, these "outside" elements always threaten to throw into question the relationship of the intended parent(s) to the projected offspring. This means that the work that occurs in the fertility clinic aims not only to create a child where such creation was not previously possible but also to ensure that the correct couple or person comes to be understood as the parent(s) of that child. Thompson has called this work *ontological choreography*, and it includes a process she describes as *strategic naturalizing*. She defines *ontological choreography* as "the dynamic coordination of the technical, scientific, kinship, gender, emotional, legal, political, and financial aspects of ART clinics" in order to produce "parents, children, and everything that is needed for their recognition as such."[6] The process is *ontological* because it involves positing and manipulating definitions of being and beings—deciding who counts as a parent, what counts as kinship, and why. The process is a type of *choreography* because it is both creative and highly staged, requiring the well-coordinated performance of a variety of actors for its ultimate success.

Crucial to the establishment of kinship is what Thompson calls *strategic naturalizing*, which she elaborates by examining patient narratives around two technically identical procedures that lead to different kinds of kinship configurations: *gestational surrogacy* and *IVF with ovum donation*. Both procedures involve the creation of an embryo through in vitro fertilization and the subsequent implantation of that embryo into a womb. In gestational surrogacy, however, the woman whose ovum is used (the genetic mother) is the intended mother; the surrogate who carries the fetus will not be the child's mother. By contrast, in IVF with ovum donation, the intended mother is the woman who gestates the fetus (the birth mother); the woman who donates the egg will not be the child's mother. Noting the different boundaries drawn in those narratives between what is *natural* or *biological* and what is *social* in conception, pregnancy, and parenting, Thompson argues that there is no fixed natural basis for establishing kinship. Rather, such relations are first constructed and then natural*ized*. Ideas of race, ethnicity and culture appear here as resources available to fertility patients in their construction of naturalizing narratives, helping to disambiguate various contributions to the child's birth and to name particular people as the child's "true" parents.

Thompson puts a fairly positive spin on the phenomenon, focusing on cases of donor egg IVF in which the intended mother (who would be carrying the pregnancy) selected a woman of her same race or ethnicity to provide the donor egg. In one case, the intended mother, Giovanna, chose as her donor a friend who, like her, was Italian American. According to Thompson, Giovanna described this shared ethnic classification as being "enough genetic similarity." In another case, Paula, an African American, declared her intention to use an African American friend or relative as her donor and assimilated the help she would be receiving from that friend to a history of shared parenting practices in African American communities.[7] In both these cases racial *similarity* between intended mother and donor becomes a resource for highlighting the connection between intended mother and child. It is not, however, among the resources used to downplay the donor-child connection.

By contrast, in gestational surrogacy, while the genetic connection between the child and the intended parents is thought to establish the child as *theirs*, the racial *difference* between the surrogate and the child gestated becomes a resource for establishing that child as *not hers*. The prevalence of attributing this kind of hereditary certainty and security to visible racial similarity and difference— also described in chapter 1 in the case of transnational gestational surrogacy—is attested to by the fact that Heléna Ragoné finds the same attitude among domestic surrogates in the United States, who reported that contracting with couples of a difference race from their own helped them to maintain a distance between themselves and the children they were carrying.[8]

Returning to the *Johnson v. Calvert* case referenced in chapter 1, we can see how race not only helped to decide who were the real parents but was used to strategically *de*naturalize certain desires and possible relations. Recall that in the case, Anna Johnson (a single black woman) fought intended parents Mark and Crispina Calvert (a white man and a Filipina woman) for the rights to a child to whom they were genetically related but whom Johnson had carried and delivered. As Hartouni describes, Anna Johnson's desire to keep the child she had carried *could* have been seen as natural. Dominant reproductive discourse tends to portray "conversion experiences" during pregnancy as natural for women; gestation, and particularly quickening, is supposed to arouse in women a "deep, biologically rooted sense of maternal desire regardless of genetic ties." If, then, this sort of bonding with a fetus is supposed to happen universally and naturally, why was Anna Johnson's claim to have bonded with the fetus she carried treated with such suspicion and disregard by the popular media and ultimately the courts? As Hartouni asks: "What rendered Johnson's claim so remarkably queer, unfathomable, deviant, or unusual—in fact, so specious as to inspire Superior Court Judge Richard Parslow to pathologize it as criminal, as a potential instrument for future emotional and financial extortion, and to dismiss it as groundless?" The answer seems to lie not merely in Anna Johnson's race but in the perceived racial *difference* between her and the child she carried. Thus the claim by the Calverts' lawyers that Johnson "had been motivated to sue for custody not, as she claimed, because of 'maternal instincts' that had 'just come out naturally,' but rather . . . because she fetishized whiteness."[9]

In other words, the same desires that are naturalized in some (white) women are denaturalized and figured as pathological in other (black) women, and the appropriateness of the desires is thought to depend on racial connection. Similarly, as discussed in chapter 1, it is "natural" for middle-class white women who have previously prioritized their career plans to decide, perhaps in the face of intense social pressure, that they deeply desire to experience motherhood; it is "pathological," however, for poor young black women without any perceived opportunities for higher education or well-paying and creative jobs to "make conscious decisions to bear children in order to convince themselves that they are alive and creative human beings."[10]

These examples suggest that, for good or ill, notions of racial similarity and difference are able to play an important and active role helping to resolve tensions about who should be considered the real parent(s) of children produced by ARTs. If, as Thompson argues, the ontological choreography involved in making parents is as much a part of the work of the fertility clinic as the making of children, then it makes sense to think of race as a technology—as just one of a number of technologies that are brought together and coordinated in ART practices in the service of their ultimate goals. Moreover, the cases in which racial difference is used to discredit reproductive relations or desires show that this technology of race can be used even where there is not agreement between all parties and well beyond the confines of the fertility clinic.

Race, Blood, and American Kinship

This technological function of race in ARTs is based on the ability of race to serve as a proxy for heredity and kinship. In cases where a donor of the same race is chosen, race stands in for shared genetic material and is used to establish a pseudobiological connection between intended parents and the children produced with donor gametes. In cases where a surrogate of a different race is chosen, race establishes a lack of kinship or "natural" connection. But how is race able to serve these functions? Recall Voegelin's distinction (in the introduction) between race *theory* (an endeavor of the natural sciences) and the race *idea* (a fundamentally political concept). The race *idea* does not attempt to *describe* reality but rather uses symbols to *construct* political realities by defining and shaping communities. Contrary to what our focus on race *theory* may lead us to believe—that race is the sort of thing that can be proven scientifically true or false—the point of a race *idea* is not to simply identify differences between groups (or define intragroup similarities) but rather to actively establish and maintain those differences (or similarities). This understanding of the race idea suggests that even in the ostensibly medical and scientific context of the fertility clinic, facts about the genetic reality or unreality of race will be of little use in identifying the constructive function of race in ART practices. Instead, I would argue, we should pick up on our exploration of the historical and technological relationships between concepts of race and heredity in order to investigate an aspect I have not yet thematized—the political and symbolic connections between ideas of race and notions of kinship.

As mentioned in the previous chapter, around 1800, when theories of monogenesis dominated discourses of natural history, theories of racial difference developed as "a second counter movement against universal biological brotherhood" (the first counter movement being theories of polygenesis, which, as we shall see, were given new life by American ethnologists in the nineteenth century).[11] The racialization of particular physical similarities allowed them to function in the nineteenth century "as a primary visible cue of group identity," compelling emotional loyalties through metaphors of family, blood, and the social body.[12] While this function of race is properly understood in the previous chapter as political, it is important to recognize that the use of these metaphors for political purposes has created an enduring relationship between the notions of race and kinship. In other words, before race could become available as a proxy for kinship on the small scale of negotiating parentage within the ART clinic—or in the courts or the media—the connection between the two concepts was established on a larger, political scale. This occurred in a variety of national and nationalist projects in the nineteenth and early twentieth centuries, where race as a political idea served the "function of creating the image of a group as a unit," constructing and constituting political communities.[13] While I draw on and reference some European thinkers of race here, however, my primary focus is on the American case.

In his seminal work, *American Kinship*, David Schneider argues for the centrality of the "blood relationship" in contemporary American conceptions of kinship. Schneider identifies relation *by blood* (or *substance*) and relation *by marriage* (or *law*) as the two key, contrasted categories of the American kinship system. The blood relationship in American kinship "is formulated in concrete, biogenetic terms" with the idea that "both mother and father give substantially the same kinds and amounts of material to the child, and that the child's whole biogentic identity or any part of it comes half from the mother, half from the father." Schneider points here to a duality in the realm of kinship similar to Voegelin's between symbolic *idea* and scientific *theory*, arguing that this basic understanding of kinship as concretely biogenetic is, in fact, scientifically flexible. "This definition says that kinship is whatever the biogenetic relationship is," he writes. "If science discovers new facts about biogenetic relationship, then that is what kinship is and was all along, although it may not have been known at the time."[14] In other words, the symbolic meaning of kinship may use science to legitimate itself, but it is not established in conformity to science, nor is it destroyed or necessarily reshaped by changes to scientific theory.

Schneider's description of American kinship suggests that one way to think about the complex historical relationship between ideas of kinship and race is through their shared metaphor of blood. Ideas of racial blood and family blood (along with an intermediary notion of national blood) seem to carry much the same symbolic meaning and force (though they operate at different levels), representing forms of kinship that are different only in degree, rather than kind.[15] At the level of family, biological relations are described as "blood relatives," certain traits, temperaments or talents are described as being "in one's blood," and expressions like "blood will tell" imply that even aspects of one's heredity that one hides or of which one is unaware will eventually make themselves known. Schneider describes several elements of the blood metaphor. He argues (1) that the blood relationship "is culturally defined as being an objective fact of nature, of fundamental significance and capable of having profound effects, and its nature cannot be terminated or changed;" (2) that "blood relatives are 'related' by the fact that they share in some degree the stuff of a particular heredity" and each "has a portion of the natural, genetic substance;" and (3) that because "blood is a 'thing' and because it is subdivided with each reproductive step away from a given ancestor, the precise degree to which two persons share common heredity can be calculated, and 'distance' can thus be stated in specific quantitative terms." Additionally, related to the unalterable nature of the blood relationship is the sense that a blood relationship is one of common or shared *identity* such that "aspects like temperament, build, physiognomy, and habits are noted as signs of this shared biological makeup, this special identity of relatives with each other."[16]

At the level of race, racial blood represents common or shared identity that is not only physiological or morphological in nature but also deeply social or cultural. George Stocking describes the nineteenth-century sense of race as a "richly connotative" one in which accumulated cultural differences were thought to be carried somehow in the blood—a "blood" that for many was "a solvent in which all problems were dissolved and all processes commingled."[17] As an example, he points to the intervention of G. Stanley Hall at an 1895 meeting of the American Antiquarian Society. Hall, who was generally opposed to race mixture, was arguing for the unusual benefits of crossing Scotch and Irish stocks and described the combination of racial bloods as "not a mere matter of biology or physiology," not "mere physical mingling of the bloods, but [also] that subtle atmosphere of associations, of home traditions, of family recollections and ideals and aims, that are so inseparable."[18] John Nale aptly demonstrates that Gobineau's understanding of racial blood was also deeply metaphorical, referring not to the literal blood in the veins of individual members of a race but rather "designating a spiritual and historical substance accounting for the unity of a people."[19] Racial blood is, for Gobineau, an element of the metaphorical "social body" or "body politic"—a way of conceptualizing peoples that understands the life, health and death of societies as analogous to the life, health, and death of the individual, the understanding of which Gobineau appropriated from French physiologist Xavier Bichat.[20] The blood of Gobineau's social body or organism, Nale writes, "is not a quantity of material but a quality of thought, a purity and homogeneity of [its] principles."[21] Within Gobineau's body and health metaphor, racial or social degeneration is described as resulting from the adulteration of the racial "blood" through race "mixing," but "blood" and "mixing" must not be taken as literal materials or processes. "What dies in blood mixing is the spiritual texture of a collective group, the values residing in the 'veins' of the body public."[22] Racial blood is symbolic of body, mind, and spirit.

By operating at the levels of family, nation, and race, the symbol of blood links these concepts. Ultimately, notes Voegelin: "The symbol of blood relations is so powerful that it is frequently forgotten that even when the symbol comes closest to reality, i.e., when it is applied to the family consisting of parents and children, even in this case the unit includes normally at least two persons who are not blood relatives—I mean the parents."[23] Relation by blood (at levels of family, nation, or race), thought to be rooted inescapably in nature itself, is figured as more powerful than relationships established through human social codes—a figuring that obscures the role of human social codes in establishing the supposedly natural rules of blood. Among the moves essential to the development of the race idea, on Voegelin's account, is the "closing" of the essential substances—such as organism, person, society—such that they are seen as fixed.[24] This movement toward fixity in the race *idea* is particularly evidenced in the common American understanding of racial identity (even as the supposed fixity is belied by the actual records of multiple and shifting criteria for racial classification throughout American history). The sense of inflexibility that permeates American notions of race is part of what Smedley argues is distinctive about the evolution of the American race system:

> First, the dichotomous race categories of black and white are set and inflexible. Unlike in South Africa or Latin America, there is no legal or social recognition of a "racial" category in between ("mixed-race"); and one cannot belong to more than one race. Second, the category "black" or "African-American"

is defined by any known descent from a black ancestor, thus conflating and socially homogenizing individuals with a wide range of phenotypes into one racial category. Third, one cannot transcend or transform one's "race" status; in other words, no legal or social mechanism exists for changing one's race. Under the system of apartheid in South Africa, a government board existed that reassigned hundreds of people every year to different racial categories.... In the United States, neither social class, education, wealth, nor professional or governmental or business achievements evoke a change in racial identity.[25]

The explanation offered by Schneider that links the American view of blood relationships as natural, determinative, and unchanging to the fact that blood is conceived of as a natural substance can help begin to explain why Americans have viewed race as fixed and important in this way.

Yet, as Randall Kennedy and other race historians show us, such a contemporary American understanding of race relies in large part on a significant forgetting, not only of histories of contestations over racial categories and rules for categorization but also of histories of interracial sexual violence and intimacy.[26] Nevertheless, it is this understanding of fixed divisions—also exemplified in the metaphor of "the color line"—that we see reflected in Ruby Lacks's disavowal of the black Lackses as kin. Blood metaphors at the racial level serve to manage this forgetting of blood relationships at the family level. In the Lacks case, a blood relationship on the family level is imagined to be impossible due to essential differences in racial blood and the deep separation such differences are supposed to engender. The social metaphor of racial blood serves its social purpose by not actually describing the sociohistorical reality (which is full of race mixing) but instead *constructing* a reality of natural and necessary racial segregation. Of course, beyond the deliberate denial and forgetting of black-white mixing in America's history, the literal idea of races as large, biogenetic kinship groups existing naturally in the United States is challenged by the reality that a variety of different ethics groups have arrived in America from a variety of geographic locations during a variety of different periods. This sociohistorical reality is metaphorically disguised in the process of what Paul Spickard calls *panethnic formation*: "the lumping together of formerly separate ethnic groups, frequently in a new geographical setting."[27] As Spickard points out, once in the United States, people who might have been members of a variety of different ethnic groups become members of about five larger panethnic groups that are understood as races: Native, Asian, African, Latin, and White Americans.[28] These formations are what, through the constructive work of the race idea, come to be understood in the US context as fixed groups based on shared blood or ancestry.

Of course, no discussion of the role of the blood metaphor in American race concepts would be complete without mention of the biologized discourses of racial purity and contamination that have depicted black blood as especially dangerous, such that any known or revealed black ancestry may be seen as tainting a "white" person's racial pedigree, endangering that person's access to white racial privilege. This phenomenon is exemplified by the infamous hypodescent or "one-drop" rule that defined as black anyone with any amount of "black blood"—that is, anyone with even a single known black ancestor. Though deeply significant in its symbolism and quite powerful in a number of social and legal contexts, Kennedy hastens to remind us that "the one-drop rule never monopolized the drawing of racial lines," pointing, as just one example, to the fact that Virginia did not adopt the one-drop rule until 1924. (Before 1910 a "white" person could be up to 24 percent black in Virginia; between 1910 and 1924 the limit was lowered to 15 percent.)[29] The one-drop rule has been widely and understandably viewed as a sign of the irrationality of racial classification, as unfair and asymmetrical, and as an instrument of oppression wrongly wielded against people of mixed racial backgrounds. While Christine B. Hickman agrees that it is all these things, however, she argues that it is something else as well: "The Devil fashioned [the one-drop rule] out of racism, malice, greed, lust, and ignorance, but in so doing he also accomplished good: His rule created the African-American race as we know it today, and while this race has its origins in the peoples of three continents and its members can look very different from one another, over the centuries the Devil's one drop rule united this race as a people in the fight against slavery, segregation, and racial injustice."[30] With her Faustian metaphor, Hickman points here to a positive symbolic role that a notion of racial blood has played in constructing African Americans as a people, demonstrating how (in my parlance) technologies of race can be taken up in ways not envisioned or desired by their "inventors."

Another notable use of the blood metaphor in American racial history is found in the notion of *blood quantum* as applied to American Indians. Blood quantum—or the description of one's ancestry in terms fractional amounts like one-half, one-quarter, or one-sixteenth—can be traced back to an ancient rule of English common law that "distinguishes between 'whole blood' and 'half blood' relatives for purposes of inheritance," but in more recent history it has been used in British colonies (and later states) "to define the legal status of mixed-race people for various purposes."[31] Such language is certainly familiar to the description of black-white mulattoes, but whereas descriptions of mixed-race people with black blood eventually slid toward a one-drop rule that classified anyone with any known black ancestry as black, Indian blood quantum measurements have in many contexts become *more* fixed and precise, rather than less. This is because the US government has had a different (and evolving) relationship with Indian tribes than it has with black slaves (or former slaves).

As Paul Spruhan describes, one "foundational contradiction in Federal Indian law" is the fact that "Indian tribes are autonomous governments with federally-recognized sovereignty over their territories, but Indians are dependent wards of the federal government subject to detailed controls over their lives."[32] This contradiction has facilitated various forms of oppression of American Indians and various appropriations of their lands. Such oppression and appropriations have only sometimes been served by allowing more people to qualify as Indian; often they have called for denying individuals official Indian status. For example, when the US government was in the habit of signing treaties with Indian tribes (often to obtain tribal lands), the votes of "mixed-blood" tribal members might help or hinder tribal agreement to the treaty, and, subsequently, Indian status might determine who was eligible to receive benefits or payments in accordance with treaty obligations.[33] While the language of blood was used by the US government and by courts during this time to decide who was and was not an Indian or a member of a particular tribe, blood quantum was not consistently applied. It was only in the late nineteenth century, "primarily in the context of the distribution of Indian property and the allotment of Indian lands," that Congress used blood quantum to attempt to define Indian status.[34] When carrying out the General Allotment Act of 1887—an act that divided reservation lands and assigned them to individual tribal members in an effort to dissolve tribes as collective entities and force Indian assimilation to individual property holding and family farming—it was in the government's general interest to limit the number of Indians who qualified for allotments, since the remaining land would be granted to white settlers. Still, the government often followed tribal decisions on membership in these cases.[35]

Though blood quantum was not the most salient factor in deciding allotment cases, the Allotment Act occasioned the creation of tribal rolls, in which tribe members' names, ancestors, and blood quanta were recorded.[36] Subsequently, provisions in congressional acts in 1906 and 1908 rendered the blood quanta listed in these rolls conclusive and beyond attack based on outside evidence.[37] In fact, blood quantum became most useful to the US government *after* allotments had been made, when it was used as justification for releasing mixed-blood holders of allotments from paternalistic government restrictions on the selling of that land. A series of moves by the government at the beginning of the twentieth century allowed mixed-blood Indians with increasing amounts of "Indian blood" to be considered competent to sell their land, with the effect of making such land subject to US taxation.

Since that time, the notion of blood quantum has become extremely important, not only in the federal government's dealings with Indians and various Indian tribes but also in the internal affairs of many tribes themselves, as blood quanta were further codified in various forms in many of the tribal constitutions and bylaws written as a result of the Indian Reorganization Act of 1934. While it is never the *sole* basis for determining tribal membership, "among federally recognized tribes in the United States, blood quantum (often 25 percent) is the most common criterion." While blood quantum is properly understood as a technology of colonialism, in the American Indian case (by contrast to the African American one), it has also become a technology of resistance to US political and cultural hegemony. Though the sovereignty of Indian tribes has frequently been disregarded or compromised, the very notion of a right to indigenous sovereignty imbues the metaphor of Indian blood with connotations of cultural identity and political right, along with that of racial essence. Because Indian blood carries those symbolic meanings and because uses of blood quantum remains institutionalized at the tribal and federal government levels, the concept has been and continues to be "central to individuals' and communities' struggles for existence, resources, and recognition."

Like the one-drop rule for African Americans, blood quantum for American Indians has been a double-edged sword.[38] Yet, as I discuss at the end of this chapter, when it comes to resistance, blood quantum may be the wrong weapon altogether. By basing tribal belonging (or Indian kinship) primarily or significantly on blood (or substance), American Indians deemphasize other viable and perhaps more desirable bases for cultural and political unity and resistance. In other words, they legitimate understandings of kinship and race that emerged as political technologies intended to contain them and dispossess them of their lands and heritage. The blood metaphor in the United States has been a tool for emphasizing racial separation, and this separation has never been characterized by equality.

Denying Common Origins—the American Polygenists

If an important function of the race *idea*, especially in American history, has been to argue for the separation or deep lack of kinship between people of different races, it should come as no surprise that the United States provided fertile ground for debates over a particular race *theory*: polygenesis, or the idea that human beings were of multiple origins. At its core, this theory provided the ultimate challenge to any notion of universal human brotherhood. It suggested that there was no ancestral or biological relation between different races whatsoever, no matter how far back in history. Moreover, rather than simply seeing race mixing as a social or moral failure, it predicted that race mixing would be a biological failure. In other words, polygenesis represented the ultimate in lack of kinship between races—there was no deep history of kinship between races, and any attempted future of kinship between races would weaken and ultimately destroy both the white and, less importantly, the black species.

While some eighteenth-century Anglo-European thinkers advanced early articulations of polygenesis, it was the nineteenth century and the United States that saw the greatest debate on the subject. The US debate "began early and lasted late," writes C. L. Brace, and was "characterized by a degree of stridency and *ad hominem* argument entirely lacking in the Old World," largely due to the fact that in North America, "three major population blocks [white, black, and Indian] confronted one another under conditions of manifest political and social inequality."[39] The men who would come to represent the *American School* of what was then known as *ethnology* (or, the *American Polygenists*) took advantage of the developing notion of racial types and of the increasing scientific challenges to the biblical chronology to advance the idea that the different human races in fact constituted different species. The key figures of the "school" were Samuel George Morton (1799–1851), Ephraim George Squier (1821–88), George Robbins Glidden (1809–57), and Josiah Clark Nott (1804–73)—though I will focus here on Morton and Nott. One definition of ethnology accepted by Nott was that of Luke Burke, editor of the *London Ethnological Journal*: "a science which investigates the mental and physical differences of mankind, and the organic laws on which they depend; and seeks to deduce from these investigations principles for human guidance, in all the important relations of social existence."[40] Note that the second part of this definition explicitly seeks in the understanding of scientific laws some form guidance for human action in the social realm.

Of the key members of the American School, Samuel George Morton was perhaps the most genuine scientist. In 1939, Morton, a physician and anatomist, published *Crania Americana*, the result of a nearly two-decade fascination with skulls. As Morton amassed a larger and larger collection of human skulls, he became convinced that cranial capacity and conformation were distinctive racial characteristics. Morton also concluded, based on the fact that the Negro and the Caucasian could be found depicted as distinct "races" in three-thousand-year-old Egyptian monuments, that biblical chronology did not afford enough time for the development of human beings into separate races through environmental factors only. Not yet being inclined to question the chronology itself, Morton adopted the "reasonable conclusion" that "each Race was adapted from the beginning to its peculiar local destination"—in other words, that there must have been multiple Creations. Though far from the first to postulate human specific diversity, Morton was the first to provide for the thesis the sort of "objective" evidence that was becoming synonymous with "science." This evidence came in the form of tables of cranial measurement. Morton also derived from his study descriptions of the chief physical and moral characteristics of each race. Not surprisingly, the Caucasian was awarded the highest intellectual endowments. *Crania Americana* was followed five years later by *Crania Aegyptiaca* (1845), which, among other things, "discovered to anthropology the great age of the races and noted that slavery was 'among the earliest of the social institutions in Egypt.'" It also concluded that: "The social position of Negroes had been the same as it was in the nineteenth century, that of servants and slaves."[41] Such "findings" would serve not only to justify continued enslavement of African-descended blacks—since they were thought fit for nothing else—but also to show how, while the Caucasian race was defined by its civilization and progress, the African race was doomed to stagnation or perhaps eventual extinction.

If Morton was the chief scientist of the American School, Josiah Clark Nott, a physician from Mobile, Alabama, was its greatest ideologue. (And if one is searching for a clear villain in the history of race, Nott certainly fits the bill.) Nott's interest in racial theory was sparked in 1842 by an anonymous letter to the editor of the *Boston Medical and Surgical Journal* on the "Vital Statistics of Negroes and Mulattoes." The author, identified simply as "Philanthropist" purported to show, by means of the 1840 US Census statistics, that the life expectancy of mulattoes and free Negroes (reasoned to have a high number of mulattoes among them) was much lower than that of either "pure Africans" or whites.[42] Nott, however, moved the discussion in a more "biological" direction by arguing against not only the longevity but also the fertility of black-white "hybrids" and thus in favor of blacks and whites as separate species. By 1843, Nott had published his first ethnological article arguing to this effect in the *American Journal of the Medical Sciences*, aptly titled "The Mulatto a Hybrid—Probable Extermination of the Two Races If the Whites and Blacks Are Allowed To Intermarry."[43]

In 1844, Morton and Nott began a correspondence, and Nott first delivered his "Two Lectures on the Natural History of the Caucasian and Negro Races" to a group of gentlemen in Mobile. Though Nott opened his lectures by stating, "The Unity of the Human Race is a question appertaining to Natural History, which should be left open to fair and honest investigation, and made to stand or fall according to the facts," objective adherence to facts was not Nott's forte.[44] The 1840 census on which Nott based many of his arguments was slanted in a blatantly proslavery manner and filled with unverifiable claims and gross errors of which Nott could hardly have been ignorant since the problems associated with the data of the census had been exposed in the very same *Boston Medical and Surgical Journal*; "he used them anyway without apology or qualification."[45] Indeed, though the Congress had not yet repudiated the census data when Nott first began using it, he continued to make use of the same data well after it fell into disrepute.[46] Nott made little effort to conduct or gather any further scientific research in support of his claims, preferring instead simply to continue to deliver his writings and talks to his receptive Southern audiences. That Nott recognized the interests of these audiences and the attention he could garner by playing to those interests is also made clear in his private correspondence. "The subject attracts and all the title articles I have written on niggerology have been eagerly sought for at the South," he wrote to Squier on February 14, 1849, "and in the present excited state of the political world I think the thing will go well, though I have never [written] to please the crowd, but for the advancement of truth."[47]

Unfortunately for Nott, just when he had finally convinced Morton to fight more firmly and clearly for the specific diversity of human races and more strongly against the biblical account of a single creation, Morton died in the spring of 1851. This left Nott to lead the battle and its remaining soldiers on his own. By 1853, Nott and Glidden had managed to produce *Types of Mankind*, "a ponderous volume of over eight hundred pages, dedicated 'to the Memory of Morton,'" which also included a chapter by Louis Agassiz, an internationally recognized Swiss paleontologist, glaciologist, and geologist who had come around to the American School's polygenist views after moving to Boston in 1846.[48] *Types of Mankind* received international recognition, and the essentials of Nott and Morton's hybridity argument were adopted by French anthropologist Paul Broca for his *Hybridity in the Genus Homo*. For his part, Nott was deeply impressed by the work of a different Frenchman, Arthur de Gobineau, and Nott engaged Henry Hotz, a Swiss man working for a newspaper in Mobile, to translate selected sections.[49]

In truth, there was quite a bit in Gobineau's extensive work that Nott *did not* find useful for his cause. Nott clearly appreciated the way that Gobineau's account placed race at the center of history; he also found Gobineau's pessimism surrounding race mixing in its current phase (after all, for Gobineau, race mixing had been productive of civilization up until a certain point in history) useful in his portrayal of amalgamation as peril. In their translation, however, Nott and Hotz excised as much of Gobineau's thought as they retained. Gobineau's original work, whose title properly translated would be *Essay on the Inequality of the Human Races*, was twelve hundred pages long. Nott and Hotz's translation, entitled *The Moral and Intellectual Diversity of Races*, did not quite reach four hundred pages. Gobineau himself was displeased with their "translation," as he revealed in a 1856 letter to a friend: "Do you not wonder . . . at my friends the Americans, who believe that I am encouraging them to bludgeon their Negroes, who praise me to the skies for that, but who are unwilling to translate the part of the work which concerns them?" Gobineau certainly did not hold the Negro race in high regard, describing it as the "most humble" and as lagging "at the bottom of the scale." Yet he held no great respect for the American whites either, whom he regarded as "a very mixed assortment of the most degenerate races of olden-day Europe" or "the human flotsam of all ages." He found it "quite unimaginable that anything could result from such horrible confusion but an incoherent juxtaposition of the most decadent kinds of people."[50] Nor was he a supporter of American slavery, castigating "the inconsistency of those who advocated slaveholding while proclaiming liberal and egalitarian doctrines in other spheres."[51]

Gobineau's wider views on race were also greatly simplified in the translation. As Michelle Wright describes: "In his discussion of the peoples that comprise Africa, Gobineau makes a multitude of distinctions based on geography, migratory history, civilization, religion, and a host of bizarre physical determinations that effectively serve to deconstruct the meaning of the 'Negro' through obsessive categorization." That these divisions and subdivisions of both the Negro and Aryan races are not included, Wright argues, serves to polarize Gobineau's discussion "into a race war between white and black in which the American nation is at stake."[52] This polarization is further accomplished by Hotz's claim, in his introduction to the work, that when one compares the white and black races: "The whole history of the former shows an uninterrupted progress; that of the latter, monotonous stagnation."[53] For Gobineau, "mankind lives in obedience to two laws [with respect to other races], one of repulsion and one of attraction," and it is only those races who can overcome the repulsion and act on the attraction to other races (that is, white races) who will be capable of development.[54] As Nale puts it: "The tragedy of Gobineau's story lies in this exceptionalism of the white race, as their propensity for society ironically leads to civilization's death by miscegenation."[55] Nott and Hotz, of course, downplay this law of attraction and its positive results.

Questions of attraction and repulsion were tricky ones in discussions of hybridity. For example, in 1846 Morton had written an extended paper on hybridization in which, in order to show that human races could constitute different species in spite of their ability to produce fertile progeny, he quoted James Cowles Prichard's *Researches into the Physical History of Mankind* as arguing that while the "separation of distinct species is sufficiently provided for by the natural repugnance between individuals of different kinds" it can be "overcome in the state of domestication, in which the natural propensities cease, in a great measure, to direct their actions." Humans, as the most domesticated of the animals, Morton concluded, would thus be able to reproduce between different human species (e.g., between races). Eager not to imply that this made race mixing a good or appropriate advance, however, Morton called attention to the "fact" that "the repugnance of some human races to mix with others, has only been partially overcome by centuries of proximity, and, above all other means, by the moral degradation consequent to the state of slavery."[56] This last point of Morton's calls attention to the way the issue of race mixing became so central to debates about race in the United States that it was used to argue both for and against slavery. As Wallenstein describes, in the years leading up the Civil War, anti-amalgamationist logic and fears were used both by defenders of slavery who argued that "any softening of the slave power would bring together white women and black men" *and* by abolitionists who pointed to the frequent sexual encounters between white male slave owners and slave women as proof that ending slavery would in fact reduce race mixing.[57]

Ultimately, Nott and Hotz were invested in the idea of natural repugnance as a mark of specific diversity between the races and saw race mixing in only one way (in contrast to Gobineau's two): as a dangerous path of degradation. "Philanthropist's" letter and Nott's subsequent work can be seen within the history of race as "the decisive step in the biologization of the case against race mixing."[58] They can also be seen as important influences with respect to race and kinship. Arguing for the separate origins of the various human races allowed for the justification of slavery not only in terms of the natural inferiority of the black race but because white and black were seen as naturally and entirely separate. If whites were not related to blacks, even in the most distant past—and if attempts to bring the two races together in the present were doomed to biological failure— then the enslavement of the latter by the former need not be seen as morally abhorrent. According to Nott, even the reality of a great deal of race mixing did not and would not make black and white kin. Moreover, such a view of human origins allowed for the belief that no matter what their recent provenance, all members of each race were related by blood to each other (but not to any members of other races). Nott's relative success in the field of race theory, despite the notable lack of strong evidence or reasoning to support his claims, demonstrates the political needs his ideas fulfilled. People wanted to believe that they were fulfilling their familial, national, and racial duties by upholding systems of slavery and, later, segregation rather than shirking some sort of larger duty to humanity. Thus, while the idea of members of one's own race being family may hold appeal in certain contemporary contexts, the divisive, exploitative provenance of the concept should give any committed antiracist pause.

Discouraging Intimacy and Disallowing Kinship

Indeed, many of the laws and customs that have operated over the past three hundred years to establish and maintain a racial hierarchy and myths of racial purity in the United States (both well before and well after the life of the American School of ethnography) can also be understood as establishing or disestablishing bonds of kinship. For example, the 1662 Virginia law that read: "Whereas some doubts have arisen whether children got by any Englishman upon a Negro woman should be slave or free, be it therefore enacted and declared by this present Grand Assembly, that all children born in this country shall be held bond or free only according to the condition of the mother; and that if any Christian shall commit fornication with a Negro man or woman, he or she so offending shall pay double the fines imposed by the former act."[59] According to this law, everything depended on the mother and her status (as slave or free); the father's identity, race, and status were deemed legally irrelevant for the child.[60] Besides establishing the free or slave status of the children in question and punishing those whites whose interracial sexual relations resulted in pregnancy, however, this law and others like it should be seen as literally making or breaking bonds of blood kinship. As Hickman describes, through such laws white fathers "escaped responsibility not only for including these children in their families but also for including them in their larger family of the White race."[61] As mentioned earlier, within the system of chattel slavery, such laws meant that the child produced by a (likely nonconsensual) sexual union between a slave woman and her white owner was seen as bearing a kinship relationship only to its mother, thus rendering the child a slave. The relationship between this child and its biological father was a property relationship rather than a family one. In other words, the lack of kinship determined by the racial difference between the father and the mother-child pair was capable of overriding any relation we might now take to be established by the simple fact of sexual reproduction. Such separation was further supported by the difference in legal standing between white male master and enslaved woman and child. While the former was a property owner, the latter were considered property. Just as slaves themselves, as property, were considered legally unable to establish bonds of kinship through marriage, it was difficult, if not impossible, for the law to consider the child of a slave and a slave owner as *both* that slave owner's property *and* his kin.

For the law, the relationship between property and kinship is navigated through estate cases, in which the court weighs the competing inheritance claims by various relatives of a decedent or considers relatives' claims to inheritance that was willed to other parties by the decedent. Adrienne Davis documents a number of cases in the antebellum and postbellum South in which race, sex, and estate law intersected, forcing the state to deal with questions of race and kinship. Focusing on cases that emerge from sexual relationships between white men and black women, Davis argues that the challenge for private law during those periods lay in "negotiating and reconciling what sometimes appear to be contradictory imperatives of preserving private property and maintaining racial hierarchy, while maintaining the legitimacy of the legal system." This involved drawing distinctions "between those sexual or biological relationships that yield legal obligations and entitlements and those that do not" or, as I would argue, determining which sexual or biological relationships would produce *kinship*. While the intergenerational transfer of private wealth normally serves to *maintain* racial hierarchy by keeping wealth and the privilege that goes along with it in white hands, when elite white men sought to leave money or property to black or mulatto mistresses or mulatto children, or to free those women and children held as slaves, a conflict emerged between respecting the sovereign choices of the property holder and maintaining the social order.[62]

While Davis notes that "all postmortem conveyances of emancipation and wealth to the enslaved affected the racial distribution of individual wealth," she argues that such conveyances to "concubines and offspring by them" posed a particular social threat in that they acknowledged blacks as "sexual family" (and might even disinherit white heirs in favor of that family). This public acknowledgement, documented in a will, represented postmortem defiance of the racial sexual order, which called for discretion in miscegenational relations and the denial of enduring companionate and filial bonds between ruling whites and the enslaved class.[63] Though five Southern state legislatures passed statutes prohibiting testamentary emancipations and devises of bequests to slaves, between 1841 and the end of slavery many courts admitted such wills into probate, endorsing the decedents' testamentary capacity authority but tempering that endorsement with strong condemnation of the testators' sexual conduct. Meanwhile, "the feelings that gave rise to the testamentary transfers were pushed into a special, pre-social set of 'natural sentiments,' laudable in their way, but reflective of charity rooted in animal sympathy rather than ethical duty rooted in law."[64] Though the relationships may have involved emotion, they did not and ought not to rise to the level of legally or socially sanctioned kinship.

While laws enacted with respect to children of mixed racial parentage—that is, laws that made or unmade bonds of blood kinship—were important during slavery because they protected white property holdings and officially discouraged interracial intimacy, laws restricting kinship *by marriage* on the basis of race were not as important at that time. During slavery, enslaved persons were not afforded the legal right to enter into marriage contracts regardless of the race of the persons they wished to marry (and were therefore not entitled to inherit "family" property). After emancipation, however, the locus of antimiscegenation regulation shifted from the policing of interracial sex to the policing of interracial marriage. Immediately after the end of the Civil War, those Southern states that had not explicitly prohibited interracial marriage did so while those Southern states that had existing statutes strengthened them, enhancing penalties and broadening the scope of prosecution.[65] Because the federal Civil Rights Act of 1866 granted blacks rights equal to those of whites to make and enforce contracts, the upholding of antimiscegenation statutes required shifting the legal approach to marriage away from "marriage-as-contract" and toward "marriage as social institution." In the words of the Supreme Court of North Carolina in 1869: "when formed, [marriage] is more than a civil contract; it is a relation, an institution, affecting not merely the parties, like business contracts, but offspring particularly, and society generally."[66]

At least thirty-eight US states had antimiscegenation laws at some point, and they were enacted, changed, or repealed at a variety of different times. For example, Pennsylvania repealed its law in 1780, but Rhode Island inaugurated one soon after. Massachusetts repealed its law in 1843, but the new state of California adopted one. Indeed, throughout the nineteenth century, the states in which interracial marriage was restricted would change and also shift toward the south and west. Every state in which blacks amounted to at least 5 percent of the population eventually enacted an antimiscegenation law. While some statutes included members of other races or ethnic groups in their provisions (and the groups included varied), *every* antimiscegenation law prohibited marriage between blacks and whites.[67] Such laws were concerned both with ideological issues like establishing racial identity and maintaining racial purity and with practical ones like state comity and inheritance of property. As Ian Haney López puts it: "Antimiscegenation laws, like lynch laws more generally, sought to maintain social dominance along specifically racial lines, and at the same time, sought to maintain racial lines through social domination."[68] Moreover, as I would like to emphasize, they were describing who could or ought to be considered family and who would not.

Of course, as with any use of race, the use of racial difference to deny or prohibit kinship was not limited to the state or the broader maintenance of the social order. Individual parties in court-mediated disputes (both black and white) made or attempted to make use of race and race-based laws to further their agendas. This occurred in estate cases, divorce or annulment proceedings, and, later, custody battles. "Theoretically," writes Kennedy, "if a spouse could show that his or her marital partner was of a different race, he or she could leave the marriage free of obligations, since in the eyes of the law, the parties had never been lawfully wed in the first place." Though, he also notes, this was not always effective, as "judges displayed a striking solicitude toward women whose white husbands sought separation on such grounds" and were not inclined to release "cads" from their matrimonial and parental responsibilities lightly. Nevertheless, if one had been deceived as to the racial identity of one's spouse, one might be deserving of sympathy or legal redress.

Indeed, even adoptions could be annulled when white parents mistakenly adopted children of a different race, if the parents were found not to have known about the children's race beforehand.[69] This possibility within adoption during an earlier time foreshadows the public and private discomforts that result from "racial mix-ups" in more contemporary ART practices (as discussed in chapters 1 and 5). Racial difference is seen as disrupting kinship and, while families may choose to ignore or attempt to overcome this disruption, such a challenge must be chosen. By default, families are seen as having a natural expectation of and right to *intra*racial reproduction.

Separation after Slavery

Perhaps nothing more clearly demonstrates the importance placed on preventing interracial marriage as a matter of social necessity than the wide variety of instances in which the threat of interracial marriage was invoked to oppose civil rights measures or legislation. (The threat was typically phrased in a tellingly gendered way as something like, "Do you want your daughter to marry a Negro?"[70]) In 1804, a white Pennsylvanian claimed that allowing black men to vote would lead to intermarriage. In 1841, a number of white Ohioans felt allowing blacks to testify against whites in court would bring about the same result. In 1857, Chief Justice Roger B. Taney's opinion in *Dred Scott v. Sandford* referenced laws against interracial marriage (and its "unnatural and immoral" nature) to argue that blacks (free or no) were never meant to be citizens of the United States. In fact, the term *miscegenation* itself was coined in this spirit during the 1864 presidential campaign when: "Seeking to provoke outrage and mislead white public opinion, Northern opponents of Abraham Lincoln published and distributed a pamphlet suggesting that Lincoln and his Republican party encouraged interracial marriage."[71] During the Reconstruction period, interracial marriage became "the *reductio ad absurdum* of congressional debates," raised whenever anyone "proposed measures for the protection of Negro rights."[72] Fears of interracial marriage were essential to the maintenance and justification of Jim Crow segregation and, as Ruby Lacks alluded to at the beginning of this chapter, appeared in the debates leading up to *Brown v. Board of Education*.[73]

Indeed, Ruby Lacks's remarks bear a striking resemblance to those made nearly 150 years earlier by W. W. Wright in his article "Amalgamation," which appeared in *De Bow's Review* in 1860. Wright was a regular contributor to the *Review*, which, having previously established itself as the antebellum South's most prominent economic journal, shifted focus after 1854 to become "a public forum for angry southerners who resented northern attacks on slavery and other southern institutions."[74] Following up on his series on "Free Negroes" around the world and "Free Negro Rule" as a whole (which he found lacking in genuine civilization), in "Amalgamation" Wright responds to the hypothesis that race mixing between blacks and whites would civilize the black race or possibly even result in a superior form of man. After reciting Nott's view on the "probable ultimate infertility of human hybrids of the mulatto type"[75] and offering a variety of other "facts and observations" about blacks and mulattoes, Wright describes "aversion to hybridity" as "the safeguard of the people" and warns: "But do away with the social and political distinctions now existing, and you immediately turn all the blacks and mulattoes into citizens, co-governors, and acquaintances: and acquaintances, as Wilberforce aptly remarks, are the raw material from which are *manufactured friends, husbands and wives*. The man whom you associate with is next invited to your house, and the man whom you invite to your house is the possible husband of your daughter, whether he be black or white."[76]

The racially constructed understanding of kinship on which this racial anxiety rests, and which allows its use as a racist political scare tactic, is highlighted in James Baldwin's response to the issue on national television one Sunday in the 1960s. John Oliver Killens recounts how Baldwin "stared long and hard at John Kilpatrick, Southern genteel aristocrat from old Virginia, and stated matter-of-factly: 'You're not worried about me marrying *your* daughter.

You're worried about me marrying your *wife's* daughter. I've been marrying your daughter ever since the days of slavery.'"[77] White men's *white* progeny—legitimated by their production within *intra*racial, state- and socially sanctioned marriages—are their *daughters* and are in need of protection from black men to preserve racial purity. White men's *nonwhite progeny*, on the other hand, may be their property or the object of their charity, but they are consigned to *the larger family of the black race* and must be left out of political rhetoric about appropriate race relations.

In the period of racial and social anxiety following the end of slavery, this racialized construction of individual kinship relations worked alongside and in conjunction with a larger, metaphorical relationship between race and kinship. D. Marvin Jones describes how, in the American mind in the wake of slavery's abolition: "Race reverberated as a metaphor of kinship, denying that there was the requisite brotherhood between blacks and whites, and denying that blacks and whites could co-exist on the same social status plane."[78] By figuring racial difference as natural and unchangeable, the kinship metaphor provided justification for the codification of racial separation in law. The inconsistency of needing to enforce through law a separation thought to be natural and inevitable was, of course, covered over. Taking a hermeneutical approach to the idea of race, Jones seeks to show the role of various metaphors in the creation and reification of US race ideas after slavery. Echoing several thinkers in the previous chapter, Jones argues that "we visualize race not through actual observations but through the mind's eye, by 'seeing' human populations as naturally parsed into distinctive subgroups," but emphasizes how the "lens though which the meaning of race is illuminated . . . is ultimately our sense of who we are . . . our sense of identity—as an alternating image of those who are like us . . . and those who are not." For Jones, it is this subjective aspect of how we see race that holds together and disguises what are ultimately contradictory sets of criteria for racial identity: (1) "a historical approach that defines race according to lineage and emphasizes connectedness over time," and (2) "a classificatory approach that emphasizes common characteristics or traits."[79] Each of these sets of criteria is represented and supported by a different metaphor—the former by the metaphor of *blood* and the latter by the metaphor of *color*—both of which have been reified through American law.

The metaphor of blood was perhaps most famously reified in *Plessy v. Ferguson* in 1896, in which the Supreme Court found that, though Homer Plessy *appeared* white, what mattered "was not what could be seen—his skin color—but what could not be seen: the problem, in a word, was his 'blood.'" Thus: "Even Plessy's small degree of African consanguinity sufficed to make him black. Black blood was, and still is, conceived of as a kind of taint."[80] What is figured in this case as being *discovered* or *uncovered* is actually being *created* in the blood metaphor and in the court decision that employs that metaphor. What is a *conditioned* way of viewing identity and the world is transformed into a *fact of nature* and then into a rule of law, all of which mutually support and sustain each other. In Jones's words:

> Blood in this narrative is the carrier of racial character, something deep within that determines one's social identity. . . . By blood, social differences are converted into natural differences. As a result of this conversion, evil traits often associated lexically with certain races are not products of socialization, nor even products of individual choice: they are inherent—"in the blood". . . . *Plessy* mobilizes this magical idea of "blood" to create an order for the post-Reconstruction world that paralleled the slave regime; blood demarcated a boundary not merely between different "races," but concomitantly between different spheres of social life.[81]

Here, ideas about blood serve a naturalizing function that helps to shore up social differences that are perceived to be dissolving with potentially negative consequences for the previously privileged.

Whereas the "blood metaphor creates a rule of differentiation; the metaphor of color valorizes or gives normative content to the differentiation." The metaphor of color in race thinking creates and defines both *black* and *white* by setting them against each other as essential opposites, not merely in terms of appearance but in terms of character and civilization. Whiteness and European identity have been figured as heroic, civilizing, and moral precisely through the simultaneous act of figuring Africa as "not merely nature" but "the heart of darkness, a place of evil." Carrying these ideas forward into the American postslavery context helps to explains the need for segregation, where the "belief that races must not mix is based on a notion of black racial identity as something so opposite to whiteness—to order and reason—that it must be kept at a distance."[82] The metaphor of color, in opposing the terms *black* and *white* (which, of course, do not actually refer to the literal skin colors of the populations in question), posits a deep opposition between people of different races that goes well beyond the physical.

For Jones, it is Darwin's theory that, though undermining the previous bases for many racial beliefs, actually allowed for a reframing of those beliefs such that the two metaphors he describes could finally be brought together in social Darwinism. The social Darwinian view holds conflict and opposition between groups to be a natural mechanism by which human evolution occurs as human beings move from one generation to the next, with the "best" always being favored for and deserving of survival. Such a view brings the blood metaphor, emphasizing the ultimate importance of heredity, together with the color metaphor, which figures physical difference in terms of the opposition between good and evil. The result is reinforcement both of the justification of social inequality as stemming from natural and inevitable difference on the one hand and of the perceived danger of race mixing and contamination on the other. Thus, with slavery over, the use of race both as a visible sign of kinship—and especially of *lack thereof*—provided ideological support for continued segregation.

Even when one adopts a more benevolent model for race relations in society than "survival of the fittest," family metaphors and ideals may be used to justify inequality. Collins, for example, points to the fact that "racial ideologies that portray people of color as intellectually underdeveloped, uncivilized children require parallel ideas that construct Whites as intellectually mature, civilized adults," which in turn naturalizes White authority within the US national "family" as akin to the "natural" (and supposedly benevolent) authority of parents over children.[83] Race thinking, then, should be seen as integral and intimately connected (through law, theories, and social practice) to the development of our understanding of kinship in the United States. It should be seen not only as helping to form the central metaphors (like that of blood) that frame our thinking about kinship but also, I will argue, as travelling along with these metaphors as they are extended and reworked for different scientific contexts, bringing with them unspoken layers of racialized meaning that are not always consciously recognized.

The "Blood" in Our "Genes"

Quiroga has argued that the use of racial categorization in ART practices is one example of how twenty-first-century hereditarianism substitutes the idea of *genes* for that of *blood*. She writes: "The metaphor of blood was, and still is, code for race, with connotations regarding the 'sanctity of blood, mixing blood, white blood, black blood, and pure versus tainted blood.'" The linking of race and heredity is, as I have argued, foundational to the American racial hierarchy, which today relies both on the idea that "intrinsic to whiteness are so-called superior traits that are linked to success" and the idea that those traits are heritable—in other words, that "whiteness itself is heritable." Despite contemporary scientific evidence to the contrary, Quiroga finds that "the folk idea that race is reducible to biological features remains prevalent." With respect to much of our current popular understanding of heredity, then, updated scientific terminology has simply been pasted onto our old metaphorical understanding, which retains much of its historical baggage. We do not question our biological determinism; we simply make it *genetic* determinism. We abandon the idea of "good" or "bad" *blood* only to replace it with "good" or "bad" *genes*, with no real need to change our sense of which "groups" carry and transmit these good or bad qualities—or to complicate our understanding of heredity itself. Today, "genes rather than blood will tell."[84]

This means that even where the deployment of race as a metaphor for kinship can be considered consensual and is used to affirm a kinship relation that is the desired outcome for all involved parties, there remains a symbolic cost to be considered. Despite the fact that the race idea appears to be tied to scientific theories of race, and that those theories seem to be moving away from the scientific racism of the past, that which is essential to the political race idea remains in many ways impervious to scientific changes. Its symbolic and metaphorical uses in assisted reproduction thus carry with them many pernicious beliefs and assumptions. Furthermore, even as scientific race theories fail to alter the essence of the race *idea*, the race *idea* has influenced and shaped—and continues to influence and shape—both the popular interpretations of scientific theories (of race, heredity and genetics) and the framing and development of those theories themselves.

As Bob Simpson points out, "the narratives, concepts and terms which are routinely thrown into the wider society by this burgeoning area of [genetics] do not simply bounce off a thick skin of ignorance and indifference but become woven into popular discourses surrounding human behavior and interaction." That is to say that when analyzing the public understanding of the new genetics, one must pay attention to "the active presence of lay beliefs and values brought to bear when making sense of new technologies and not merely the absence of technical knowledge." We must pay attention not only to what people *do not* know but in fact to what they are quite certain that deep down inside they *do* know. Even if the idea of blood as literally responsible for hereditary transmission and for race seems dead in our time, there is strong evidence that popular conceptions of genetics, especially in terms of race, continue to be influenced by the logic of the blood metaphor—the logic of hereditary substance. As Simpson explains, "ideas about consubstantiation through blood have formed the basis of ideologies of descent which not only provide the basis of symbolic unity of a people but also underpin their claims to territory and land." Although "with the rise of new genetics comes a new vocabulary for grounding difference and similarity as 'blood' is displaced by DNA as the essential marker of shared identity and attribute," this does not mean that the idea of "unity through shared substance" has actually been significantly altered. To demonstrate this, Simpson cites the example of a reaction in Scotland to press coverage about sperm being imported from Danish sperm banks to compensate for a shortage of local donors. The importation of the sperm was described as a "Viking Baby Invasion," and, following the press coverage, new Scottish donors stepped forward. Simpson speculates that it was a belief that genes form the substance of a community and that their community would be undermined by the introduction of "foreign" genes that recruited new donors.[85]

Such an analysis of popular perceptions and motivations accords with Kimberly TallBear's discussion of the prevalence of old racial ideology among American Indian communities, where, she reports, "Blood talk and, increasingly, talk of DNA have unfortunately infiltrated tribal political life and are used to help justify cultural and political authority." According to TallBear, to look to DNA testing as a new and "better" means of authenticating claims to tribal identity is to reify the concept of race on which the old blood quantum policy was based: "It is to accept that the blood of races are somehow fixed and divided, rather than being asserted as part of a political or ideological stance."[86] In other words, it is to take American Indian identity to be biologically rather than culturally based—as being the result of shared substance rather than shared tradition. In these examples, the logic of blood as substance lives on within the language of "genetics" and "DNA." The race idea continues to serve its symbolic function much as it has previously but with updated reference to contemporary scientific theories, resulting in understandings of those theories that are shaped by that organizing symbolism.

Conclusion

Race, I have argued, acts as a technology in the ART clinic and beyond, interacting with other technologies and being actively manipulated by human actors in order to "make parents." This technology, I claim, operates using race as a proxy for kinship, a relationship that is available in ART contexts only because of its earlier construction and deployment during America's slavery and postslavery eras. Race in that time was employed as a political technology to create and support a system of white privilege and supremacy. The threat of racial contamination and the idea of essential racial difference were used to justify racial separation and subjugation. In these legal, social, and political movements, however, ideas about and rules for kinship were also constructed and reinforced. Thus an understanding of race as a proxy kinship that emerged from a broad political context is now being deployed on a more intimate level in ART practices. In the next chapter, I will consider more closely what it means to shift concepts of race and reproduction from public political, legal, and scientific arenas to more individualized and privatized sites.

Notes

1. Skloot, *Immortal Life of Henrietta Lacks*, 123–24.
2. Ibid., 78–79.
3. Ibid., 122.
4. Ibid., 125.
5. Thompson, *Making Parents*, 5.
6. Ibid., 8.
7. Ibid., 156–58.
8. Ragoné, "Of Likeness and Difference," 66–67.
9. Hartouni, *Cultural Conceptions*, 91, 94.
10. Angela Davis, "Outcast Mothers and Surrogates," 362.
11. Figal, *Heredity, Race, and the Birth of the Modern*, 61.
12. Ibid., 76.

13. Voegelin, "Growth of the Race Idea," 28.

14. Schneider, *American Kinship*, 23.

15. Stocking, "Turn-of-the-Century Concept of Race," 8.

16. Schneider, *American Kinship*, 25.

17. Stocking, "Turn-of-the-Century Concept of Race," 6.

18. Ibid., 5.

19. Nale, "Arthur de Gobineau on Blood and Race," 106.

20. Ibid., 115.

21. Ibid., 118.

22. Ibid., 119.

23. Voegelin, "Growth of the Race Idea," 285.

24. Ibid., 303.

25. Smedley, *Race in North America*, 9.

26. Kennedy's *Interracial Intimacies* (2003) seeks to counter this forgetting by documenting the history of interracial sex, marriage, and procreation in the United States.

27. Spickard, *Almost All Aliens*, 17.

28. Ibid., 18–19.

29. Kennedy, *Interracial Intimacies*, 223.

30. Hickman, "The Devil and the One Drop Rule,"1166.

31. Spruhan, "A Legal History of Blood Quantum," 4.

32. Ibid., 48.

33. Ibid., 9–18.

34. Ibid., 9.

35. Ibid., 23–39.

36. Strong and Van Winkle, "'Indian Blood,'" 557–58.

37. Spruhan, "A Legal History of Blood Quantum," 42–43.

38. Strong and Winkle, "'Indian Blood,'" 554–59.

39. Brace, "The 'ethnology' of Josiah Clark Nott," 512.

40. Ibid., 514.

41. Stanton, *The Leopard's Spots*, 29–33, 51.

42. A reprint of "Vital Statistics of Negroes and Mulattoes" can be found in Bernasconi and Dotson, *Race, Hybridity, and Miscegenation*.

43. A reprint of "The Mulatto a Hybrid—Probable Extermination of the Two Races If the Whites and Blacks Are Allowed To Intermarry" is also available in Bernasconi and Dotson.

44. Nott, *Two Lectures*, 1.

45. Brace, "The 'ethnology' of Josiah Clark Nott," 517. For more on the problems with the 1840 census, see Harriet Washington, *Medical Apartheid*, chapter 6.

46. Stanton, *The Leopard's Spots*, 79.

47. Brace, "The 'ethnology' of Josiah Clark Nott," 518.

48. Stanton, *The Leopard's Spots*, 162.

49. Brace, "The 'ethnology' of Josiah Clark Nott," 522.

50. Wright, "Nigger Peasants from France," 832–33, 837–38.

51. Biddiss, *Father of Racist Ideology*, 145.

52. Wright, "Nigger Peasants from France," 838–40.

53. Hotz, "Analytical Introduction," 32.

54. Gobineau, *Inequality of Human Races*, 30.

55. Nale, "Arthur de Gobineau on Blood and Race," 113.

56. Morton, "Hybridity in Animals and Plants," 286–87.

57. Wallenstein, *Tell the Court I Love My Wife*, 53.

58. Bernasconi, "The Policing of Race Mixing," 210.

59. Hening, *The Statutes at Large*, 170.

60. Wallenstein, *Tell the Court I Love My Wife*, 15.

61. Hickman, "The Devil and the One Drop Rule," 1176.

62. Adrienne Davis, "The Private Law of Race and Sex," 225–27.

63. Ibid., 254.

64. Ibid., 251, 251n93, 257.

65. Ibid., 240–41, 274.

66. Quoted in Adrienne Davis, "The Private Law of Race and Sex," 275.

67. Kennedy, *Interracial Intimacies*, 219–20.

68. Haney López, *White by Law*, 117.

69. Kennedy, *Interracial Intimacies*, 235–36, 450.

70. Avins, "Anti-Miscegenation Laws and the Fourteenth Amendment," 1227.

71. Kennedy, *Interracial Intimacies*, 20–22, 20n.

72. Avins, "Anti-Miscegenation Laws and the Fourteenth Amendment," 1227.

73. Kennedy, *Interracial Intimacies*, 24.

74. Kvach, *De Bow's Review*, 6.

75. Wright, "Amalgamation," 3.

76. Ibid., 14, original emphasis.

77. Killens, *Black Man's Burden*, 127.

78. Jones, "Darkness Made Visible," 438.

79. Ibid., 448–50.

80. Ibid., 452.

81. Ibid., 453.

82. Ibid., 455, 469–70.

83. Collins, "It's All in the Family," 65.

84. Quiroga, "Blood Is Thicker than Water," 145–46.

85. Simpson, "Imagined Genetic Communities," 3–4.

86. TallBear, "DNA, Blood, and Racializing the Tribe," 83, 96.

5   Race and Choice in the Era of Liberal Eugenics

Hey B—,

There is no way this isn't a weird question, so I'm just going to acknowledge that up front.

Remember when I visited you and we went to that house with all the beautiful tile. And the partner of the owner of the house was a black guy, whose name I no longer remember. Anyway, I'm wondering if he is still in your circle of friends.

Basically, R— and I are looking at trying to start a family in the next little while and, for political and personal reasons I can go into more later if you want, we were hoping to find a black, gay sperm donor. Sadly, we don't know any black gay people at the moment, so we're looking into some websites but are also kind of asking around.

Okay, so yeah, that was a weird question.

Anyway, how's it going? We should definitely catch up on the phone soon. Have any exciting Christmas plans?

—Private Facebook message from me to a longtime friend (December 8, 2011)

Aᴛ ᴛʜᴇ ᴇɴᴅ of 2011, my partner and I were beginning in earnest our search for donor sperm. As reproductive technologies go, donor insemination, which we initially pursued at home rather than at a clinic, is relatively low-tech. Because it involves obtaining donor gametes, however, it brings into relief the element of choice in reproduction. This element of choice includes (though is not limited to) racial choice. I say "brings into relief" in an attempt to avoid naturalizing and thereby erasing the elements of racial choice involved in nontechnological reproduction. Such choice is often obscured because *individual* choice (which serves as our privileged ideal for the concept of choice in general) can be severely circumscribed by *social* and *legal* choices outside the immediate control of the individual.

Take, for example, my aforementioned short white mother and her marriage to a tall black man in 1974, which, in 1978, resulted in the birth of a visibly mixed-race child who would grow to be 5'9" (and thus able to use her mother's shoulder for an armrest). Not to question this interracial relationship—as I did not for many, many years—is to miss the context in which it took place: Wyoming in the 1970s. That my mother even managed to find a black man to fall in love with and marry in Wyoming at that time was a considerable feat. By several family accounts, there were literally no black families in Gillette, Wyoming, when my mother grew up there. Things were different in Laramie (my father's hometown) because the University of Wyoming (where my parents met) was located there. Still, when I asked my dad how many black people lived in Laramie at that time, it made sense for him to begin counting the local black families on his hands. Of course, the relative unavailability of nonwhite men was not the only constraint on my mother's romantic and, ultimately, reproductive choices. There was also her mother's disapproval to contend with. My grandmother did not even need to *meet* my father in order to assert (at least to my aunt and perhaps to my mother herself) that my mother's marriage to a black man would destroy my grandfather's already failing health and ultimately lead to his premature death. When my mother chose to marry my father anyway, her parents chose not to attend her wedding.

My mother's sister did attend the wedding, however, as did my father's parents, who gave their support to the union. My mother walked herself down the aisle. Rumors of my grandfather's delicate constitution and moral outrage turned out to be greatly exaggerated. In fact, it was he who kept open the lines of communication with my mother during the first years my parents' marriage, calling her on Sundays while my grandmother was at church. He lived to see my birth and the reconciliation that event brought about between my mother and her mother. Though my grandmother did not see me often, everyone agrees that she doted on me. My father and my grandmother even came face to face once, though not until a couple years after my parents' divorce. The encounter was brief but civil.

Aside from adding a bit of local color (pun intended), the point of this story is to illustrate that, in spite of the increasing visibility of interracial marriages and of children born within them, we should not forget that the vast majority of people still marry *intra*racially and that this represents a form of social choice. According to a Pew Research study based on the 2010 US census, interracial marriages accounted for about 15 percent of *new* marriages, bringing interracial marriages to 8 percent of *all* US marriages. Though this represents a major jump in interracial marriage, it hardly indicates the disappearance of the kind of informal barriers that faced my parents. Moreover, further breakdown of these statistics indicates that White Americans are statistically quite unlikely to marry interracially. Only 2.1 percent of married white women and 2.3 percent of married white men had nonwhite spouses.[1] In short, the sociopolitical reproduction of racial categories through the bodily reproduction of children in racially endogamous marriages in not accidental, nor does it lie in the past.

Nevertheless, there is a certain starkness to the identity-based choices on offer to people like my partner and me in search of donor gametes. It is virtually impossible not to know the racial/ethnic background of a sperm donor (whether he is an acquaintance or anonymously catalogued by a sperm bank). And, indeed, it would not be my or my partner's preference to leave such elements to chance by, say, picking donor names or ID numbers out of a hat. Like many others in our position, our discussion of who exactly might constitute a desirable donor was based on what we see as our own key identity characteristics. Far from being merely a personal choice, however, our decision to seek out a black, gay donor was highly political—and would have been political, I would argue, whether we recognized it as such or not.

At the beginning of the last chapter, where I discussed the deployment of race as a proxy for kinship within the ontological choreography of the fertility clinic, IVF with ovum donation and gestational surrogacy served as privileged examples. In this chapter, I shift to artificial insemination as a privileged example in order to explore race as an identity feature—one that, I will argue, is becoming increasingly individualized, privatized, and therefore depoliticized. Sperm donation does not seem to provoke the same sort or level of anxieties about parental authority and legitimacy as surrogacy does. This is most likely because, especially in its anonymous form, sperm donation seems to entail very little involvement or intimacy. Accordingly, donor sperm is relatively cheap. With decreased concern about the potential disruption of a sperm donor to one's intended family life, selection of sperm seems, then, to be more focused on the perceived characteristics of that sperm—thought of these days in terms of "genetics." As mentioned in chapter 1, a typical default assumption is that these characteristics (including race) will be chosen to "match" those of the nongestating partner (man or lesbian), who, in an ideal procreative world, would have been able to provide his or her own genetic material to the intended child. Indeed, some researchers are attempting to develop new reproductive technologies in which embryonic stem cells from women would be used to create sperm cells and embryonic stem cells from men would be used to create eggs. The market for such technologies is seen as gay and lesbian couples—who would then be able to create children who were biogenetically related to both of them.[2] Such attempts serve as yet another example of how the view that biogenetic relation provides the best basis for kinship shapes the development of reproductive technologies.

In this chapter, I would like to inquire about the role race is playing in assisted reproduction in a reproductive era of what we might call *liberal* or *neoliberal eugenics*. If we live in such an era, it is explicitly characterized by at least two things: (1) the increasing availability of what Lee M. Silver has dubbed *reprogenetics*—"the use of genetic information and technology to ensure or prevent the inheritance of particular genes in a child;" and (2) the belief that use of reprogenetics—insofar as they are safe and available—should be understood as a matter of personal choice.[3] Implicitly, however, I would argue, along with Dorothy Roberts, that the era is further characterized by the sense that there exists a social duty to exhibit a form of *personal responsibility* when procreating, such that one must try to avoid bearing any children with genetic "flaws" that might prove a burden on society. At first blush, it is hard to understand how a sociohistorical and ultimately nongenetic concept like race fits into such an era. Indeed, with the emergence of something we might call *genetic identity*, racial identities may appear anachronistic—outdated, if not outright harmful. I will argue, however, that race and notions of racial identity have not become irrelevant in this era. Rather, I will claim that the era of liberal eugenics does something specific to the notion of race—personalizing and depoliticizing it—while at the same time making use of race as a boundary concept, marking the limits both of individual choice and of the new eugenics.

Having already elaborated Foucault's concept of technologies in general in chapter 2, in what follows I discuss his observations on neoliberalism in particular in order to show why I am using his work as the theoretical grounding of this chapter. I argue that the arena of reprogenetics and assisted reproduction is best understood in terms of what Foucault calls *technologies of the self*, and I describe a few of the ways in which power operates through such technologies in this arena. With that in mind, building on discussions of the use of race in reproductive technology practices from chapter 1, I then consider some examples of how identity features, including race, are used by people and couples in donor selection. While the privacy afforded to people in making reproductive decisions is important, I argue that, seen as technologies of the self, these decisions (and their privatization) also serve political (and indeed depoliticizing) purposes. Finally, I suggest that pressure for racial matching in assisted reproduction serves not only to renaturalize notions of race, as argued in chapter 1, but also, in keeping with the opening discussion of chapter 3, to defend the new liberal eugenics from the old eugenics by denying that the former possesses any racialized agenda.

The Neoliberal Regime of Truth

I turn to Foucault at this juncture because, beyond his understanding of technologies with respect to the formation of subjects and power, he offers a critique of neoliberalism that I find particularly illuminating when trying to reflect on the role of race in reprogenetics and the era of liberal eugenics.[4] In *The Birth of Biopolitics*, Foucault defines the question of liberalism as the question of frugality of government—the attempt to govern just enough, with the fear of governing too much dominating any fear of not governing enough. Here: "Government's limit of competence will be bounded by the utility of government intervention." This concern with frugality is connected to a change in the perception of the market. Whereas previously it was believed that markets should be regulated in order to serve as a site of justice, argues Foucault, in the middle of the eighteenth century "the market appeared as something that obeyed and had to obey 'natural,' that is to say spontaneous mechanisms . . . [whose] spontaneity is such that attempts to modify them will only impair and distort them." As such, a liberal rationality of government sees government's interventions into markets themselves as having no utility and therefore as completely beyond its proper sphere. Whereas a previous regime of truth sought to set juridical limits on the exercise of power by appeal to the natural or original rights of individuals, in liberalism the "natural" that serves as a limit on government is the natural, spontaneous functioning of the market, which produces truth almost *by virtue of* its invisibility and unknowability. Insofar as these mechanisms cannot be understood and must not be interfered with, they are believed to produce an objective, self-regulating truth. In a sense, then, Foucault argues, this liberalism is a sort of naturalism.[5]

However, the label of "liberalism" fits in the sense that it is defined in terms of its particular relationship to freedom. This new relationship to freedom should not be seen as simply an increase in freedom whereby government becomes more tolerant and flexible as part of some sort of progression toward a universal ideal of freedom. Rather, Foucault argues that liberal governmental practice "is a consumer of freedom inasmuch as it can only function insofar as a number of freedoms actually exist: freedom of the market, freedom to buy and sell, the free exercise of property rights, freedom of discussion, possible freedom of expression and so on." Because it must consume freedom, it must also produce and organize freedom, such that "at the heart of this liberal practice is an always different and mobile problematic relationship between the production of freedom and that which in the production of freedom risks limiting and destroying it." In other words: "Liberalism must produce freedom, but this very act entails the establishment of limitations, controls, forms of coercion, and obligations relying on threats, etcetera." Calculations regarding the production and limitation of freedom are, according to Foucault, based on the principle of security. Whereas freedom requires individual interests to be protected against the encroachment of collective interests, security requires that collective interests be protected against individual interests. One consequence of this interplay between security and freedom in liberalism is the stimulation in individuals of the fear of danger, which will move individuals to limit their own field of action. Examples of this political culture of danger, which emerges in the nineteenth century and which is a necessary correlative of liberalism, include campaigns around disease and hygiene and "what took place with regard to sexuality and the fear of degeneration: degeneration of the individual, the family, the race, and the human species."[6]

The emergence of neoliberalism is not simply the resurgence or recurrence of old forms of liberal economics in response to new contexts. Instead it is marked by a reversal of the relationship between the market and the state such that it calls for "a state under the supervision of the market rather than a market supervised by the state." In neoliberalism, which Foucault discusses in its German and American forms: "What is at issue is whether a market economy can in fact serve as the principle, form, and model for a state which, because of its defects, is mistrusted by everyone on both the right and the left, for one reason or another." In order to give a positive answer to this question, Foucault argues, it was necessary to carry out certain shifts, transformations, and inversions of earlier liberal doctrine: (1) "a shift from exchange to competition in the principle of the market" such that the focus is not on "a free exchange between two partners who through this exchange establish the equivalence of values" but rather on the power of competition to ensure economic rationality by forming prices and regulating choices; (2) a shift from the belief that the role of the state is to *laissez-faire* (since competition is a natural phenomenon) to the belief that the (essentially unobtainable) objective of pure competition does not arise naturally but must be pursued through the careful and artificial construction of certain optimal conditions, requiring permanent vigilance, activity, and intervention; and (3) a shift from the idea that market and state represent different domains to the idea that government exists *for* the market, with the needs of the market providing the rule of all governmental action.[7]

Speaking specifically of American liberalism, Foucault argues that it "was not just an economic and political choice formed and formulated by those who govern and within the governmental milieu" but "a whole way of being and thinking" with disputes between individuals and government appearing as the problem of freedoms. Liberalism in the American context goes beyond a critique of or technical alternative for government; it is "a general style of thought, analysis, and imagination" that offers its own utopia. Given this different context, one distinguishing factor of American *neo*liberalism, on Foucault's account, is its theory of human capital, which represents two processes: "one that we could call the extension of economic analysis into a previously unexplored domain, and second, on the basis of this, the possibility of giving a strictly economic interpretation of a whole domain previously thought to be non-economic."[8] Rather than an economic theory that sees human labor as a mere cog in processes of capital, investment, and production, the theory of human capital sees economics, in the words of Lionel C. Robbins, as "the science which studies human behavior as a relationship between ends and scarce means which have alternative uses"[9]—in other words, as "the analysis of the internal rationality, the strategic programming of individuals' activity." Labor is not an object in this theory but an active economic subject. *Human* capital, seen as belonging to and essentially inseparable from the individual, is "everything that in one way or another can be a source of future income" or "the set of all those physical and psychological factors which make someone able to earn this or that wage." The neoliberal American worker, then, "appears as a sort of enterprise for himself" or "as entrepreneur of himself, being for himself his own capital, being for himself his own producer, being for himself the source of [his] earnings." Further, on this model, "we should think of consumption as an enterprise activity by which the individual, precisely on the basis of the capital he has at his disposal, will produce something that will be his own satisfaction." Consumer and producer are no longer divided, then, but exist together in the *enterprising subject*.[10]

Human capital, Foucault argues, is made up of innate and acquired elements, and it is at this point in his lectures that Foucault speaks most directly to the interests of this chapter. Acquired elements are easy to understand in terms of the economic calculations of the enterprising subject. They are things like education and training, in which the individual can choose to invest his or her limited time and money in order to secure greater earnings and, subsequently, greater satisfaction. By contrast, innate elements—that is, features of an individual that are inherited or otherwise biologically given—might initially be seen as beyond the control of the individual and, therefore, as uninteresting in an economic analysis concerned only with capital that is "formed thanks to the use of scarce means, to the alternative use of scarce means for a given end." If we do not have to pay for our genetic makeup, then such an innate element may seem to exist outside the realm of rational economic calculation. Yet, as Foucault recognized over thirty years ago, "one of the current interests in the application of genetics to human populations is to make it possible to recognize individuals at risk and the type of risk individuals incur throughout their life." Though there is less individuals can do after their parents made them as they are, "when we can identify what individuals are at risk, and what the risks are of a union of individuals at risk producing an individual with a particular characteristic that makes him or her the carrier of a risk," then parents themselves are put in a position to make rational economic decisions with respect to the genetic capital of their intended offspring.

> Putting it in clear terms, this will mean that given my own genetic make-up, if I wish to have a child whose genetic make-up will be at least as good as mine, or as far as possible better than mine, then I will have to find someone who also has a good genetic make-up. And if you want a child whose human capital, understood simply in terms of innate and hereditary elements, is high, you can see that you will have to make an investment, that is to say, you will have to have worked enough, to have sufficient income, and to have a social status such that it will enable you to take for a spouse or co-producer of this future human capital, someone who has significant human capital themselves.[11]

Foucault claims it is neither interesting nor useful to translate the genetic anxieties of such scenarios into the "traditional terms of racism," and this may be true if we are thinking in terms of the fears of racial degeneration and projects of racial hygiene exemplified by eugenics programs. If, however, we think in terms of the social mores against interracial marriage that tie race to social class and privilege and that represent marrying outside the white race as harmful to future children, I believe there are similarities to be drawn. Whiteness (as Roberts, Quiroga, and others were seen to argue in earlier chapters) is a significant source of human capital, the maintenance and reproduction of which requires white people to marry other white people.

The framing of individual genetic profiles in terms of risk, which Foucault identifies, persists and is therefore a crucial observation linking applications of genetics with neoliberal rationality. Foucault was not in a position at the time of these lectures, however, to address the forms of reprogenetic technology and intervention that would become available, taking the possibility of economic investment in reproduction beyond positioning oneself to procure one of a scarce number of mates with a privileged genetic status. Options like prenatal genetic testing, sex selection, gene therapies, hormone therapies, drug therapies, and other technologies that allow for selection and enhancement of one's projected or existing offspring can, however, be fruitfully examined and critiqued in terms of Foucault's insights. These insights include: (1) the tendency of American neoliberalism to generalize the economic form of the market throughout the social body into areas not usually thought to be governed by monetary exchanges; (2) its use of market rationality "as a principle of intelligibility and a principle of decipherment of social relationships and individual behavior;" (3) its framing of the subject as acting on himself or herself as an enterprise (or site of multiple enterprises); and, (4) its conception of the relationship between parents and children "in terms of investment, capital costs, and profit—both economic and psychological profit—on the capital invested."[12]

Technologies of the Self

As described in chapter 2, Foucault uses notions of technologies, techniques, and practices to carry out genealogies and critiques of power, of subject formation, and of the variety of ideas and institutions through which power can be exercised. When uncovering and critiquing a particular regime of truth, he points not only to the ideas and assumptions that characterize the regime but also to the concrete means, instruments, rules, and practices through which that regime of truth emerges, is instantiated, and is maintained. These means and practices can be understood in terms of four major (overlapping and intersecting) types of technologies: (1) technologies of production; (2) technologies of sign systems; (3) technologies of power; and (4) technologies of the self. It is this last type, *technologies of the self*, that are of particular importance in the study of reproductive and reprogenetic technologies. Though the operations being affected in these cases are not simply on the self but on actual or projected offspring, I would argue that both the sense that the work is being performed within the private space of the family and the sense that it is importantly voluntary place reproductive technologies squarely within this final type. We should also note, as Foucault did, that such practices of self "are nevertheless not something that the individual invents by himself" but rather "patterns that he finds in his culture and which are proposed, suggested and imposed on him by his culture, his society and his social group."[13]

With its focus on the enterprising subject and other aforementioned features, one can see how neoliberalism is a regime of truth in which technologies of the *self* play a symbolically significant role in the governing of civil society. As Nikolas Rose describes, in "advanced" liberal democracies, the governing of individuals and of the population is in large part achieved through means and in arenas that are deliberately designated as nonpolitical. Sites of reproductive and reprogenetic intervention should therefore be seen as part of "a complex apparatus of health and therapeutics ... concerned with the management of the individual and social body as a vital national resource, and the management of 'problems of living', made up of techniques of advice and guidance, medics, clinics, guides and counsellors." Such "strategies of regulation that have made up our modern experience of 'power'" must be understood as "complexes that connect up forces and institutions deemed 'political' with apparatuses that shape and manage individual and collective conduct in relation to norms and objectives but yet are constituted as 'non-political.'" In advanced liberal democracies, then, the strategies of rule must not "seek to govern through 'society', but through the regulated choices and aspirations to self-actualization and self-fulfillment."[14] Insofar as national or social prosperity is thought to be achieved through individual prosperity, and insofar as individual prosperity is thought to require personal freedom, the state is believed to be taking a back seat while individuals are not simply *left* but rather *exhorted* to govern themselves. Consider, for example, the increasing popularity of employee "wellness" programs, which may be mandated by employers or made appealing to individuals through reductions to insurance premiums. Such programs exhort individuals to govern their own health by submitting to tests of various health metrics and then following standardized advice from health experts. This project is undertaken in the name of *both* the individual's own well-being and institutional productivity.

As I noted in chapter 3, it is important for proponents of so-called *liberal* eugenics that their practices of making "better" children be distinguished from reviled former practices of eugenics in virtue of a lack of state-sponsored coercion (and, as I will discuss later, a lack of a racially motivated agenda). Reproductive and reprogenetic technologies must be chosen and used without state intervention so as to escape obvious forms of power and domination.[15] Yet, as recourse to Foucault's notion of technologies of the self helps make clear, these "private" interactions involve the exercise of great deals of power. To offer just a few examples, we can consider Rose's discussion of the intrinsic relation of liberal rule to the authority of expertise, Sandel's discussion of compliance and hyper-responsibility in human enhancement, and Roberts's discussion of the link between privatization and punishment in reprogenetics (which serves to depoliticize social inequalities).

As Rose points out, public distaste for state intervention does not necessarily lead to the banishment of authorities from our "private" lives. Rather, political forces can utilize and instrumentalize "forms of authority other than those of 'the State' in order to govern—spatially and constitutionally—'at a distance.'" In this process, "authority is accorded to formally autonomous expert authorities and simultaneously the exercise of that autonomy is shaped through various forms of licensure, through professionalization and through bureaucratization." Where this succeeds, "politics" and the state are rendered "absent," but the "authority of expertise" remains firmly in place. In Rose's words: "The regulation of conduct becomes a matter of each individual's desire to govern their own conduct freely in the service of the maximization of a version of their happiness and fulfillment that they take to be their own, but such lifestyle maximization entails a relation to authority in the very moment it pronounces itself the outcome of free choice."[16] That is to say, the parent who is an enterprising subject and seeks to employ reprogenetic technologies as an investment in his or her child—or, increasingly, any parent at all—finds himself or herself very much dependent on the expertise of doctors or other fertility experts to carry out his or her project. Indeed, most parents rely on medical experts even to understand what it is *possible* to desire and pursue in the field of reproduction through reprogenetics.

Practices around prenatal genetic testing demonstrate the major role of authority in a technology of the self. As disabilities theorists point out, many doctors simply expect women to undergo prenatal genetic testing and do not take time to discuss what it is, why it is being done, or what the potential consequences of an "abnormal" result would be. It is only after an "abnormal" result has already appeared that women or couples speak to a physician or genetic counselor about their "options." Studies indicate, however, that the presentation of these options favors therapeutic abortion of fetuses who will be born with disabilities and that these experts do not provide prospective parents with important forms of information that might make continuing the pregnancy feel more viable—for example, information about the wide range of severity in certain conditions or information from parents currently raising children with disabilities about their experiences.[17]

In his discussion about the ethics of all forms of human enhancement, including so-called designer children, Michael Sandel argues that the language of autonomy, fairness, and individual rights that permeates discussion of the issue fails to capture much of our deep uneasiness about the "pursuit of perfection." Where some opponents fear that genetic enhancements will "undermine our humanity by threatening our capacity to act freely, to succeed by our own efforts, and to consider ourselves responsible—worthy of praise or blame—for the things we do and for the way we are" (as in athletes who succeed via biotechnological enhancement of their skill), Sandel argues that the "deeper danger" enhancements represent is a kind of *hyperagency*. On Sandel's account, "what the drive to mastery misses and may even destroy is an appreciation of the gifted character of human powers and achievements." Far from simply allowing people to do as they like or to freely pursue their individual projects, the availability of enhancements and biotechnological fixes appears as "a bid for compliance—a way of answering a competitive society's demand to improve our performance and perfect our nature."[18] In other words, the enterprising subject has no one but herself to blame if she fails to take advantage of any means available to her for increasing her human capital. Ultimately, Sandel feels the real threat of human enhancement is the transformation of three key related features of our moral landscape: humility, responsibility, and solidarity. Where we believe we fully control our or our children's traits and abilities, we lack an appreciation for the role of luck in our lives, for chance as a factor in our successes and the failures of others. Rather than acknowledging what Sartre called our *facticity* even as we recognize that we have freedom in how we take up those givens in life, the availability of genetic enhancement suggests that there are no givens with which one must contend. This leads to an overheightened sense of responsibility according to which, though we may also be praised for our skills and successes, we must be blamed for any lacks or failures. Sociohistorical factors shaping one's life possibilities and outcomes fade into the background. In the face of this dogmatic belief in individual responsibility, social solidarity is diminished. After all, if everyone is personally responsible for his or her own lot, there is little reason to respond with sympathy to those who are suffering or in need. Insurance markets, for example, can mimic solidarity only when people do not know or control their own risk factors. If genetic testing were capable of reliably predicting each person's medical future and life expectancy, those assured of good health and long life would have little reason to participate in the pool, and heath costs would not be dispersed among the whole population. In the end, our supposed meritocracy, "less chastened by chance, would become harder, less forgiving."[19]

In a similar vein, Dorothy Roberts argues that there are crucial similarities between the reprogenetic technologies aimed at middle- and upper-class women whose reproduction is generally encouraged and those contraceptive technologies aimed at poor and nonwhite women, which she understands as *privatization* and *punishment* respectively. "Both population control programs and genetic selection technologies," she suggests, "reinforce biological explanations for social problems and place reproductive duties on women that shift responsibility for improving social conditions away from the state." She continues:

"Placing responsibility for ending health disparities on individual reproductive decisions can reduce the sense of societal obligation to address systemic inequities. Reliance on eradicating illness through genetics can divert attention and resources away from the social causes of disability and disease, as well as social norms that impair social participation by sick and disabled people." Roberts's term for the neoliberal regime of truth we have been describing is the *ownership society*, which values "responsibility, liberty and property" and in which "patients control their own health care, parents control their own children's education, and workers control their retirement savings." She argues, in keeping with the aforementioned disability critique, that "new genetic technologies have generated greater surveillance of women, the ones primarily responsible for making the 'right' genetic decisions."

Ultimately, insofar as they retain control over their own reproductive decisions, women become "gatekeepers of new social order."[20] The many real problems plaguing poor and minority communities have long been blamed on "irresponsible" reproductive decisions within those communities, rather than on an extensive and continuing history of marginalization, exploitation, and discriminatory social policy. The contemporary focus on genetic correction and enhancement seems to exacerbate rather than reverse this trend. A focus on individually accessed technological solutions renders social and political solutions aimed at structural inequalities misguided or unnecessary. A privatization of the sources of inequality thus depoliticizes them.

The Personal and the Political in Assisted Reproduction

The old feminist slogan "the personal is political" points to the way in which seemingly individual problems experienced within putatively private realms like the family (and the seemingly individual choices made within those realms) are in fact conditioned by and productive of broader social inequalities and systems of power. But while the recognition of this fact is vitally important for feminist projects and for wider social justice work, it is unclear precisely what sort of interventions ought to be made. To what extent does the recognition of the political nature of family life justify public or state involvement in the lives of families? In the broader reproductive context, for example, the assertion of a right to privacy has been instrumental in securing (or fighting to maintain) control for women over their own bodies, particularly with respect to the ability to obtain a safe, legal abortion. It therefore becomes hard to imagine arguing against this sort of privacy or against the same sort of privacy with respect to assisted reproductive technologies.

According to Charis Thompson, *reproductive privacy* concerns both protections on access to and use of procedures by individuals, and the public apparatuses that maintain and protect these privacy boundaries. She points to the notorious fragility of privacy in the realms of intimacy, sexuality, and reproduction—"a fragility that is immediately apparent when the word *illegal* or *unwanted* is placed before those terms." She notes that: "Feminists have long argued that the preservation of this private sphere is both essential and deeply problematic for women and that the boundary construction of this sphere is highly political."[21] This tension between the need to preserve privacy and the need to contest the depoliticization of the private sphere is a major feature of the ART landscape, captured eloquently in the title of Lynda Fenwick's 1998 book exploring the complex issues surrounding reproductive technology: *Private Choices, Public Consequences.* The role of racial identity in private ART choices and the potential public or political consequences of these choices, however, has gone undertheorized.

In her description of reproductive privacy, Thompson offers several ethnographic narratives in which conceptions of identity play a role in the choices made by couples using reproductive technologies. The two I excerpt here involve lesbian couples choosing sperm donors:

> 1. *[The birth mother] Naomi was, at least since the 2000 census, multiracial. Jules was white and Jewish. . . . While they agreed that a Jewish donor would have been acceptable, Naomi chose a donor who matched her own predominant racial identity as she experienced it, which was African American. Jules supported her in this decision, speculating that it stemmed from wanting in part to preserve or pass on this identity visibly and in part to pass on their cultural advantages to a child of that racial minority. Mostly, however, Jules explained that she felt that it was none of her business why Naomi chose the way she did.*[22]
> 2. *Beth and Pat were also anxious because their friend who had previously agreed to be the sperm donor had been turned away by the clinic because according to the National Institutes of Health guidelines, his sexual orientation meant that he was at high risk for HIV. This meant that they had to pick from commercially available anonymous sperm donors. Instead of picking a donor to match certain culturally and phenotypically salient characteristics of the nongestational mother, as several of their friends had done who had used a sperm bank, they decided that in the new procedure they would "match" Beth, the gestational mother, because the egg was going to come from Pat.*[23]

Both of these narratives involve reference to particular visible and invisible identities, and both employ a concept of matching. The couples are not seeking just any sperm donor but one that relates in particular ways to their own self-identification.

Such decision-making seems particularly apparent among people or couples who self-identify with some type of minority group. Citing an unpublished paper presented at the 2010 meeting of the American Sociological Association, Carol Walther notes that in sperm selection, race "was often discussed among interracial couples or people of colour, but not among white families." This should not, I would argue, be taken to indicate that white couples do not care about race but rather that whiteness functions as a sort of default in donor gametes. As Walther recounts: "Ryan, Moras and Shapiro (2010) found that although rarely discussed explicitly, race and ethnicity largely informed lesbian couples' decisions of donors. They argued that gay and lesbian families reflect institutional scripts of families infused with racial biases and suggest that the lack of discourse about race within white, lesbian families serves to normalize a narrative of whiteness."[24] This conclusion was supported anecdotally by a white woman I met at a conference who had used a sperm donor to conceive with her same-sex partner. After hearing my presentation on the role of race in assisted reproductive technologies, she approached me to say that she and her partner (both white) had opted to use sperm from a nonwhite donor. This action was not received by others in "color-blind" terms or understood as a neutral personal choice; rather, she reported, many of their friends, family, and acquaintances had not understood or approved of their choice. The default status of whiteness is also reflected and supported in terms of the sperm available: "Donor pools in the USA are made up of predominately white, college-aged men; some sperm banks have no African American donors to choose from while other banks have very few African American donors and other donors of colour."[25]

It is important to acknowledge, however, that people of color seeking sperm donors do not necessarily conceive of race in simplistic terms or in terms that match the understandings of their doctors. In her ethnographic work on ARTs, Quiroga notes: "Race was always a subtext in Native American, African American, Asian American, and Latino narratives. References surfaced at varying levels, in different contexts and in response to interactions which primed that particular aspect of the self. One notable area in which race surfaced was when respondents described problematic interactions with biomedical practitioners who attempted to monitor their access to donor gametes and to make decisions for them."[26] She offers several narratives that illustrate this point, discussing both conflicts with practitioners and the reasoning that patients employ when left to make their own choices:

1. When discussing how she chooses a donor without physician input, Beatriz mentions trying to match Ted's characteristics. . . . However, what is most striking is that Beatriz does not refer explicitly to the race of the donor. They do not search for an Asian or Hispanic donor but for "brown eyes and brown [hair] and medium skin," which could match either Beatriz or Ted. While they adhere to the aspect of the kinship model that focuses on appearance, their aim is not to ensure racial purity. Instead, Beatriz narrates her choices in terms of "blending" and not in terms of racial matching. Furthermore, she explicitly rejects the

notion of passing off a child born using donor sperm as Ted's biological offspring.[27]

2. Raeshell [describing an interaction with the first physician she consulted]: We talked briefly and he asked me whether or not I had any questions. Well, I just said, "Well, how do you try to match the physical characteristics of the husband?" And he says, "Well, you know unless your husband has any real distinguishing features, usually it's not difficult to do that." And I said, "Well, I think my husband's most distinguishing feature is the fact that he's black." . . . And he goes, "Oh, I don't have any black donors in the program." . . . And immediately in my mind, I kind of moved past it. I said, "Okay, well, I'll take anything in, you know, in the color range." I said, "If you have, you know Hispanic, Puerto Rican, you have somebody, I mean, a tangent. I mean, those are all people with African descent over history and time; hey, I'm not going to be too flipped out or too choosy about it. I'm open. It's only sperm. And the baby is gonna be half black or something because it's going to be my baby, right? So, I didn't trip off of it. And he says to me, "Oh, no, I do not think that would be appropriate at all."[28]

3. Raeshell consulted another fertility specialist, Dr. S, who counseled her, "Don't try to have too much control over this," which contributed to her feeling that she was helpless in this process.

Raeshell: I would take a fair-skinned donor over a dark-skinned black male, but what I am getting from the medical side is that they don't feel that that's appropriate. As long as there's any black male available, that person as a donor is preferential to any other donor out there, and I don't feel that way.

Raeshell wants the donor to look as much as possible as her husband Tom, who is light-skinned. She is frustrated with the physician's view, which ignores the fact that a wide variation in skin tones exists in black communities. Her bitter appraisal of their attitude that "any black male available" will be an appropriate donor regardless of physical attributes calls up the prejudiced phrases "can't tell them apart" or "they all look alike." . . . Raeshell interprets the interchangeability of her husband with any black donor as reflective of a typical white depersonalizing stance. This angers her and contributes to her feeling of not being in control. It suggests that a different, unspoken standard of donor matching holds for African Americans and other nonwhites, where race outweighs all other physical attributes. Raeshell's physicians are not concerned with matching her husband's physical characteristics; they are only interested in her using black sperm.[29]

These narratives demonstrate that even if, as I contend, race is an important factor for nearly all people using ARTs (whether they acknowledge its importance or not), the constructions of that importance and the choices that result from those constructions vary.

In a document written to a potential sperm donor, my partner and I constructed our own decision to seek a gay, black donor as follows:

> We have given a great deal of thought to our racial and sexual identities and the role we want them to play in our reproductive decisions. Though we believe race and sexuality are better understood as socially constructed than biologically determined, they are, nevertheless, important labels in our society. Our decision to seek out a black, gay sperm donor can perhaps be best understood, then, as a desire to place value on those people and lives which society has typically undervalued in matters of reproduction. Insofar as there are contemporary markets for children (or gametes), white children have always been considered more valuable and desirable than black ones. Similarly, gay men have been largely excluded from sperm donation due to unfounded fears related to HIV/AIDS and perhaps because it is thought that we'd best avoid the transmission of any "gay genes." By contrast, we wish to assert that black people and gay men have much to contribute to our biological future and we hope that our donor might appreciate an opportunity to make such a contribution.
>
> Our concerns are not only political, however, but also personal and practical. Though we do not care whether our child is gay or straight, we hope, on some level, this decision will ensure that our child will reflect important parts of our identity and life experience. On the practical side, we also recognize that Camisha's claim to a mixed-race child is much less likely to be questioned than her claim to a white one. Given the legal uncertainties of lesbian parenting, such details take on even more importance.[30]

While my partner and I explicitly emphasize the political in our reasoning—due in no small part to the nature of my research and of my intellectual commitments—the political and the personal are interwoven in this and all the other narratives presented thus far. To read any of the narratives as merely individual reflections on (racial) identity and explications of personal choices would be to fail to recognize the way in which social and political histories and contexts necessarily provide (and limit) the language in which one may describe oneself and make oneself intelligible to oneself and to others. Moreover, where histories and contexts of oppression and discrimination are concerned, narratives of selfhood may be consciously or unconsciously constructed as forms of opposition or resistance.

Returning to the question of privacy and the tension it engenders, we can see concretely in these examples the importance of control and choice to people seeking sperm donors, especially those who self-identify with one or more minority statuses. The narratives constructed by these women draw, as all narratives do, on shared social meanings, but they also result in meaningful decisions that are ultimately quite personal. The interference of medical professionals or others in these decisions may therefore constitute a quite personal form of harm, making reproductive privacy and autonomy something of great value to women using reproductive technologies. In what remains of this chapter, however, I will attempt to uncover some of the risks and consequences of personalizing and privatizing notions of race within the field of reproductive technologies. Perhaps chief among these risks is the covering over of the political elements so evident in these narratives, such that race is depoliticized and renaturalized.

Technologies of the Self as Technologies of Race

In chapter 2 I pointed out that race—like madness, disease, delinquency, and sexuality (all sites of exploration for Foucault)—can be seen as a sort of nonexistent and yet very much existent object, established and continually reestablished through a set of practices, emerging from and upholding particular regimes of truth, and serving particular political functions that are nevertheless disguised by the ways in which rules and practices surrounding race act as if it is real. Using the Foucauldian understanding of technologies, I argued, we might speak of *technologies of race* in two different but overlapping and co-constituting senses: first, as the technologies or practices through which concepts of race are created, reinforced, and given important social reality—the technologies which produce race. Second, as the ways in which concepts of race are deployed in the service of political ends—the means by which race becomes productive. Included in the first sense of technologies of race, we might also speak of practices that shift or transform notions of race. So, how is the notion of race shifted or transformed by the technologies of the self that characterize assisted reproduction in the era of liberal eugenics?

Rose, in keeping with Foucault, rejects views that place "the resurgence of interest in race and ethnicity in contemporary genomic medicine . . . within the trajectory of 'racial science'" or see it as "simply the most recent incarnation of the biogenetic legitimation of social inequality and discrimination." He argues instead that "race now signifies an unstable space of ambivalence between the molecular level of the genome and the cell, and the molar level of classification in terms of population group, country of origin, cultural diversity, and self-perception" and that "a new genomic and molecular biopolitics of race, health, life is taking shape" within this space. While he acknowledges and explores a number of ethical and sociopolitical (as well as scientific and methodological) difficulties that arise with respect to the use of race and ethnicity in contemporary genomic medicine, he concludes that uses of race and ethnicity here "are not undertaken in the name of constituting and legitimating a hierarchy of differences, or with the hope of the improvement of the quality of the population."[31] In other words, they do not operate in the same way as the bad old eugenics.

There is much in Rose's discussion that I find helpful. It is indeed important when examining current practices surrounding race (as it is when examining past practices) to attend to the specificities of different contexts, rather than insisting on their unity or continuity. Nor is Rose simply defending or excusing all practices concerning race in contemporary genomic medicine; like any good Foucauldian, his lens is critical. Yet, while this critical lens operates well when pointed at things like ethnic categorization in health research and the racialization of pharmaceuticals or pharmacogenomics, when it comes to technologies of the self, I often find Rose's tone to be overly optimistic. Speaking of the use of DNA analysis technologies to provide commercial genetic ancestry testing, Rose writes that "in advanced liberal democracies at least, the biopolitics of identity is very different from that which characterized eugenics. The molecular rewriting of personhood in the age of genomics is linked to the development of novel 'life strategies' for individuals and their families, involving choice, enterprise, self-actualization, and prudence in relation to ones [sic] genetic makeup. And these genetic practices of individuation provide new ways in which individuals are locating themselves within communities of obligation and self-identification delineated by race."[32] Certainly, it is important to recognize the active and deliberate role that people play in constructing their own identities using the social meanings and scientific tools at their disposal. Indeed, such construction is at play both in the examples from the previous chapter where race is used to construct kinship and in the discussions of identity and sperm donor choice above. We must also consider, however, the way that individual and group constructions of identity stem from and interact with forms of power beyond the individual or group.

Roberts, for example, takes a more critical view of commercial genetic ancestry testing, even as she recognizes how and why its use in "recovering African origins" has become so important to many African Americans. She points first to the many ways in which ancestry testing is incapable of delivering the definitive genealogical results so many consumers believe they are getting. This includes the problem of sampling limitations, which mean that *contemporary* populations from many parts of the globe are not included in company databases, let alone the fact that such populations are not static and cannot truly represent the genetic makeup of historical populations. More significantly, however, Roberts believes that "the explosion in genetic ancestry testing is perpetuating a false understanding of individual and collective racial identities that can have widespread repercussions for our society." She points to the use of genetic testing by white-skinned people to lay claim to minority status in order to show how genetic definitions of race strip it of its political meaning. "Applying for benefits under a genetic alias distorts the purpose of affirmative action policies designed to remedy institutionalized racism." She contrasts such uses with the use of genetic ancestry technologies by African Americans in support of legal claims seeking reparations for slavery. In the latter, the tests are used as one part of a political movement for racial justice (rather than a personal bid for preferential treatment). She also notes that some African Americans want to use genetic connection to Africa as a basis for pan-African political solidarity or ancestral pride. Crucially, she argues: "The way African Americans creatively incorporate genetic genealogy into their lives is a far cry from a reductionist notion that genetics determines one's race or one's fate. They embed test results in the family history they have already begun to construct, interpret them to fit their political and spiritual viewpoints, and integrate them into their collective customs. The work of constructing an identity rooted in African ethnicity starts with the "Certificate of African Ancestry"; it is not determined by it." While Roberts understands and respects these both personal and political attempts, she nevertheless worries about the use of genetic genealogy as "the linchpin of identity and affiliation." Political vision, she reminds us, cannot be replaced by a DNA test. She is troubled by the way that such tests are "being used by some African Americans, as well as people from other groups, as the basis for collective identity that lacks the shared political values and goals needed to fight racial oppression."[33]

I believe something is captured in Roberts's critique of ancestry testing, and in her aforementioned critique of prenatal genetic testing, that is absent from Rose's analysis, and it is a danger I also see in the choice of sperm donor based on identity characteristics: the danger of the depoliticization of race. Roberts tends to describe this danger in terms of the establishment of a false genetic definition of race, which establishment Rose explicitly rejects. For my purposes, in asking what neoliberal technologies of the self do to the concept of race, I see the depoliticization Roberts points to in terms of the personalization and privatization of racial identity. The construction of racial identity and kinship *are* political, but they are not always seen as such, especially in cases where members of a privileged group (like people racialized as white) are acting within the established racial norms (that is, marrying and reproducing *intra*racially). One way to try to disrupt the naturalization of the reproduction of race is to point to its social (or technological) construction. I would argue, however, that one neoliberal answer to that disruption is to acknowledge the social construction of identities (including race) while at the same time concealing that construction behind a veil of private choice. Yes, people chose the racial identity of their donors when they choose donor sperm, and yes, they do so believing they are choosing the race of their future child, but people should be free to make private reproductive choices for the good of themselves, their families, and their families' futures.

This personalization and depoliticization of race in reproduction is aided by and contributes to an ideal of colorblindness. In stating that a person's race does not determine her intellectual, psychological, or moral worth, the color-blind ideal invites us to see race as an ethically neutral characteristic. One says, "Race does not matter! All people are equally valuable and deserving of respect." The problem comes when the words "race does not matter," are taken to describe a political reality. One is taken to have said, "Race does not matter! Everyone in society has a fair shot no matter who they are." The two statements are very different and come into conflict with each other when it comes to questions of political action. An ethical commitment to the idea that people should not be mistreated on the basis of race in fact *requires* that one recognize the myriad ways in which race proscribes people's opportunities and life chances. When we fail to recognize that racial choice in reproduction does not simply create "a child that looks like us" but takes part in a larger political reproduction of racialized inequality, the problem is not just the way in which we may still be operating with a biogenetic notion of race but also the way in which we have reduced race to a *merely* biological phenomenon. When, for example, John Harris, defender of the right (and even duty) of parents to produce the "best" possible children, insists that "phenotypical traits such as hair, eye and skin color, physique, stature, and gender are examples of . . . morally neutral choices," he also implies that people could or ought to make any of these choices—race, height, hair color—equally freely.[34] As if each is simply a matter of personal preference and will have no significant effect on the lives of one's children.

Ultimately, then, features of the neoliberal approach—the emphases on privacy, liberty, choice, and the individual's right and power to create himself through technology and consumption—serve not only to depoliticize inequalities through their emphasis on personal responsibility but also to depoliticize race itself. Neoliberal technologies of the self become technologies of race in this sense. In keeping with the ideal of color blindness, by asserting the moral equality of all individuals regardless of race—even perhaps by arguing that racial difference is constructed rather than natural—neoliberal practitioners, patients, and bioethicists can label as irrelevant the actual social and political consequences of the construction of racial difference and render it, in the present, as simply another option on the biogentic menu.

Yet, even within the discourse that defends the right of intended parents to choose the "race" of their technologically assisted offspring, the choice is construed less as free than as natural. "White men, especially, get very upset when you start questioning their right to have children," says Roberts in a *Ms. Magazine* interview. "People get very defensive when you suggest that their decisions about having children might have some racial implications. The response I get all the time is, 'This has nothing to do with racism. I just want children like me.'"[35] As noted in the previous chapter and in the earlier ethnographic narratives, there is a strong expectation that people will choose to have children who match them racially, and the idea of a nonwhite person choosing to have a white child in order to confer social advantage upon that child is not well received. Thus while the *ostensible* defense is one of rights or liberty (accompanied by a downplaying of the continued importance or relevance of race in today's society), the *actual* discursive grounding of that right seems to be based on the right-holder's own possession of the racial identity she or he will bestow upon the child to be created, especially where that identity is one of privilege (i.e., white).

Take, for example, Berkowitz and Snyder's argument that, in order to avoid perpetuating racism in medically assisted conception, choice of donor gametes should follow the bioethical guideline of "Reasonable Phenotypic Approximation." In a troubling combination of neoliberal and antidisability language, Berkowitz and Snyder describe how, given a racist and sexist society, "any product of conception other than a white male may be viewed by potential parents as disabled," such that "parents seeking optimum products of conception" may wish to use ARTs to have only white male children, which they might justify by invoking a right to "enjoy the benefits of scientific progress and its applications." To be clear, Berkowitz and Snyder oppose granting this neoliberal free choice to prospective parents; their opposition, however, rests both on a naturalizing and depoliticizing of race and racial selection in *nonassisted* reproduction and on an individualizing of racism. On their account, preconceptive race selection "is racist because it forces one to think in terms of race, to place a value upon race, and to prefer one race over another," a way of thinking that is both "in conflict with larger societal goals directed against racism which urge individuals to be race-blind" and is thought to represent "racism *in its purest form* as prior to conception, a child's worth is based in part upon its race."[36] Implied in this description of the problem are the beliefs that people do not think about race when not using donor gametes to reproduce, that not thinking in terms of race is the solution to racism, and that judgments of individual worth made on the basis of race are more purely racist than are structural or institutional mechanisms that create and maintain racial inequality.

Based on their understanding of racial selection as a "relatively new" issue that manifests only in cases where "some parents desire to bear a child whose race differs from their own," Berkowitz and Snyder conclude that: "Racism in MAC [medically assisted conception] can be prevented by insisting that MAC conceived children only represent a Reasonable Phenotypic Approximation (RPA) of their parents." They emphasize skin color but allow consideration of "ethnic attributes of the infertile couple" as long as one remembers that "those physical attributes which are readily perceptible to the casual observer and define and individual's racial heritage deserve increased fidelity." They continue, "For instance, an infertile Hispanic female and an infertile Caucasian male desire a child. To produce the best racial RPA, sperm and ovum can be procured from a Caucasian male donor and a Hispanic female donor whose respective skin colors best approximates that of the infertile couple. This combination would produce a child whose skin color, while not perfectly matching the theoretical combined skin color of the infertile couple, approximates the color that would have resulted had the couple not been infertile."[37] Note, of course, that the decision-making process they describe is one that might be deliberately adopted by a mixed-race couple as an attempt to express aspects of their identity through their intended child. I have attempted to argue, however, that such a decision would be *both* personal *and* political and would most certainly involve *thinking about race.*

By contrast, Berkowitz and Snyder see their rule as one that takes race out of the decision-making process by attempting to "recapitulate nature without human bias." This can be achieved only, they argue, by limiting the choices of prospective parents in favor of "careful selection of donors by disinterested, objective health care professionals," which aims to approximate "what nature would have provided had the couple not been infertile." Ostensibly separating the physical/visual from the social/political, they favor the former, arguing that "since ethnicity is usually not an obvious physical characteristic, more emphasis should be placed on choosing donors of similar skin color rather than on choosing donors of similar ethic heritage."[38]

Aside from the fact that this view reflects gross ignorance of the wide variation in skin tone (and more general phenotype) that exists in nonwhite populations even between full genetic siblings, the view is troubling because it strips racial identities of their political meanings (whether good or bad). It ignores all the racial politics and racist practices that gave the individual couple the racial classifications they possess today and tells us that the ethical thing to do is to reproduce as best we can what is already there. Moreover, since Berkowitz and Snyder explicitly "assume that the choice of race, like sex, will be based upon anticipated gain," the rule seems implicitly aimed at nonwhite people who might attempt to have white children to confer social advantage.[39] In other words, disadvantaged nonwhites become the potential perpetuators of racism. The argument makes the same sort of move that is made under the color-blind ideal when something like affirmative action is deemed "racist." Noticing race and acting on the basis of it is construed as inherently wrong, even when that action is in response to historical and continuing forms of institutional and structural racism. Such a view tries deliberately to ignore existing inequality in the ostensible hope that it will simply go away. In reality, however, the color-blind ideal is serving as justification for allowing the inequalities (which tend to significantly benefit the holders of the color-blind ideal) to remain in place. By disallowing any racial selection that goes against one's racial phenotype, Berkowitz and Snyder believe they are rejecting the idea of racial privilege, but they are also denying any potential attempt by prospective parents to gain racial privilege (in the case of nonwhite parents choosing a white child) or to forfeit racial privilege (in the case of white parents having a nonwhite child). In this sense, they are refusing to question or challenge the link between the political reproduction of racial privilege and biological reproduction itself.

Thus, while Berkowitz and Snyder frame their discussion as intervening in a "conflict between an individual's right to reproductive privacy and society's desire to eradicate racism" and see themselves as supporting the good of society over the rights of the individual, I would argue that their proposal for Reasonable Phenotypic Approximation is far from a simple opposition or resistance to neoliberal free choice.[40] Rather, it operates within many of the same assumptions. First, their focus on matching physical (racial) appearance participates in the personalizing and depoliticizing of racial identity, focusing on perceived phenotypical difference as a biological phenomenon rather than a sociohistorical one. Second, their identification of racial choice as a new problem naturalizes the existence of racial categories and severs contemporary decisions from their historical context. And, finally, in their very desire to restrict free choice in the name of social goods, Berkowitz and Snyder reinforce the notion that free choice is a powerful player in social justice, implying that individual racism is a leading source of racial inequality and that it is individuals rather than institutions who must be acted upon to reduce injustice.

A recent case involving a private Calgary sperm bank demonstrates a slightly different interplay of some of these same assumptions while also pointing to the typically implicit role of white privilege in public reaction to race issues in assisted reproduction. In July 2014, a story broke about a single white Canadian woman, Catherine, who was told by a private Calgary sperm bank that she could purchase sperm only from donors of her "same ethnicity" (i.e., white donors). Calvin Greene, the doctor who directly forbade Catherine from selecting the sperm of the nonwhite donors in whom she had expressed interest, cited an explicit clinic policy, available on its website at the time that the story broke, that stated "it is the practice of the Regional Fertility Program not to permit the use of a sperm donor that would result in a future child appearing racially different than the recipient or the recipient's partner."[41] (This copy was removed from the website the following week, and the clinic released a statement saying that the policy, in place since the 1980s, had been discontinued a year earlier. Dr. Greene's statements to Catherine and to the press, it said, represented only his individual opinion.[42]) Greene is quoted as explaining, "I'm not sure that we should be creating rainbow families just because some single woman decides that that's what she wants. That's her prerogative, but that's not her prerogative in our clinic."[43] He further likened the rationale behind the "ethnic" matching policy he defended to provincial policies in adoption and foster care that try to match "cultural backgrounds," with the idea that such matching is in the potential child's best interest.

By contrast, Catherine's reasons for wanting to be free to choose a nonwhite donor are described as focused around increasing the pool of donor candidates who met her other selection criteria so that she could find a suitable donor whose sperm had not already been used by numerous other women. The reporter writes: "While many people do want children who will look like them, [Catherine] said she is less concerned with the colour of her potential child's skin than the demeanour, personality and health history it might inherit from its biological father." Note that the descriptions given of Catherine's reasoning are ambiguous with respect to whether race did not matter to her *at all* (i.e., she is "color-blind") or whether race was simply not the most important of her criteria (i.e., she considers a nonwhite donor acceptable in the absence of equally suitable white donors). Indeed, Dr. Greene dismissed Catherine's stated reasons, claiming that: "She needs to look harder, because I can tell you reasonable people can easily find a suitable [white] donor."[44]

How should we think about this case? I am not necessarily interested in condemning anyone's actions, not even the doctor's, despite the fact that his own employers felt fit to distance themselves from his views. There are, of course, some neoliberal approaches to the legality of the issue. Considerations of freedom and privacy place the rights of the fertility clinic (as a private business) to create and enforce their own policies on one side while Catherine's desires and her ability to make (consumer) choices based on her own criteria are placed on the other. Ultimately, however, it is ideas about race, culture, and multiculturalism that catch public interest and make the story memorable. These, too, could be matters of law. According to Dr. Greene, the Alberta Human Rights Commission upheld the clinic's policy five years earlier after a white couple—who were not infertile but were seeking nonwhite sperm—brought a complaint against the clinic.[45] The decision in that case, however, would not dictate that such a policy (were it still held by the clinic) would be upheld in other cases or could not be challenged on the basis of other Canadian antidiscrimination statutes.

Indeed, putting aside legal concerns to pursue ethical questions, Canadians' sense of their country as a nondiscriminatory, multicultural nation seems to color many of the responses to the case (pun intended). Most experts asked by the press to comment on the case argue against the policy on the grounds that it is discriminatory, "archaic," and mistaken in its conflation of biology and skin color with culture.[46] Several people leaving online comments describe Dr. Greene as racist. Yet I see no reason to assume that Dr. Greene is any more racist than the average person. Rather, I suspect he is reflexively accused of racism for insisting that race and racial difference matter in people's lives; at the same time, Catherine is automatically deemed ethical and progressive because she is understood as not caring about race (returning again to the individual as the perpetrator and measure of racism). By framing his argument about race/ethnicity in terms of culture—and thereby allowing his opponents to claim race/ethnicity are mere biology—Dr. Greene allows race/ethnicity to be depoliticized and thus distracts from the actual merit of his concerns (and of similar concerns in the realm of interracial adoption).[47] Without taking a stance one way or the other, I would argue that, at the very least, questions of racial identity and classification and of their effects on lives ought to be a serious concern for white parents of nonwhite children. I can therefore understand why Greene might have viewed Catherine's motives with some suspicion. Just as I can understand why, in the earlier case of the white couple who were not infertile but hoped to use nonwhite sperm, Dr. Greene had them evaluated by the clinic's psychologist.[48] I can well imagine "good" reasons for deliberately choosing sperm from nonwhite donors, but I would expect those reasons to include significant political awareness. Moreover, the fact that people so readily defend the right of white people to have legal access to nonwhite children in this and other cases (while we do not see such eager support for nonwhite people to *legally* parent white children) seems to me a clear indication of white privilege. In questioning reproductive decision-making as both an ethical *and* political matter, and especially in a neoliberal context in which personal freedom and responsibility are emphasized, it is important not to allow whiteness and the entitlement it may afford to go unquestioned.

It is also interesting to note that arguments cited in the press both for and against the ethnic matching policy invoke "the spirit of Canada's Assisted Human Reproduction Act, which demands doctors place priority on the well-being of potential children and refrain from producing 'designer' babies." Greene argues that choosing sperm donors with whom one has "no cultural relationship" constitutes designing one's baby. Meanwhile, Tim Caulfield, a University of Alberta law professor and legal expert in assisted reproduction, notes that the clinic's policy itself could be argued to produce designer children by virtue of its own restrictions.[49] This dual use of the specter of "designing" children once again illustrates the ubiquity of racial choice in reproduction. Though both arguments imply that there is a correct, non-"designer" method (mimicking "nature" on the one hand and "ignoring" race on the other), the reality is that a neutral choice free from racial histories and complexities is impossible—racial selection is always taking place. By imagining one can combat racism by controlling the individual actions taken by doctors and consumers of assisted reproduction—and thereby detracting attention from the political history and continuing relevance of race—one operates within and reinforces the neoliberal logic that personalizes and depoliticizes race and racial identity.

Yet for all that the views of liberal eugenicists and those who oppose "racial selection" have in common, it is politically important that they be seen as opposing each other, as providing each other with limits. This is how technologies of the self can be understood as technologies of race in the second sense—that is, as deploying concepts of race in the service of political ends. As I have mentioned, the wide variety of technologies that allow for what some like to call "liberal eugenics" must constantly be defended against accusations of constituting a return to or providing a "back door" to the discredited eugenics of the early twentieth century. Of course, proponents of liberal eugenics remind us, the science is better these days, although one must do little more than scratch the surface to discover that the science of genetics is not yet all that people have hoped and continue to hope it will be. But might not good science be misused? Did not the old eugenicists believe they were acting for the greater good of humanity? How, then, to assure us that this new eugenics has not been or will not be corrupted?

One way that liberal eugenicists might respond to such worries is to discourage the involvement of the state. Neoliberalism distrusts the state and prefers that reprogenetics be pursued as technologies of the self so that morally neutral market mechanisms can act through enterprising subjects in order to bring about maximum satisfaction with maximum efficiency. Leaving the state out of the new eugenics is thought to keep it liberal and noncoercive. But, of course, massive state coercion is not the only problem we associate with Nazi Germany—there is also racism. We must be assured, then, that liberal eugenics is not racist. By restricting the role of the state, we eliminate racial purity as a state eugenic project, but perhaps we still need to be concerned with the racism of non-state actors and individuals. This is why people like Berkowitz and Snyder suggest disallowing assisted reproductive decision making based on race. Of course, one way to do this, which they do not explore, would be by removing any racial labeling from donor gametes so that every choice of gamete was essentially a racial lottery. Yet such an action remains virtually unthinkable. To destabilize and denaturalize the transmission of racial privilege in this way would call into question the entire American social and political landscape. The preferred solution, then, becomes the removal of racial choice by insisting on approximating the way we believe nature works with respect to race (as described by Berkowitz and Snyder as well as Dr. Greene). Doing so is seen as preventing us from crossing a moral line in reprogentics. Indeed, Berkowitz and Snyder wax quite poetically in their conclusion about the dangers their policy will prevent. "At best, the predetermination of race and sex reflects cultural bias," they write. "At its worst, racial engineering is a harbinger of racial purity." Fortunately, they assure us, "it is not too late to prohibit the predetermination of race and sex" and, in so doing, help assure that "our labors will not find a home in the arsenal of evil."[50]

Race, then, becomes that which is crucial in reprogenetics but whose importance and relevance to questions of social justice and the reproduction of injustices is disguised by its construal as a nonchoice. Even, or perhaps *especially*, when race is not explicitly discussed, I suggest that it serves as an implicit limit in reprogenetic practices and debates in at least two ways. First, race thinking is thought to serve as a sign that a eugenic project has gone too far, such that the refusal to mention race is taken as proof of the benevolence of contemporary eugenic undertakings. Second, the transmission of race from parent to child is construed in reprogenetics as natural and inevitable (and tampering with it as unnatural and immoral), such that the way in which race has always been policed in reproduction and the social consequences of that policing are obscured.

Conclusion

The era of *liberal* or *neoliberal eugenics* is characterized both by an emphasis on personal choice in reproductive technologies and by a corresponding emphasis on personal responsibility. While race may seem like an outdated or irrelevant concept in this era—simply a personal trait or identity to be chosen in one's offspring if one wishes—in fact the race idea continues to play important social and political roles. By personalizing and depoliticizing race, this neoliberal approach turns race into a Foucauldian technology of the self—that is, a technology of power that masks political operations of power and persistent social inequalities beneath the idea of free, individual preferences and actions. A strong social expectation of racial matching in assisted reproduction is naturalized and thus removed from scrutiny, leaving the impression that no racial choice is occurring. The ostensible absence of racial choice is then used as proof that the new eugenics possesses no racialized agenda and therefore escapes the immorality of the old eugenics. At the same time, any choice that defies racial matching—particularly by a person of color—is vilified, serving to normalize, naturalize, and defend the status quo of racialized social inequality.

Notes

1. Wang, *Rise of Intermarriage Rates.*
2. Highfield, "Sperm Cells Created from Female Embryo."
3. Silver, "Reprogenetics," 375.
4. Though not explicitly taken up in earlier chapters, Foucault's work on technologies of subject formation and power would certainly offer a strong alternative lens through which to see that work.
5. Foucault, *Birth of Biopolitics*, 28–29, 31, 39–40.
6. Ibid., 63–66.
7. Ibid., 116–21.
8. Ibid., 218–19.
9. Robbins, *Nature and Significance of Economic Science*, 16.
10. Foucault, *Birth of Biopolitics*, 223–26.
11. Ibid., 227–28.
12. Ibid., 243–44.
13. Fornet-Betancourt et al., "The Ethic of Care for the Self as a Practice of Freedom," 122.
14. Rose, "Governing 'advanced' Liberal Democracies," 37–38, 41.
15. Buchanan et al. are in favor of state *regulation*, however.

16. Rose, "Governing 'advanced' Liberal Democracies," 46, 58–59.

17. See Parens and Asch, *Prenatal Testing and Disability Rights*; or Shakespeare, "The Social Context of Individual Choice."

18. Sandel, "The Case Against Perfection," 78, 82.

19. Ibid., 87.

20. Roberts, "Privatization and Punishment," 1344, 1349, 1352, 1355, 1357.

21. Thompson, *Making Parents*, 214.

22. Ibid., 215, original italics.

23. Ibid., 216–17, original italics.

24. Walther, "Skin Tone, Biracial Stratification and Tri-racial Stratification among Sperm Donors," 2, 4.

25. Ibid., 4.

26. Quiroga, "Blood Is Thicker than Water," 151.

27. Ibid., 154.

28. Ibid., 155.

29. Ibid., 156–57.

30. Excerpt from private document.

31. Rose, *Politics of Life Itself*, 160–61.

32. Ibid., 177.

33. Roberts, *Fatal Invention*, 250, 252–53, 255.

34. Harris, *Enhancing Evolution*, 7.

35. Brennan, "Interview with Dorothy Roberts."

36. Berkowitz and Snyder, "Racism and Sexism in Medically Assisted Conception," 28–29, 33, my emphasis.

37. Ibid., 33–36.

38. Ibid., 36–37.

39. Ibid., 34.

40. Ibid., 40.

41. Barrett, "No 'Rainbow Families.'"

42. Higgins et al., "Can Fertility Clinics Refuse to Create 'Rainbow Families'?"

43. Barrett, "No 'Rainbow Families.'"

44. Ibid.

45. Ibid.

46. See both Barrett and Higgins et al.

47. For detailed discussion of this debate, see Kennedy.

48. Barrett, "No 'Rainbow Families.'"

49. Ibid.

50. Berkowitz and Snyder, "Racism and Sexism in Medically Assisted Conception," 42–44.

Conclusion

*"Race no longer talks about race," but is sublated into normative discourses of
privacy, intimacy, bourgeois domesticity, marriage, family and kinship.*
—*David Eng*, The Feeling of Kinship: Queer Liberalism
and the Racialization of Intimacy

In many ways the role of race in assisted reproductive technologies seems to
hide in plain sight. We tell ourselves that race is not a biogenetic trait, that people
are not determined by their racial identities, that racial identities are made-up
things, that everyone should be treated equally—and all these things are true. Yet
we find that we cannot and do not *want* to make decisions with respect to assisted
reproduction that do not take race into account. The existence of drop-down
menus for race and ethnicity on sperm bank web pages are, on the one hand,
a stark reminder of the deep social practices that have divided and continue to
organize people in terms of race. The fact that the existence of such drop-down
menus is not seen as strange or regressive, on the other hand, reveals how race is
still fundamentally viewed as the natural outcome of reproduction. We just *know*
that a child's race is the product of the race or races of her parents, and even when
technology must intervene to correct or improve upon nature, we do not believe
it should change this most essential of realities.

The Normative Question

When I speak to people about my project and my insights into the role of race in
assisted reproductive technologies, they often want to know how people *should*
behave. If ART practices are essentially racist, they wonder, how could one utilize
ARTs in a nonracist or more ethical fashion? What sorts of policies could we
enact to fight racism in ARTs? I am not at all convinced that it is useful to think
about ART practices and choices in terms of (individual) racism. I understand the
impulses behind these sorts of questions, but actually find it difficult to imagine a
world in which assisted reproductive technologies are rendered racially "neutral."
As I have shown, racial selection is always taking place in ARTs—whether it is
doctors or patients who choose, and whether that choice is to create children
whose racial classifications match those of the intended parents or specifically
not to do so. Suppose, then, that no racial or ethnic information was ever asked of

donors, ever recorded by fertility services, or ever given to consumers involved in ART procedures. Suppose that surrogates were never selected or paid but rather volunteered their services and were assigned to intended parents anonymously on a first-come-first-served basis. Would this make ARTs less racist and more ethical?

I am convinced that this is the wrong question. It seems to form yet another iteration of the attempts described in the introduction to reason our way out of the political reality of race. It attempts to locate or create a position of innocent and moral purity from which to act. Yet such a position simply is not possible, and enforcing a sort of race "blindness" in ART would, for me, constitute the enactment of a troublesome policy at the wrong site. The *policy* would be troublesome because, as poor people and people of color would be the first to point out, (more) government intervention into matters of reproduction is always risky. Moreover, such a policy would show a lack of respect for the fact that, no matter what their history, the categories of race and ethnicity *can* have rich cultural meanings. Such cultural meanings are deserving of our attention and protection. The *site* would be wrong because, as I have tried to demonstrate, the role of race in *assisted* reproduction does not stand apart from its role in *nonassisted* reproduction. As long as race, racism, and racial privilege continue to operate in the larger contexts of sex, marriage, reproduction, and kinship, it will do little good to regulate the reproductive behavior of that portion of the population who must seek assistance in having children. Furthermore, just as the problems of structural and institutional racism will not be eliminated through scientific clarification of the race concept, they will not be eliminated through reproductive interventions. I have argued that reproductive choices and behaviors both reflect and perpetuate social and sociohistorical views on race, making reproduction in general (and assisted reproduction in particular) interesting sites for the *critical study* of race. However, that does not make them (or other intimate contexts) ideal sites for antiracist *intervention*.

Indeed, the only "proposed" actions I have come across that suit the "problems" described in this work are those that would function to somehow disrupt both the assumptions about race that seem to inhabit many ART practices and the taken-for-granted ability of white people to pass white privilege to their children. I describe these actions in a previous essay:

> In Charis Thompson Cussins's "Confessions of a Bioterrorist"—a fictional essay based on her work in a variety of reproductive technology settings—three imagined women share their fantasies of reprogenetic transgression. A lesbian embryologist and lab technician imagines fertilizing one egg with another, forgoing the use of sperm. A white zoo technician who had herself sterilized after the birth of her second child imagines using her still functional womb to gestate endangered bonobos. A black Englishwoman and sociologist

with a northern European lover worries about bearing a child that is too white and imagines selecting an embryo for its blackness. Elsewhere, in a chapter titled "Owning the Self in a Disowned World (A Menagerie of Nightmares and Hallucinations)," Patricia Williams imagines a new program of guerilla warfare for a technological age, in which white male college graduates "smuggle small hermetically sealed vials of black sperm into the vaulted banks of unborn golden people."[1]

These imagined reproductive technological choices are framed by their imaginers as acts of "bioterrorism" or "guerilla warfare," and I suspect their imaginers are less interested in actively promoting these specific actions than in illustrating the sorts of "choices" that are not generally on offer, even in a "free," neoliberal era. In my earlier words: "Each potential choice, in the deviancy of the desires it reflects, challenges the social norms surrounding reproduction, thereby revealing the social context in which all reproductive choices—both those identified as choices and those obscured as merely natural—take place."[2]

The aim, then, is to better understand the *design* and *functions* of the technology of race in any given context. Only through this critical work will we position ourselves to think about disrupting these functions. As David Eng puts it, we must "develop a critical vocabulary and analysis of the ways in which racial disparities and property relations embed and recode themselves within the private realm of family and kinship relations, only to seep back into circulation within the public domain."[3] Though I believe policy-focused efforts are better suited to more public realms, keeping Eng's words in mind, I would argue that the analysis of assisted reproduction within Critical Philosophy of Race can point our thinking, and perhaps even our action, in a number of interesting directions, some of which have already been described.

Review of Key Points

I am sympathetic to anyone who argues that we must stop talking about race because she genuinely believes that complete repudiation of the very idea of race would be crucial to ending racism, but I have argued that such attempts to banish race are normally based in a persistent misunderstanding of what race *is*. In an effort to shift our thinking on race from debates over *what race is* to investigations of *what race does* (and *how*), I have suggested that race be considered *technologically*. I have claimed that using technology as a theoretical lens for thinking about race provides a useful way of looking at race in the context(s) of ART. It is my hope that it might prove useful in other contexts as well. I do not contend that this is the only (or even the best) lens for thinking about race, nor do I claim to offer a single or unified way of thinking about race as technology. Rather I have made use of several different (though not fully distinct) conceptions of technology and have examined how race might be considered as technology in several different (though not fully distinct) contexts. Most simply put, my aim has been to highlight the fact that race is both *produced* and *productive*. That is, it is not a natural biogenetic fact; nor is it simply a means of human categorization. The race idea and the race science that was used to support it are human inventions, and those inventions have been used (and continue to be used, whether consciously or unconsciously) to carry out a variety of political projects.

I have offered a "technological" history of race in which I argued against the idea that the existence of pure races was considered a biological fact until that was disproven in the twentieth century. I described the growth of racial science as undergirded by beliefs both in the power of race to drive history and in the need to *take control* of this power. Such beliefs, I claimed, take part in a technological worldview that Heidegger has argued defines the modern period. In this sense, technologies of eugenics should not be seen as the disturbing culmination of a century or so of bad racial science but as essential to development of the race concept in the modern period. I also discussed how notions of race have organized the American concept of kinship and were used to structure political racial inequality. It is this history of the association of race and kinship in the American imaginary that, on my account, allows race to serve as a proxy for kinship in the contemporary fertility clinic and related reproductive and legal contexts. When race is used in this way, I claimed, drawing on Charis Thompson's notion of ontological choreography, we can see it as another technology operating in conjunction with and alongside other ARTs.

Finally, I looked at our current era of (neo)liberal (repro)eugenics and argued that race is operating within and being transformed by what Foucault called technologies of the self. In this era, racial identities are increasingly individualized and privatized, the effect of which is to depoliticize racial inequalities. Race is portrayed as just another feature to be chosen as an expression of one's personal identity. At the same time, however, the overwhelming expectation of racial matching serves as a limit on individual choice, as a justification of social inequalities, and as a means of showing that new eugenic technologies are not coercive projects of racial purification. Indeed, this question of the relationship between contemporary ARTs and old eugenic projects runs throughout the project, and I hope I have explored that relationship in a way more nuanced than either the "back door to eugenics" view or the view that sees the two as entirely separate. On my account, they are connected by the continuing drive to master nature and by a persistent desire to assign scientific explanations to social and political inequities.

Further Directions

I have no wish to condemn ARTs in their entirety or to deny people the opportunity to make choices about race in reproduction. Rather, my recommendation here is for the ongoing practice of social- and self-critique among those who use, administer, legislate and think about ARTs. "A critique is not a matter of saying that things are not right as they are," Foucault reminds us. "It is a matter of pointing out on what kinds of assumptions, what kinds of familiar, unchallenged, unconsidered modes of thought the practices that we accept rest. . . . It is a question of making conflicts more visible, of making them more essential than mere confrontations of interests or mere institutional immobility."[4] In that vein, let me close by suggesting a few further assumptions, modes of thought, and conflicts that can be seen as underlying or intersecting questions and problems of race in assisted reproduction.

One way to think about the needs and desires that fuel what Michele Goodwin calls "baby markets" is in terms of insecurities. Baby markets, under Goodwin's definition, include not only the exchange of materials and services for assisted reproduction but also adoption systems operating domestically or across borders.[5] The concept of insecurity, which is relevant to so much of our contemporary sociopolitical landscape, serves in the case of baby markets to bridge the gap between the realm of personal decision making and the broader context of social and economic inequality in which they operate.

Such markets are both permeated with and driven by insecurities. On the supplier or seller side, we have women who donate or sell eggs for use in IVF (with donation being the preferred language to describe what typically amounts to a sale), women who agree to serve as surrogates, pregnant women who make arrangements for their children to be adopted, parents who surrender or lose custody of their children, and orphanages. (We also have men who donate or sell sperm, but because of the lesser time, energy, and payment involved, insecurity seems less likely to play a significant role.) In the adoption cases, a personal feeling of insecurity, financial or otherwise, may factor into both the woman's decision not to keep the child and the woman's need to contract with an adopting person or couple in order to cover expenses. In egg donor and surrogate cases, the worldwide demand for these materials and services is unlikely ever to be met by women acting altruistically. Rather, reproductive markets seem to rely on domestic and international structural inequalities to place significant numbers of women in positions of at least relative insecurity such that "donating" eggs or serving as a surrogate appears as an attractive or reasonable way to make money. It does not have to be the case that such women are desperate or entirely without other options to say that insecurity plays a role; it need only be the case that a perception of limited options be a major factor in the decision to sell reproductive goods or services. An obvious example, as discussed earlier, were the Indian women who chose to serve as surrogates for a foreign couple because they could earn the equivalent of nearly five years of total family income by doing so and had few other earning opportunities available to them. These insecurities, then, are significantly political in nature, in the sense that they are products of global political and economic histories and contemporary practices.

By contrast, the insecurities that mark the buyer or demand side of baby markets are more likely to be personal, social, or legal in nature, though also financial in a different sense. While people seeking babies in baby markets are likely to have greater financial resources than those selling reproductive goods or services, those resources are often not inexhaustible. Driven by a personal (but socially mediated) desire to parent children, and often emotionally taxed by a diagnosis of infertility, buyers (men and women, heterosexual and homosexual couples, or aspiring single parents) will often be concerned and feel insecure about obtaining a child by a method they can afford, having that child be healthy, and being assured of their right to keep that child. Reliance on persons beyond the intended parent or parents, like gamete donors, surrogates, or birth mothers, introduces elements of uncertainty and unpredictability into having a child that buyers will seek to mitigate. This risk may be mitigated through the use or mediation of third parties like fertility clinic operators, lawyers, or adoption brokers. Broader questions of social and legal standing may also come into play, as with same-sex couples. Gay couples may choose to hire surrogates and lesbian couples to use donor sperm in order that at least one parent has a biological connection to the intended child and thus the legal recognition of parenthood that that connection brings.

It should be clear by this point that both the concept and the political realities of race can play roles in both creating and answering various insecurities. Obviously, an entire system and history of global White Supremacy and colonial exploitation should be understood as the root cause of the economic inequalities that underlie contemporary baby markets. Eng describes this relationship as an ever-increasing outsourcing of the reproductive labor costs of the Global North to Third World women in the Global South.[6] More specifically, I have argued that the use of ARTs (and, I would add, the turn to transnational adoption) must be at least partly understood as responses to a shortage of white babies available for domestic adoption. A white infant for a white adopting couple provides the security of not having to account for the child's origin to others, of believing the child to be as-yet undamaged, and of knowing the child will move through the world with white privilege. By contrast, for a white adopting couple, a nonwhite child (perhaps particularly an African American child) requires explanation; may, the American social imaginary suggests, have been irreparably damaged by an unfit birth mother; and may be harmed by the continuing racism that many white couples would be reluctant to acknowledge until faced with the prospect of raising and caring for a nonwhite child. The fact that many white people turn to transnational adoption as a more expensive but preferred alternative to domestic transracial adoption only further underscores America's troubled racial history.[7] The view of Asian Americans as model minorities helps to make Asian babies an attractive option, but even a black baby from Africa appears as safer than one from Alabama.

Several of the arguments made for race as a technology in ARTs could be reframed in terms of insecurity. For example, racial similarity (serving as a proxy for kinship) and racial difference (thought to demonstrate a visible lack of kinship) are tools that serve to alleviate the insecurities of various parties in reproductive procedures by naming the "correct" person or people as the true parent(s) of a child produced. In transracial surrogacy, there is some sense of extra (perhaps legal) safety achieved by contracting with a surrogate that "anyone can see" is not the "true" mother of the child in question. In transnational gestational surrogacy, differences not only in race or color but also in class, material resources, and global positionality provide extra security to contracting couples, who are likely to believe their surrogate will not have the desire, power, or means to keep the child she gestated. In this sense, it is the surrogate's material insecurities that are leveraged to relieve the psychological insecurities of the contracting parents.

If we step back from ARTs to consider science and technology in general with respect to insecurity, we might describe them as part of an ongoing battle of humankind against the insecurity represented by nature. Science attempts to alleviate the unpredictability of nature by discovering its laws. Technology harnesses natural materials and powers in the service of human security and the fulfillment of human desires. At bottom, I have argued, science and technology seem to represent a human drive for mastery. Ironically, despite this underlying technological impulse, individual technologies or types of technology often come to be seen or described as "out of control," and calls are made to get them back under control. Appeals to a concept of the natural in these cases often represent a conservative desire to resist forms of social change that technologies seem to have made possible or desirable. Religiously based opposition to ARTs, for example, may seek to preserve "natural" reproduction as a way to maintain the heterosexual, monogamous couple as the dominant reproductive (and therefore social) unit. Yet use of ARTs by same-sex couples may also represent a particular conservative approach of the sort that Eng calls "queer liberalism."[8] Granting marriage rights to same-sex couples and permitting or encouraging them to produce and raise children is both an expansion of marriage rights and a shoring up of those rights, along with a shoring up of the family formations they produce as the most legitimate social formations, which are most deserving of social support and legal protection. Security, in this case, is extended to cover additional citizens, but conformity to certain standards is still required, and security is far from universalized.

In chapter 1, I appealed to a series of questions from philosopher of technology Neil Postman concerning for what and for *whom* technologies are intended, and the unintended consequences that may flow from their use. There I tried to answer his questions in reference to assisted reproductive technologies, with respect to their impact on racial identities and the institutions of race and racism. What might we gain by explicitly thematizing *insecurity* in a similar set of questions? We could ask, for example: What insecurities does this technology aim to address? Whose insecurities are they? Will the social structures surrounding the use of this new technology create, exacerbate, or rely upon insecurities of other groups? Are there other approaches to this technology or other technologies that do not create, exacerbate, or rely upon the insecurities of others? Are there non-technological solutions with more equitable or fewer negative effects?

Asking such questions might lead us to focus medical, technological, and social efforts on different, wider-spread causes of infertility like untreated STDs, poor medical treatment during an earlier birth, or workplace and environmental toxins. Fighting these causes of infertility (and insecurity) would involve different technologies. We might also consider social solutions to the problem of delayed fertility in the first world among professional and white-collar workers. What would it take to restructure public and private life in the United States, for example, such that childbearing and rearing did not stand in conflict with career success and did not require the outsourcing of household and childcare labor (let alone reproductive material and labor) to poorer women? Similarly, for the case of transnational (or even domestic) adoption, when we focus on the insecurities of those who supply children rather than those who demand them, we might follow Twila Perry in asking whether, "rather than transferring the children of the poor to economically better-off people in other countries, there should be a transfer of wealth from rich countries to poor ones to enable the mothers of poor children to continue to take care of their children themselves?"[9]

Notes

1. Russell, "Limits of Liberal Choice," 103.
2. Ibid., 104.
3. Eng, *Feeling of Kinship*, 6.
4. Foucault, "Practicing Criticism," 154–56.
5. Goodwin, *Baby Markets*, xx–xxi.
6. Eng, *Feeling of Kinship*, 95.
7. Ortiz and Briggs, "Culture of Poverty, Crack Babies, and Welfare Cheats," 52–54.
8. Eng, *Feeling of Kinship*, 27–28.
9. Perry, "Transracial and International Adoptions," 155.

Bibliography

Alcoff, Linda, and Elizabeth Potter, eds. *Feminist Epistemologies*. New York: Routledge, 1993.

Alpern, Kenneth D., ed. *The Ethics of Reproductive Technology*. New York: Oxford University Press, 1992.

Appiah, K. Anthony, and Amy Gutmann. *Color Conscious: The Political Morality of Race*. Princeton, NJ: Princeton University Press, 1996.

Augstein, Hannah Franziska, ed. *Race*. Bristol, UK: Thoemmes, 1996.

Avins, Alfred. "Anti-Miscegenation Laws and the Fourteenth Amendment: The Original Intent." *Virginia Law Review* 52 (1966): 1224–55.

Bailey, Alison. "Reconceiving Surrogacy: Toward a Reproductive Justice Account of Indian Surrogacy." *Hypatia* 26, no. 4 (2011): 715–41.

Bailey, Ronald. *Liberation Biology: The Scientific and Moral Case for the Biotech Revolution*. Amherst, NY: Prometheus Books, 2005.

Banerjee, Amrita. "Race and a Transnational Reproductive Caste System: Indian Transnational Surrogacy." *Hypatia* 29, no. 1 (2014): 113–28.

———. "Reorienting the Ethics of Transnational Surrogacy as a Feminist Pragmatist." *Pluralist* 5, no. 3 (2010): 107–27.

Banton, Michael. *Racial Theories*. Cambridge: Cambridge University Press, 1998.

Barrett, Jessica. "No 'Rainbow Families': Ethnic Donor Stipulation at Fertility Centre 'Floors' Local Woman." *Calgary Herald*, July 25, 2014. http://www.calgaryherald.com/health /rainbow+families+Ethnic+donor+stipulation+fertility+centre+floors+local+ woman/10063343/story.html.

Bartels, Dianne M., ed. *Beyond Baby M: Ethical Issues in New Reproductive Techniques*. Clifton, NJ: Humana, 1990.

Beack, Joan. "There Are Far Worse Things a Parent Can Be than Old." *Chicago Tribune*, January 2, 1994.

Beauchamp, Tom L., and James F. Childress. *Principles of Biomedical Ethics*. New York: Oxford University Press, 2009.

Berger, Michele Tracy. "Discussion with Global Approaches to Intersectionality Reading Group." Lecture, Penn State University, University Park, PA, 2011.

Berkowitz, Jonathan M., and Jack W. Snyder. "Racism and Sexism in Medically Assisted Conception." *Bioethics* 12, no. 1 (1998): 25–44.

Bernasconi, Robert. "Critical Philosophy of Race." In *The Routledge Companion to Phenomenology*, edited by Sebastian Luft and Søren Overgaard, 551–62. London: Routledge, 2012.

———. "Nature, Culture, and Race." In *Södertörn Lectures*. Edited by Apostolis Papakostas. Stockholm: Södertörn University, 2010.

———. "The Philosophy of Race in the Nineteenth Century." In *The Routledge Companion to Nineteenth Century Philosophy*, by Dean Moyar, 498–521. Milton Park, UK: Routledge, 2010.

———. "The Policing of Race Mixing: The Place of Biopower within the History of Racisms." *Journal of Bioethical Inquiry* 7, no. 2 (2010): 205–16.

———. "Race and Earth in Heidegger's Thinking during the Late 1930s." *Southern Journal of Philosophy* 48, no. 1 (2010): 49–66.

———. "Who Invented the Concept of Race? Kant's Role in the Enlightenment Construction of Race." In *Race*, edited by Robert Bernasconi, 11–36. Malden, MA: Blackwell, 2001.

———. "With What Must the Philosophy of World History Begin?" *Nineteenth-Century Contexts* 22, no. 2 (2000): 171–201.

Bernasconi, Robert, and Kristie Dotson, eds. *Race, Hybridity, and Miscegenation*. Bristol, UK: Thoemmes, 2005.

Bernasconi, Robert, and Tommy Lee Lott, eds. *The Idea of Race*. Indianapolis: Hackett, 2000.

Bernier, Francois. "A New Division of the Earth." In *The Idea of Race*, edited by Robert Bernasconi and Tommy Lee Lott, 1–4. Indianapolis: Hackett, 2000.

Beurton, Peter J., Raphael Falk, and Hans-Jörg Rheinberger, eds. *The Concept of the Gene in Development and Evolution: Historical and Epistemological Perspectives*. Cambridge, UK: Cambridge University Press, 2000.

Bhatia, Shekhar. "Mumbai Clinic Sends Couple Email: You Have a Boy and Girl. Congratulations." *Evening Standard*, May 20, 2009. http://www.standard.co.uk/news/mumbai-clinic-sends -couple-email-you-have-a-boy-and-girl-congratulations-6771048.html.

Biddiss, Michael D. *Father of Racist Ideology: The Social and Political Thought of Count Gobineau*. London: Weidenfeld and Nicolson, 1970.

Blumenbach, Johann Friedrich. "On the Natural Variety of Mankind." In *The Idea of Race*, edited by Robert Bernasconi and Tommy Lee Lott, 27–37. Indianapolis: Hackett, 2000.

Brace, C. L. "The 'Ethnology' of Josiah Clark Nott." *Bulletin of the New York Academy of Medicine* 50, no. 4 (1974): 509–28.

———. *"Race" Is a Four-Letter Word*. New York: Oxford University Press, 2005.

Brassington, Iain. "On Heidegger, Medicine, and the Modernity of Modern Medical Technology." *Medicine, Health Care and Philosophy* 10, no. 2 (2007): 185–95.

Brennan, Moira. "Interview with Dorothy Roberts." *Ms. Magazine*, April/May 2001. http:// www.msmagazine.com/apr01/roberts.html.

Buchanan, Allen, Dan W. Brock, Norman Daniels, and Daniel Wikler. *From Chance to Choice: Genetics and Justice*. Cambridge, UK: Cambridge University Press, 2000.

"Cheaper Overseas: Surrogate Mothers." ABC News. September 28, 2007. http://abcnews .go.com/GMA/story?id=3664065.

Clarke, Adele. *Disciplining Reproduction: Modernity, American Life Sciences, and "The Problems of Sex."* Berkeley: University of California Press, 1998.

Cohen, Margot. "A Search for a Surrogate Leads to India." *Wall Street Journal*, October 9, 2009. http://online.wsj.com/article/SB10001424052748704252004574459003279407832 .html.

Collins, Patricia Hill. *Black Feminist Thought: Knowledge, Consciousness, and the Politics of Empowerment*. New York: Routledge, 1991.

———. *Black Sexual Politics: African Americans, Gender, and the New Racism*. New York: Routledge, 2005.

———. "It's All in the Family: Intersections of Gender, Race, and Nation." *Hypatia* 13, no. 3 (1998): 62–82.

Corea, Gena. *The Mother Machine: Reproductive Technologies from Artificial Insemination to Artificial Wombs*. New York: Harper and Row, 1985.

Cowan, Ruth Schwartz. "Francis Galton's Statistical Ideas: The Influence of Eugenics." *Isis* 63, no. 4 (1972): 509–28.

———. "Nature and Nurture: The Interplay of Biology and Politics in the Work of Francis Galton." *Studies in the History of Biology* 1 (1977): 133–208.

Crenshaw, Kimberlé, Neil Gotanda, Gary Peller, and Kendall Thomas, eds. *Critical Race Theory: The Key Writings That Formed the Movement*. New York: New Press, 1995.

Da Cal, Enrique Ucelay. "The Influence of Animal Breeding on Political Racism." *History of European Ideas* 15, no. 4–6 (1992): 717–25.

Darwin, Charles. *The Descent of Man, and Selection in Relation to Sex*. Edited by Adrian J. Desmond and James R. Moore. London: Penguin, 2004.

———. *Origin of Species*. New York: Bantam Books, 1999.

Darwin, Erasmus. *The Temple of Nature, Or, The Origin of Society: A Poem, with Philosophical Notes*. London: J. Johnson, 1803.

———. *Zoonomia; Or, The Laws of Organic Life*. Vol. 1. Dublin: P. Byrne, 1800.

Davis, Adrienne D. "The Private Law of Race and Sex: An Antebellum Perspective." *Stanford Law Review* 51, no. 2 (1999): 221–88.

Davis, Angela Y. "Outcast Mothers and Surrogates: Racism and Reproduction Politics in the Nineties." In *American Feminist Thought at Century's End: A Reader*, edited by Linda S. Kauffman, 355–66. Cambridge, MA: Blackwell, 1993.

Davis, F. James. *Who Is Black?: One Nation's Definition*. University Park: Pennsylvania State University Press, 1991.

De Beistegui, Miguel. *The New Heidegger*. London: Continuum, 2005.

Deitrich, Heather. "Social Control of Surrogacy in Australia: A Feminist Perspective." In *Issues in Reproductive Technology: An Anthology*, edited by Helen Bequaert Holmes, 367–80. New York: Garland, 1992.

Dick, Philip K. *The Collected Stories of Philip K. Dick*. New York: Carol, 1992.

Disraeli, Benjamin. *Lord George Bentinck: A Political Biography*. London: Colburn, 1852.

Dreyfus, Hubert L., Paul Rabinow, and Michel Foucault. *Michel Foucault, beyond Structuralism and Hermeneutics*. Chicago, IL: University of Chicago Press, 1983.

Dubow, Saul. *Scientific Racism in Modern South Africa*. Cambridge, UK: Cambridge University Press, 1995.

Durbin, Paul T. *Philosophy of Technology: Practical, Historical, and Other Dimensions*. Dordrecht: Kluwer Academic, 1989.

Dusek, Val. *Philosophy of Technology: An Introduction*. Malden, MA: Blackwell, 2006.

Duster, Troy. *Backdoor to Eugenics*. New York: Routledge, 2003.

Edelman, Ezra, dir. *O.J.: Made in America*. "Part 3." Aired June 23, 2016, on ESPN.

Edin, Kathryn, and Maria Kefalas. *Promises I Can Keep: Why Poor Women Put Motherhood before Marriage*. Berkeley: University of California Press, 2005.

Edwards, Jeanette, Sarah Franklin, Eric Hirsch, Frances Price, and Marilyn Strathern, eds. *Technologies of Procreation: Kinship in the Age of Assisted Conception*. New York: Routledge, 1999.

Einsiedel, Edna F. *Emerging Technologies: From Hindsight to Foresight*. Vancouver: UBC Press, 2009.

Eng, David L. *The Feeling of Kinship: Queer Liberalism and the Racialization of Intimacy*. Durham, NC: Duke University Press, 2010.

Farquhar, Dion. *The Other Machine: Discourse and Reproductive Technologies*. New York: Routledge, 1996.

Feder, Ellen K. *Family Bonds: Genealogies of Race and Gender*. Oxford: Oxford University Press, 2007.

Fenwick, Lynda Beck. *Private Choices, Public Consequences: Reproductive Technology and the New Ethics of Conception, Pregnancy, and Family*. New York: Dutton, 1998.

Ferré, Frederick. *Philosophy of Technology*. Englewood Cliffs, NJ: Prentice Hall, 1988.

Ferrell, Robyn. *Copula: Sexual Technologies, Reproductive Powers*. Albany: State University of New York Press, 2006.

Figal, Sara Eigen. *Heredity, Race, and the Birth of the Modern*. New York: Routledge, 2008.

Fineman, Martha Albertson., and Terence Dougherty, eds. *Feminism Confronts Homo Economicus*. Ithaca, NY: Cornell University Press, 2005.

Fornet-Betancourt, R., H. Becker, A. Gomez-Muller, and J. D. Gauthier. "The Ethic of Care for the Self as a Practice of Freedom: An Interview with Michel Foucault on January 20, 1984." *Philosophy and Social Criticism* 12, no. 2–3 (1987): 112–31.

Foucault, Michel. *The Archaeology of Knowledge*. Translated by Alan Sheridan. New York: Pantheon Books, 1972.

———. *The Birth of Biopolitics: Lectures at the Collège De France, 1978–79*. Edited by Michel Senellart. Translated by Graham Burchell. Basingstoke, UK: Palgrave Macmillan, 2008.

———. *The Birth of the Clinic: An Archaeology of Medical Perception*. New York: Vintage Books, 1994.

———. *The Care of the Self*. Vol. 3. The History of Sexuality. New York: Pantheon Books, 1978.

———. *The History of Sexuality*. Vol. 1. New York: Vintage Books, 1990.

———. *Madness and Civilization: A History of Insanity in the Age of Reason*. New York: Vintage Books, 1988.

———. *The Order of Things: An Archaeology of the Human Sciences*. New York: Vintage Books, 1994.

———. *Power*. Edited by James D. Faubion. New York: New Press, 2000.

———. "Practicing Criticism." In *Politics, Philosophy, Culture: Interviews and Other Writings, 1977–1984*, edited by Lawrence D. Kritzman, 152–58. New York: Routledge, 1988.

———. *Sécurité, territoire, population: Cours au Collège De France (1977–1978)*. Edited by François Ewald, Alessandro Fontana, and Michel Senellart. Paris: Gallimard, 2004.

———. *Technologies of the Self: A Seminar with Michel Foucault*. Edited by Luther H. Martin, Huck Gutman, and Patrick H. Hutton. Amherst: University of Massachusetts Press, 1988.

Fox, Dov. "Racial Classification in Assisted Reproduction." *Yale Law Journal* 118 (2009): 1844–98.

Frank, Johann Peter. *A System of Complete Medical Police: Selections from Johann Peter Frank*. Baltimore: Johns Hopkins University Press, 1976.

Franklin, John Hope. *From Slavery to Freedom: A History of Negro Americans*. New York: Alfred A. Knopf, 1980.

Franklin, Sarah. *Dolly Mixtures: The Remaking of Genealogy*. Durham, NC: Duke University Press, 2007.

———. *Embodied Progress: A Cultural Account of Assisted Conception*. London: Routledge, 1997.

Franklin, Sarah, and Susan McKinnon, eds. *Relative Values: Reconfiguring Kinship Studies*. Durham, NC: Duke University Press, 2001.

Franklin, Sarah, and Helena Ragoné, eds. *Reproducing Reproduction: Kinship, Power, and Technological Innovation*. Philadelphia: University of Pennsylvania Press, 1998.

Fraser, Nancy. *Unruly Practices: Power, Discourse, and Gender in Contemporary Social Theory*. Minneapolis: University of Minnesota Press, 1989.

Füredi, Frank. *The Silent War: Imperialism and the Changing Perception of Race*. New Brunswick, NJ: Rutgers University Press, 1998.

Friedman, David D. *Future Imperfect: Technology and Freedom in an Uncertain World*. New York: Cambridge University Press, 2008.

Galton, Francis. *Hereditary Genius: An Inquiry into Its Laws and Consequences*. Amherst, NY: Prometheus Books, 2006.

———. "Hereditary Talent and Character." *Macmillan's Magazine* 12 (1865): 157–66.

———. *Inquiries into Human Faculty and Its Development*. London: Macmillan, 1883.

Gates, E. Nathaniel. *The Concept of "Race" in Natural and Social Science*. New York: Garland, 1997.

Gerrie, Jim. "Was Foucault a Philosopher of Technology?" *Techne* 7, no. 2 (2003): 66–73.

Gobineau, Arthur De. "Essai sur l'inégalité des races humaines." In *Oeuvres*, edited by Jean Gaulmier and Jean Boissel, Vol. I., 133–1174. Paris: Gallimard, 1983.

———. *The Inequality of Human Races*. Translated by Adrian Collins. New York: Fertig, 1999.

———. "Racial Inequality." In *Gobineau: Selected Political Writings*, translated by Michael D. Biddiss, 18–176. London: Cape, 1970.

Goodwin, Michele Bratcher, ed. *Baby Markets: Money and the New Politics of Creating Families*. New York: Cambridge University Press, 2010.

Grayson, Deborah R. "Mediating Intimacy: Black Surrogate Mothers and the Law." *Critical Inquiry* 24, no. 2 (1998): 525–46.

Gregory, John. *A Comparative View of the State and Faculties of Man with Those of the Animal World by John Gregory . . . in Two Volumes*. London: J. Dodsley, 1774.

Hamilton, D. P. "She's Having Our Baby: Surrogacy Is on the Rise." *Wall Street Journal*, February 4, 2003. http://online.wsj.com/article/SB1044305510652776944.html.

Haney López, Ian. *White by Law: The Legal Construction of Race*. New York: New York University Press, 1996.

Hanson, F. Allan. "Donor Insemination: Eugenic and Feminist Implications." *Medical Anthropology Quarterly* 15, no. 3 (2001): 287–311.

Haraway, Donna Jeanne. "A Manifesto for Cyborgs: Science, Technology and Socialist Feminism in the 1980s." In *The Haraway Reader*, 7–46. New York: Routledge, 2004.

———. *Modest_Witness@Second_Millennium.FemaleMan©_Meets_OncoMouse™: Feminism and Technoscience*. New York: Routledge, 1996.

———. *Primate Visions: Gender, Race, and Nature in the World of Modern Science*. New York: Routledge, 1989.

——— "Race: Universal Donors in a Vampire Culture: It's All in the Family: Biological Kinship Categories in the Twentieth-Century United States." In *The Haraway Reader*, 251–94. New York: Routledge, 2004.

———. *Simians, Cyborgs, and Women: The Reinvention of Nature*. New York: Routledge, 1991.

Harding, Sandra G. *The Science Question in Feminism*. Ithaca, NY: Cornell University Press, 1986.

Harris, John. *Enhancing Evolution: The Ethical Case for Making Better People*. Princeton, NJ: Princeton University Press, 2007.

Hartouni, Valerie. *Cultural Conceptions: On Reproductive Technologies and the Remaking of Life*. Minneapolis: University of Minnesota Press, 1997.

Haworth, Abigail. "Surrogate Mothers: Womb for Rent." *Marie Claire*, July 29, 2007. https:// www.marieclaire.com/politics/news/a638/surrogate-mothers-india/.

Hegel, Georg Wilhelm Friedrich. *Introduction to the Philosophy of History: With Selections from the Philosophy of Right*. Translated by Leo Rauch. Indianapolis: Hackett, 1988.

———. *Lectures on the Philosophy of World History: Introduction, Reason in History*. Translated by Johannes Hoffmeister. Cambridge, UK: Cambridge University Press, 1980.

———. *The Philosophy of History*. Translated by John Sibree. Buffalo, NY: Prometheus Books, 1991.

Heidegger, Martin. *Mindfulness*. Translated by Parvis Emad and Thomas Kalary. London: Continuum, 2006.

———. *Nietzsche*. Edited by David Farrell. Krell. Vol. 3. San Francisco, CA: Harper and Row, 1979.

———. "The Question Concerning Technology." In *Basic Writings: From Being and Time (1927) to The Task of Thinking (1964)*, edited by David Farrell Krell, 307–41. San Francisco, CA: Harper, 1993.

Hening, William Waller. *The Statutes at Large Being a Collection of All the Laws of Virginia, from the 1. Session on the Legislature in the Year 1619: Published Pursuant to an Act of the General Assembly of Virginia, Passed on the 5. Day of Febr. 1808*. Vol. 11. Charlottesville: University Press of Virginia, 1969.

Herder, Johann Gottfried. *Another Philosophy of History and Selected Political Writings*. Indianapolis: Hackett, 2004.

Hickman, Christine B. "The Devil and the One Drop Rule: Racial Categories, African Americans, and the U.S. Census." *Michigan Law Review* 95 (1997): 1161–265.

Higgins, Shannon, Idella Sturino, and Peter Mitton. "Can Fertility Clinics Refuse to Create 'Rainbow Families'?" CBC/Radio-Canada. July 28, 2014. http://www.cbc.ca/radio /thecurrent/jul-29-2014-1.2907808/can-fertility-clinics-refuse-to-create-rainbow -families-1.2907809.

Highfield, Roger. "Sperm Cells Created from Female Embryo." *Telegraph*, January 31, 2008. https://www.telegraph.co.uk/news/science/science-news/3323846/Sperm-cells-created -from-female-embryo.html.

Hoffman, Paul. "The Science of Race." *Discover* 15, no. 11 (1994): 4.

Holloway, Karla F. C. *Private Bodies, Public Texts: Race, Gender, and a Cultural Bioethics*. Durham, NC: Duke University Press, 2011.

Holmes, Helen Bequaert, ed. *Issues in Reproductive Technology: An Anthology*. New York: Garland, 1992.

Hotz, Henry. "Analytical Introduction." Introduction to *The Moral and Intellectual Diversity of Races with Particular Reference to Their Respective Influence in the Civil and Political History of Mankind*, by Arthur De. Gobineau, 13–103. Philadelphia, PA: J. B. Lippincott, 1856.

Howe Colt, George. "Science and Surrogacy: Searching for a Biological Child on the High-Tech Frontier." *Life* 10, no. 6 (1987): 36–42.

Hubbard, Ruth, and Elijah Wald. *Exploding the Gene Myth: How Genetic Information Is Produced and Manipulated by Scientists, Physicians, Employers, Insurance Companies, Educators, and Law Enforcers*. Boston, MA: Beacon, 1993.

Hull, Richard T., ed. *Ethical Issues in the New Reproductive Technologies*. Belmont, CA: Wadsworth, 1990.

Ikemoto, Lisa C. "Eggs as Capital: Human Egg Procurement in the Fertility Industry and the Stem Cell Research Enterprise." *Signs: Journal of Women in Culture and Society* 34 (2009): 763–81.

———. "The In/Fertile, the Too Fertile, and the Dysfertile." *Hastings Law Journal* 47 (1995): 1007–61.

———. "Reproductive Tourism: Equality Concerns in the Global Market for Fertility Services." *Law and Inequality* 27 (2009): 277–309.

Inhorn, Marcia C. "Global Infertility and the Globalization of New Reproductive Technologies: Illustrations from Egypt." *Social Science and Medicine* 56, no. 9 (2003): 1837–51.

Jacobson, Matthew Frye. *Whiteness of a Different Color: European Immigrants and the Alchemy of Race.* Cambridge, MA: Harvard University Press, 1998.

Jones, D. Marvin. "Darkness Made Visible: Law, Metaphor, and the Racial Self." *Georgetown Law Journal* 82 (1993): 437–511.

Junker-Kenny, Maureen, ed. *Designing Life?: Genetics, Procreation and Ethics.* Aldershot, UK: Ashgate, 1999.

Kant, Immanuel. "Of the Different Human Races." In *The Idea of Race*, edited by Robert Bernasconi and Tommy Lee Lott, 8–22. Indianapolis: Hackett, 2000.

———. "On the Use of Teleological Principles in Philosophy (1788)." In *Race*, edited by Robert Bernasconi, 37–56. Malden, MA: Blackwell, 2001.

Kennedy, Randall. *Interracial Intimacies: Sex, Marriage, Identity, and Adoption.* New York: Pantheon, 2003.

Kerr, Anne, and Tom Shakespeare. *Genetic Politics: From Eugenics to Genome.* Cheltenham, UK: New Clarion, 2002.

Kevles, Daniel J. *In the Name of Eugenics: Genetics and the Uses of Human Heredity.* Cambridge, MA: Harvard University Press, 1995.

Kevles, Daniel J., and Leroy E. Hood, eds. *The Code of Codes: Scientific and Social Issues in the Human Genome Project.* Cambridge, MA: Harvard University Press, 1992.

Killens, John Oliver. *Black Man's Burden.* New York: Trident, 1965.

Klausen, Susanne Maria. *Race, Maternity, and the Politics of Birth Control in South Africa, 1910–39.* Houndmills, UK: Palgrave Macmillan, 2004.

Knox, Robert. *The Races of Men.* London: H. Renshaw, 1850.

Kuhn, Thomas S. *The Structure of Scientific Revolutions.* Chicago, IL: University of Chicago Press, 1970.

Kvach, John F. *De Bow's Review: The Antebellum Vision of a New South.* Lexington: University Press of Kentucky, 2013.

Landecker, Hannah. *Culturing Life: How Cells Became Technologies.* Cambridge, MA: Harvard University Press, 2007.

Larson, Edward J. *Sex, Race, and Science: Eugenics in the Deep South.* Baltimore, MD: Johns Hopkins University Press, 1995.

Latour, Bruno. *Science in Action: How to Follow Scientists and Engineers through Society.* Cambridge, MA: Harvard University Press, 1987.

Lesky, Erna. Introduction. In *A System of Complete Medical Police: Selections from Johann Peter Frank*, by Johann Peter Frank, edited by Erna Lesky, ix–xxiii. Baltimore, MD: Johns Hopkins University Press, 1976.

Locke, John. *Two Treatises of Government.* Edited by Peter Laslett. Cambridge, UK: Cambridge University Press, 1988.

López-Beltrán, Carlos. "Forging Heredity: From Metaphor to Cause, a Reification Story." *Studies in History and Philosophy of Science Part A* 25, no. 2 (1994): 211–35.

Mamdani, Mahmood. "Race and Ethnicity as Political Identities in the African Context." In *Keywords: Identity*, edited by Nadia Tazi, 1–23. Paris: Alliance of Independent Publishers, 2004.

———. *When Victims Become Killers: Colonialism, Nativism, and the Genocide in Rwanda*. Princeton, NJ: Princeton University Press, 2001.

Markens, Susan. "The Global Reproductive Health Market: U.S. Media Framings and Public Discourses about Transnational Surrogacy." *Social Science and Medicine* 74 (2012): 1745–53.

Marx, Karl, and Friedrich Engels. *The German Ideology*. Edited by C. J. Arthur. New York: International, 1972.

May, Elaine T. *Barren in the Promised Land: Childless Americans and the Pursuit of Happiness*. New York: Basic Books, 1995.

McCann, Carole R. *Birth Control Politics in the United States, 1916–1945*. Ithaca, NY: Cornell University Press, 1994.

Mehlman, Maxwell J. *The Price of Perfection: Individualism and Society in the Era of Biomedical Enhancement*. Baltimore, MD: Johns Hopkins University Press, 2009.

Mendieta, Eduardo. "Migrant, Migra, Mongrel: The Latin American Dishwasher, Busboy, and Colored/Ethnic/Diversity (Philosophy) Hire." In *Reframing the Practice of Philosophy*, edited by George Yancy, 147–66. Albany, NY: SUNY Press, 2012.

Millman, Arthur B., and Carol L. Smith. "Darwin's Use of Analogical Reasoning in Theory Construction." *Metaphor and Symbol* 12, no. 3 (1997): 159–87.

Mills, Charles W. *Blackness Visible: Essays on Philosophy and Race*. Ithaca, NY: Cornell University Press, 1998.

———. *The Racial Contract*. Ithaca, NY: Cornell University Press, 1997.

———. Review of *Ethics along the Color Line*. *Hypatia* 22, no. 2 (2007): 189–93.

Müller-Wille, Staffan, and Hans-Jörg Rheinberger, eds. *Heredity Produced: At the Crossroads of Biology, Politics, and Culture, 1500–1870*. Cambridge, MA: MIT Press, 2007.

Montagu, Ashley. *Man's Most Dangerous Myth: The Fallacy of Race*. New York: Columbia University Press, 1945.

Morton, Samuel George. "Hybridity in Animals and Plants, Considered in Reference to the Question of the Unity of the Human Species." *Edinburgh New Philosophical Journal* XLIII (1847): 262–88.

Nader, Laura. *Naked Science: Anthropological Inquiry into Boundaries, Power, and Knowledge*. New York: Routledge, 1996.

Nale, John. "Arthur de Gobineau on Blood and Race." *Critical Philosophy of Race* 2, no. 1 (2014): 106–24.

Nietzsche, Friedrich. *On the Genealogy of Morality*. Translated by Maudemarie Clark and Alan J. Swensen. Indianapolis: Hackett, 1998.

Nolfi, George, dir. *The Adjustment Bureau*. Hollywood, CA: Universal Studios, 2011. DVD.

Nott, Josiah Clark. *Two Lectures on the Natural History of the Caucasian and Negro Races*. Mobile, AL: Dade and Thompson, 1844.

Omi, Michael, and Howard Winant. *Racial Formation in the United States: From the 1960s to the 1990s*. New York: Routledge and Kegan Paul, 1986.

Ortiz, Ana Teresa, and Laura Briggs. "The Culture of Poverty, Crack Babies, and Welfare Cheats: The Making of the 'Healthy White Baby Crisis.'" *Social Text 76* 21, no. 3 (2003): 39–57.

Outlaw, Lucius T. *On Race and Philosophy.* New York: Routledge, 1996.

Pande, Amrita. "Transnational Commercial Surrogacy in India: Gifts for Global Sisters?" *Reproductive BioMedicine Online* 23 (2011): 618–25.

Parens, Erik, and Adrienne Asch, eds. *Prenatal Testing and Disability Rights.* Washington, DC: Georgetown University Press, 2000.

Parks, Jennifer. "Rethinking Radical Politics in the Context of Assisted Reproductive Technology." *Bioethics* 23, no. 1 (2009): 20–27.

Paul, Diane B. *The Politics of Heredity: Essays on Eugenics, Biomedicine, and the Nature-Nurture Debate.* Albany, NY: SUNY Press, 1998.

Perry, Twila L. "Transracial and International Adoptions: Mothers, Hierarchy, Race, and Feminist Legal Theory." *Yale Journal of Law and Feminism* 10 (1998): 101–64.

Peterson, James C. *Changing Human Nature: Ecology, Ethics, Genes, and God.* Grand Rapids, MI: W. B. Eerdmans, 2010.

Postman, Neil. *Building a Bridge to the 18th Century: How the Past Can Improve Our Future.* New York: Alfred A. Knopf, 1999.

———. *Technopoly: The Surrender of Culture to Technology.* New York: Knopf, 1992.

Quiroga, Seline Szkupinski. "Blood Is Thicker Than Water: Policing Donor Insemination and the Reproduction of Whiteness." *Hypatia: A Journal of Feminist Philosophy* 22, no. 2 (2007): 143–61.

Ragoné, Helena. "Of Likeness and Difference: How Race Is Being Transfigured in Gestational Surrogacy." In *Ideologies and Technologies of Motherhood: Race, Class, Sexuality, Nationalism*, edited by Helena Ragoné and France Winddance Twine, 56–75. New York: Routledge, 2000.

———. *Surrogate Motherhood: Conception in the Heart.* Boulder, CO: Westview, 1994.

Ratcliff, Kathryn Strother, ed. *Healing Technology: Feminist Perspectives.* Ann Arbor: University of Michigan Press, 1989.

Raymond, Janice G. *Women as Wombs: Reproductive Technologies and the Battle over Women's Freedom.* New York: HarperCollins, 1994.

Reardon, Jenny. *Race to the Finish: Identity and Governance in an Age of Genomics.* Princeton, NJ: Princeton University Press, 2005.

"Rent a Womb? Extreme Measure to Get Pregnant." Transcript. In *Good Morning America.* ABC News. September 28, 2007.

Rich, Adrienne Cecile. *Of Woman Born: Motherhood as Experience and Institution.* New York: Norton, 1995.

Robbins, Lionel C. *An Essay on the Nature and Significance of Economic Science.* London: Macmillan, 1935.

Roberts, Dorothy E. *Fatal Invention: How Science, Politics, and Big Business Re-create Race in the Twenty-First Century.* New York: New Press, 2011.

———. *Killing the Black Body: Race, Reproduction, and the Meaning of Liberty.* New York: Vintage Books, 1999.

———. "Privitization and Punishment the New Age of Reprogenetics." *Emory Law Journal* 54, no. 3 (2005): 1343–60.

———. "Race, Gender, and Genetic Technologies: A New Reproductive Dystopia?" *Signs: Journal of Women in Culture and Society* 34, no. 4 (2009): 783–804.

Robertson, John A. "Surrogate Motherhood: Not So Novel After All." In *The Ethics of Reproductive Technology*, edited by Kenneth D. Alpern, 45–56. New York: Oxford University Press, 1992.

Rose, Nikolas. "Governing 'Advanced' Liberal Democracies." In *Foucault and Political Reason: Liberalism, Neo-liberalism, and Rationalities of Government*, edited by Andrew Barry, Thomas Osborne, and Nikolas Rose, 37–64. Chicago, IL: University of Chicago Press, 1996.

———. *Politics of Life Itself: Biomedicine, Power, and Subjectivity in the Twenty-First Century*. Princeton, NJ: Princeton University Press, 2007.

Rothman, Sheila M., and David J. Rothman. *The Pursuit of Perfection: The Promise and Perils of Medical Enhancement*. New York: Pantheon Books, 2003.

Rousseau, G. S., and Roy Porter, eds. *The Ferment of Knowledge: Studies in the Historiography of Eighteenth-Century Science*. Cambridge, UK: Cambridge University Press, 2008.

Roy, Sujit. "Surrogate Motherhood: Should It Be Allowed?" Merinews, June 30, 2008. http://www.merinews.com/article/surrogate-motherhood-should-it-be-allowed/136765.shtml.

Russell, Camisha. "Black American Sexuality and the Repressive Hypothesis: Reading Patricia Hill Collins with Michel Foucault." In *Convergences: Black Feminism and Continental Philosophy*, edited by Maria Del Guadalupe. Davidson, Kathryn T. Gines, and Donna-Dale L. Marcano, 201–24. Albany, NY: SUNY Press, 2010.

———. "The Limits of Liberal Choice: Racial Selection and Reprogenetics." *Southern Journal of Philosophy* 48 (2010): 97–108.

Russell, Nicholas. *Like Engend'ring Like: Heredity and Animal Breeding in Early Modern England*. Cambridge, UK: Cambridge University Press, 1986.

Ryan, Maura A. "The Introduction of Assisted Reproductive Technologies in the 'Developing World': A Test Case for Evolving Methodologies in Feminist Bioethics." *Signs: Journal of Women in Culture and Society* 34, no. 4 (2009): 805–25.

Saetnan, Ann Rudinow, Nelly Oudshoorn, and Marta Stefania Maria Kirejczyk, eds. *Bodies of Technology: Women's Involvement with Reproductive Medicine*. Columbus: Ohio State University Press, 2000.

Sältzer, Rolf, ed. *German Essays on History*. New York: Continuum, 1991.

Sama Resource Group for Women and Health. *ARTs and Women: Assistance in Reproduction or Subjugation?* Report. New Delhi: Sama Resource Group for Women and Health, 2006.

———. "The Myth of Regulation: A Critique of the 2008 Draft ART (Regulation) Bill and Rules." *Medico Friend Circle Bulletin* 335–336 (2009): 8–13. http://www.samawomenshealth.in/wp-content/uploads/2015/08/MFC335-336.pdf.

Sandel, Michael J. "The Case against Perfection: What's Wrong with Designer Children, Bionic Athletes, and Genetic Engineering." In *Human Enhancement*, edited by Julian Savulescu and Nick Bostrom, 71–89. Oxford: Oxford University Press, 2009.

Sarojini, Nadimpally, Vrinda Marwah, and Anjali Shenoi. "Globalisation of Birth Markets: A Case Study of Assisted Reproductive Technologies in India." *Globalization and Health* 7, no. 27 (2011): 1–9.

Sartre, Jean-Paul. *Critique of Dialectical Reason*. London: New Left Books, 1976.

Schneider, David. *American Kinship: A Cultural Account*. 2nd ed. Chicago, IL: University of Chicago Press, 1980.

Schultz, Sandra. "The Life Factory: In India, Surrogacy Has Become a Global Business." Spiegel Online, September 25, 2008. http://www.spiegel.de/international/world/the-life-factory-in-india-surrogacy-has-become-a-global-business-a-580209.html.

Sehgal, Priti. "Reproductive Tourism Soars in India: Adoption and Surrogacy Laws Have Yet to Catch Up." The Women's International Perspective. Last modified October 7,

2008. http://thewip.net/2008/10/07/reproductive-tourism-soars-in-india-adoption-and -surrogacy-laws-have-yet-to-catch-up/.

Shakespeare, Tom. "The Social Context of Individual Choice." In *Quality of Life and Human Difference: Genetic Testing, Health Care, and Disability*, edited by David T. Wasserman, Robert Samuel Wachbroit, and Jerome Edmund Bickenbach, 217–36. Cambridge, UK: Cambridge University Press, 2005.

Shanley, Mary Lyndon, and Adrienne Asch. "Involuntary Childlessness, Reproductive Technology, and Social Justice: The Medical Mask on Social Illness." *Signs: Journal of Women in Culture and Society* 34, no. 4 (2009): 851–74.

Sheth, Falguni A. "The Technology of Race." Special issue, *Radical Philosophy Review*, 7, no. 1 (2004): 77–98.

———. *Toward a Political Philosophy of Race*. Albany, NY: SUNY Press, 2009.

Silver, Lee M. "Reprogenetics: Third Millennium Speculation." *EMBO Reports* 1 (2000): 375–78.

Simpson, Bob. "Imagined Genetic Communities: Ethnicity and Essentialism in the Twenty-First Century." *Anthropology Today* 16, no. 3 (2000): 3–6.

Skloot, Rebecca. *The Immortal Life of Henrietta Lacks*. New York: Crown, 2010.

Smedley, Audrey. *Race in North America: Origin and Evolution of a Worldview*. Boulder, CO: Westview, 1993.

Smith, Merritt Roe, and Leo Marx, eds. *Does Technology Drive History?: The Dilemma of Technological Determinism*. Cambridge, MA: MIT Press, 1994.

Spar, Debora L. *The Baby Business: How Money, Science, and Politics Drive the Commerce of Conception*. Boston, MA: Harvard Business School Press, 2006.

Spickard, Paul R. *Almost All Aliens: Immigration, Race, and Colonialism in American History and Identity*. New York: Routledge, 2007.

Spiegel-Rösing, Ina, and Derek De Solla Price, eds. *Science, Technology, and Society: A Cross-Disciplinary Perspective*. London: SAGE, 1977.

Spruhan, Paul. "A Legal History of Blood Quantum in Federal Indian Law to 1935." *South Dakota Law Review* 51 (2006): 1–50.

Squier, Susan Merrill. *Babies in Bottles: Twentieth-Century Visions of Reproductive Technology*. New Brunswick, NJ: Rutgers University Press, 1994.

Stanton, William Ragan. *The Leopard's Spots: Scientific Attitudes toward Race in America, 1815–59*. Chicago, IL: University of Chicago Press, 1960.

Stepan, Nancy. *The Idea of Race in Science: Great Britain, 1800–1960*. Hamden, CT: Archon Books, 1982.

Stocking, George Ward. *Race, Culture, and Evolution: Essays in the History of Anthropology*. New York: Free Press, 1968.

———. "The Turn-of-the-Century Concept of Race." *Modernism/Modernity* 1, no. 1 (1994): 4–16.

Strathern, Marilyn. *Kinship, Law and the Unexpected: Relatives Are Always a Surprise*. New York: Cambridge University Press, 2005.

———. *Reproducing the Future: Essays on Anthropology, Kinship, and the New Reproductive Technologies*. New York: Routledge, 1992.

Strong, Pauline Turner, and Barrik Van Winkle. "'Indian Blood': Reflections on the Reckoning and Refiguring of Native North American Identity." *Cultural Anthropology* 11, no. 4 (1996): 547–76.

Stubblefield, Anna. *Ethics along the Color Line*. Ithaca, NY: Cornell University Press, 2005.

Subramanian, Sarmishta. "Wombs for Rent: Is Paying the Poor to Have Children Wrong when Both Sides Reap Such Benefits?" *Maclean's* 120, no. 25 (July 2, 2007): 40–47.

TallBear, Kimberly. "DNA, Blood, and Racializing the Tribe." *Wicazo Sa Review* 18, no. 1 (2003): 81–107.

Taylor, Paul C. *Race: A Philosophical Introduction.* Cambridge, UK: Polity, 2004.

Ten, C. L. "The Use of Reproductive Technologies in Selecting the Sexual Orientation, the Race, and the Sex of Children." *Bioethics* 12, no. 1 (1998): 45–48.

Terral, Mary. "Speculation and Experiment in Enlightenment Life Sciences." In *Heredity Produced: At the Crossroads of Biology, Politics, and Culture, 1500–1870*, edited by Staffan Müller-Wille and Hans-Jörg Rheinberger, 253–76. Cambridge, MA: MIT Press, 2007.

Thakur, Sunita. "'Wombs for Rent' Grows in India." *Marketplace.* Last modified December 27, 2007. http://www.marketplace.org/topics/life/wombs-rent-grows-india.

Thompson, Charis (Cussins). "Confessions of a Bioterrorist: Subject Position and Reproductive Technologies." In *Playing Dolly: Technocultural Formations, Fantasies, and Fictions of Assisted Reproduction*, edited by Ann Kaplan and Susan Squier, 189–220. New Brunswick, NJ: Rutgers University Press, 1999.

Thompson, Charis. *Making Parents: The Ontological Choreography of Reproductive Technologies.* Cambridge, MA: MIT Press, 2005.

Topinard, Paul. *Anthropology.* London: Chapman and Hall, 1890.

———. *Elements d'anthropologie générale.* Paris: A. Delahaye et E. Lecrosnier, 1883.

UNESCO. "Statement of 1950." In *The Race Question in Modern Science: Race and Science*, by Juan Comas, 496–501. New York: Columbia University Press, 1961.

Unnithan, Maya. "Infertility and Assisted Reproductive Technologies (ARTs) in a Globalising India: Ethics, Medicalisation and Agency." *Asian Bioethics Review* 2, no. 1 (2010): 3–18.

Vandermonde, Charles A. *Essai sur la manière de perfectionner l'espèce humaine.* Paris: Vincent, 1756.

Voegelin, Eric. "The Growth of the Race Idea." *Review of Politics* 2, no. 3 (1940): 283–317.

———. "The Growth of the Race Idea." In *Published Essays: 1940–1952*, edited by Ellis Sandoz, 27–61. Vol. 10. The Collected Works of Eric Voegelin. Columbia: University of Missouri Press, 2000.

———. *Race and State.* Edited by Klaus Vondung. Translated by Ruth Hein. Baton Rouge: Louisiana State University Press, 1997.

Vora, Kalindi. "Indian Transnational Surrogacy and the Commodification of Vital Energy." *Subjectivity* 28, no. 1 (2009): 266–78.

Vorzimmer, Peter J. "Darwin's 'Questions about the Breeding of Animals' (1839)." *Journal of the History of Biology* 2, no. 1 (1969): 269–81.

Wallace, Alfred Russel. "The Development of Human Races under the Law of Natural Selection." In *Contributions to the Theory of Natural Selection: A Series of Essays*, 303–31. London: Macmillan, 1870.

Wallenstein, Peter. *Tell the Court I Love My Wife: Race, Marriage, and Law: An American History.* New York: Palgrave Macmillan, 2002.

Walther, Carol S. "Skin Tone, Biracial Stratification and Tri-racial Stratification among Sperm Donors." *Ethnic and Racial Studies*, 2012, 1–20.

Wang, Wendy. *The Rise of Intermarriage Rates: Characteristics Vary by Race and Gender.* Pew Research Center. Last modified February 16, 2012. http://www.pewsocialtrends.org /files/2012/02/SDT-Intermarriage-II.pdf.

Washington, Harriet. *Medical Apartheid: The Dark History of Medical Experimentation on Black Americans from Colonial Times to the Present.* New York: Doubleday, 2006.

Weikart, Richard. *From Darwin to Hitler: Evolutionary Ethics, Eugenics, and Racism in Germany.* New York: Palgrave Macmillan, 2004.

Weinbaum, Alys Eve. *Wayward Reproductions: Genealogies of Race and Nation in Transatlantic Modern Thought.* Durham, NC: Duke University Press, 2004.

Weiss, Kenneth M., and Anne V. Buchanan. *The Mermaid's Tale: Four Billion Years of Cooperation in the Making of Living Things.* Cambridge, MA: Harvard University Press, 2009.

Weiss, Kenneth M., and Stephanie M. Fullerton. "Racing Around, Getting Nowhere." *Evolutionary Anthropology: Issues, News, and Reviews* 14, no. 5 (September/October 2005): 165–69.

White, Paul. "Acquired Character: The Hereditary Material of the 'Self-Made Man'" In *Heredity Produced: At the Crossroads of Biology, Politics, and Culture, 1500–1870*, by Staffan Müller-Wille and Hans-Jörg Rheinberger, 375–98. Cambridge, MA: MIT Press, 2007.

Williams, Patricia J. *The Alchemy of Race and Rights.* Cambridge, MA: Harvard University Press, 1991.

Wilson, Philip K. "Erasmus Darwin and the 'Noble' Disease (Gout): Conceptualizing Heredity and Disease in Enlightenment England." In *Heredity Produced: At the Crossroads of Biology, Politics, and Culture, 1500–1870*, by Staffan Müller-Wille and Hans-Jörg Rheinberger, 133–54. Cambridge, MA: MIT Press, 2007.

Winner, Langdon. *The Whale and the Reactor: A Search for Limits in an Age of High Technology.* Chicago, IL: University of Chicago Press, 1986.

Wright, Michelle Maria. "Nigger Peasants from France: Missing Translations of American Anxieties on Race and the Nation." *Callaloo* 22, no. 4 (1999): 831–52.

Wright, W. W. "Amalgamation." *De Bow's Review: Industrial Resources, Statistics, Etc.* 29 (1860): 1–20.

Yanagisako, Sylvia Junko, and Carol Lowery Delaney, eds. *Naturalizing Power: Essays in Feminist Cultural Analysis.* New York: Routledge, 1995.

Young, Iris Marion. *Intersecting Voices: Dilemmas of Gender, Political Philosophy, and Policy.* Princeton, NJ: Princeton University Press, 1997.

Zenderland, Leila. *Measuring Minds: Henry Herbert Goddard and the Origins of American Intelligence Testing.* Cambridge, UK: Cambridge University Press, 1998.

Index

CAMISHA A. RUSSELL is Assistant Professor of Philosophy at the
University of Oregon.